EMPOWERED PSYCHOTHERAPY

Robert Langs

EMPOWERED PSYCHOTHERAPY

Teaching Self-Processing

A New Approach to the Human Psyche and Its Reintegration

Robert Langs

Foreword by
James S. Grotstein

London
KARNAC BOOKS

First published in 1993 by
H. Karnac (Books) Ltd.
58 Gloucester Road
London SW7 4QY

British Library Cataloguing in Publication Data

Langs, Robert
  Empowered Psychotherapy: Teaching
  Self-Processing — A New Approach to the
  Human Psyche and Its Reintegration.
  I. Title
  616.89

  ISBN: 1–85575–057–0

Printed in Great Britain by BPCC Wheatons Ltd, Exeter

CONTENTS

FOREWORD

James S. Grotstein

Over two decades have passed since Robert Langs set out on his lonely, almost quixotic journey to bring renewed vision, clarity, and integrity to the practice of psycho-analytic psychotherapy and to right the seemingly unrightable wrongs that he found dormantly festering there. Considered at first an *enfant terrible* on the fringe and then a disquieting superego to the analytic establishment and to most practising psychotherapists, he has finally come to enjoy a noteworthy acceptance and credibility for his then revolutionary ideas.

Perhaps the following would suffice to give the briefest idea of the thrust of his ideas: Beginning with his concept of the bipersonal field and culminating in the evolution of "communicative psychotherapy" and now "empowered psychotherapy" through "self-processing", there runs a red thread of continuity through the various evolutions that have characterized Langs's thinking. I believe that this red thread is that of a pragmatic idealist who has been attempting to reinstitute such ideas as truth, ethics, humility, and ontological security in psychoanalytic psychotherapy. His focus has been unswervingly directed towards what most clinicians would believe was the *background* of therapy, not the foreground — namely, the *frame* and all the considerations appertaining to its establishment, maintenance, subversion (by either the patient or the therapist), and its restoration after subversion. Langs has made this putative background more important than the traditional foreground of dynamic and genetically reconstructive psychoanalytic psychotherapy.

Thus, similarly to Bion who studied the group as an entity in its own right and who located the invariant resistance of group members that sabotaged the unity of the group functioning, Langs has chosen to examine the psychotherapeutic field as a unity, one having its own laws and regulations that the therapist as well as the patient must respect and protect. Put another way, he seems to imply that a *covenant* of trust must take place between therapist and patient to protect, maintain, and restore the frame so that the patient can feel free enough to be able to access his or her internal world ("secondary unconscious processing system") in order to propagate the veridical "free associations" (in traditional psychoanalytic psychotherapy) or self-"guided associations" apposite to Langs's newest concept of "self-processing". This covenant is of such importance that it transcends the individualities of therapist and patient, but the burden is on the therapist to be eternally vigilant for all encoded messages as to "triggers" of frame brakes so that they can be recognized and enable the restoration of the frame.

One might believe at first blush that Langs is too obsessive about these alleged frame breaks and too compulsive in his preferred protocols in insisting that they need to be recognized as "unconscious triggers" and the frame resecured. On deeper inspection of his clinical vignettes, not only in this volume but across the years of his writing, one finds incontrovertible evidence of their appearances in encoded derivatives. One soberly gathers from the evidence of his work and from those of his colleagues that what is really obsessive and compulsive is not Langs but the very unconscious itself that relentlessly monitors the self's caretakers and the authenticity and propriety of their ministrations to the patient. In short, the unconscious just seems to be constructed that way — relentlessly perceptive and eternally wary of boundary violations — if it is to be a properly engaged secret partner to the ego and to consciousness with the latter's "primary unconscious (actually pre-conscious) processing system", the latter of which functions quite differently from the secondary unconscious system of the unconscious. Ideally, the two work in complementary harmony; pathologically, in symptomatic disharmonious dissynchrony and even dissociation.

Langs demonstrates himself to be primarily an analyst in the sense that Freud himself understood — that is, one who is attempting to understand the unconscious. Langs is also a respectful psychoanalytic revisionist, however. His emphasis on the unconscious is similar to Freud's in many ways, but, like Lacan, who also "re-read" Freud revisionistically and who, like Langs, reprivileges the importance of the unconscious over the ego and consciousness, he also adds a new and important construct to the concept of the unconscious. Whereas Freud believed that the primary unconscious consisted of the drives and the secondary unconscious of repressed memories, Langs innovatively states that the profoundest component of the unconscious is *perception*! This concept is in opposition to the canons of orthodox, classical, and Kleinian thinking but has been implicit although unstated in the works of Fairbairn, Winnicott, Sullivan, and Kohut. Langs deserves the credit for first applying this insight to psychoanalytic technique, but the idea has been simultaneously emerging in infant development research, cited by Stern, in which these researchers now believe that the infant is born with a very early capacity to perceive reality as it is — and that the capacity for phantasy is delayed until the second year.[1] Langs, however, has gone a step further than the infant developmental researchers in postulating that there is such an entity as *unconscious perception*! This innovation can have vast implications for and application to infant developmental research and for infant and child rearing, to say nothing of its applicability to child abuse research and treatment.

The idea that the unconscious contains the capacity for the perception of reality (has "reality-testing" abilities) has major implications for psychoanalytic theory and technique as well. First, Langs is thereby ennobling the very status of the unconscious, as did Lacan, to that of a veritable *alter ego*, which was the original meaning of "*das Es*", as espoused first by Nietzsche and later by Groddeck. Second, it helps to understand a fundamental characteristic of human behaviour that has been all but ignored, but which Langs, following Fairbairn, emphasizes — that just as children will *introjectively identify* with their parents' failures and inadequacies *in order to protect their image of the parents* (Fairbairn's "moral defence of the superego"), so will patients do the same in terms of protecting their image of the therapist. Put another way, the infant, like the patient, looks at the world through the periscope of its mother's (therapist's) eyes.

Langs' work is ultimately existential in its message. The reason why the therapist must monitor the frame is to assure the patient that she or he, the therapist, though capable of error, can possess the integrity, courage, and concern to be able to recognize the impact on the patient of his or her error, to acknowledge it, and to repair it so as to restore a sense of safety, faith, and trust in the patient. Two examples, out of countless others, come to mind. My office is in a small two-storey building. The entrance to my office, which is upstairs, is at one end, and the exit is at the other. One day I asked a patient to leave by the entrance rather than the usual exit at the end of a session because it had been raining, and I believed that the outside exit steps would be slippery. The patient cooperatively complied and then came in the following day and included in his associations some reference to my fear of dying! I immediately understood this association to be an encoded message, a trigger, for the patient's concern about my alleged fear of dying, due to my allowing him back into my private domain rather than ushering him to his own life.

The second example happened more recently with the same patient. For some then unaccountable reason, I ended a session fifteen minutes prematurely, then caught myself at the last minute and resumed the treatment until the proper time of ending. Two sessions later the patient failed to appear at the time of his normal appointment and appeared two hours later instead. It was unusual for me to make an error like this, and I was unaware — and remained unaware — of any countertransference interferences. I was aware, however, of other pressing problems in my own life and also aware of feeling ill with 'flu and not wishing to be practising but to be recovering at home, which I had proceeded to do following my error with this patient. In the subsequent analysis of this error I noted the patient's absence as an encoded derivative of the adaptive context and interpreted to him that he had (introjectively) identified with the erring me in order to take over that quality of mine so that he could be guilty of it rather than I, so as to spare me. Following this, I interpreted how frightened he must have been about me and my error to have sought to relieve me of it. This helped considerably to rectify (secure) the broken frame.

Langs created the concept of "communicative psychotherapy" in order to highlight the importance of the background frame over the foreground dynamics. He added the concept of "communicative errors" as being significantly different from transference, but which might involve countertransference on the part of the therapist, both for initiating frame breaks and for failure to look for them in the patient's material and to rectify them. The very addition of the concept of communicative errors to our ideas of technique is noteworthy and welcome. Much of what is called transference and transference enactments might now be called results of communicative errors and should not be confused with transference. *As a matter of fact, the revelation of authentic transference occurs only in the secure frame (secured from communicative errors).*

Langs' latest contribution to psychoanalytically informed psychotherapy is the concept of "self-processing". He states that one of the principal reasons for this newest idea of his was to enable him to sharpen and hone the instrument of his craft by allowing him to define a therapeutic field whereby his concepts of frame stability could be better emphasized as the keystone of therapeutic consideration. The field is defined as one (a) in which a "teacher" ethically recruits "students" for a limited series of "class" exercises in "self-processing"; (b) same as above but for one "student"; or (c) where the "student" can become his own "teacher" by stringently following the frame rules. The "students" and "teacher" (or "instructor") are bound by covenant obligations. Students take it in turn to present. The presenting student must relate a dream or dream-like narrative ("presentation narrative") and must then associate to the key points of the narrative, but the associative process is not like the "free associations" in traditional psychoanalytic psycho-therapy; it is to follow the rules of "guided associations" to the key points of the dream narrative in order to obtain the key triggers that were perceived in the student's unconscious as registering the impact of an endangerment in their mental or physical lives, but which, according to Langs, generally involve a failure by either the student or the instructor or both to note a frame break. Once the student has presented his or her presentation narrative, the other members enter into the arena with their own comments, and finally the instructor intervenes with questions aimed at clarifying the triggers and then linking them in the narrative so as to pinpoint the student's uncon-scious perception of danger — principally frame danger. This frame danger is to be understood as death anxiety or claustro-phobic anxiety with regard to the establishment of a secure frame, and as death anxiety of another order in the event of a failure for the frame to be recognized as insecure.

What one comes away with as a result of immersing oneself in this highly evocative, innovative, and useful contribution is a renewed respect for the sensitivity of the operating conditions of therapy to refuse to stay in the background of our attention and consideration. One also comes away with a newer respect for the need for truth and ethics to be a paramount consideration in treatment. What impacts on one most profoundly, however, is the undeniable need for the therapist–instructor to recon-sider his or her role of ontological responsibility in how he or she creates, manages, and restores the frame. Langs' concepts seem to converge with the recent countertransference literature to implicate the importance of the duties of the therapist to monitor himself or herself and his or her behaviour with regard to the frame. Put another way — and I believe that Langs would agree with this — in order for psychotherapy to take place, there must be a secure frame if the unconscious is to present or generate the necessary dream work (phantasies, etc.) for the treatment. Frames are bound to be broken because of the humanness of the participants, but unconscious perception is ever alert to infractions of its safety frontier, processes them by its secondary unconscious processing system, and reveals the triggers of the awareness of its unsafety in encoded derivatives that demand recognition. In fact, Langs seems to believe that

the frame psychology *is* the essence of treatment! Even if the
reader is sceptical, he or she will come away from reading this
book with an enhanced realization of the importance of his or
her frame awareness. I certainly have.

NOTE

1. Parenthetically, Langs also deserves credit for being unusu-
    ally painstakingly meticulous and graciously generous in
    his citations of the works of others on whom he depended
    for formulating his ideas.

EMPOWERED
PSYCHOTHERAPY

INTRODUCTION

Regardless of orientation, every mental health professional strives deeply to understand and help his or her patients or clients. In the spirit of the never-ending search for new ways to support and expand these pursuits, this book strives to present some uncommon lines of clinical observation and thought that hopefully will shed new light on the work and thinking of the full range of helping professionals — whatever their background and persuasions.

This unusual hope for broad applicability for the insights and techniques that characterize the empowered form of psychotherapy that is the subject of this book stems from several sources. Chief among them are the quasi-educational/quasi-therapeutic foundation of this new treatment form; its basically dialectical, adaptive, interactional, and evolutionary orientations; its concern with the fundamental architecture and design of the human psyche; its grounding in a formal science of psychoanalysis and psychotherapy; and its attention to the moment-to-moment details of emotionally charged human communication. This devotion to basics seems to open almost magically new vistas into the human psyche and its adaptive resources; hopefully, the reader will find these new vistas both informative and exciting to behold.

In more concrete, clinical terms, much of this hoped-for freshness has its source in an aspect of *self-processing therapy*, as it is called, that is especially unique to its structure. I refer to the obligation of the presenting patient or student[1] in each and every class to carry out an explicit, emotionally charged adaptive task. Stated as simply as possible, the requisite is that the student, using his or her resources alone, develop the means of accessing his or her own deeply unconscious world of experience, needs, and wisdom and bring to the conscious light of day the contents and workings of these dark and powerful strata of the mind.

In essence, the student's *conscious system* (the system of the mind that is attached to awareness) of the *emotion-processing mind* (that part of the human psyche designed to adapt to and communicate about emotionally charged stimuli) is asked to find the torturous route to his or her *deep unconscious system* (the system of the emotion-processing mind that operates entirely without awareness). This assignment proves to be no easy task, yet it is one that is extremely illuminating — and vital to emotional health.

This particular adaptational activation of the emotion-processing mind provides an especially well-defined and fortuitous opportunity to observe the human psyche in living action. Surprisingly, both the surface and the depths, the *conscious system* and the *deep unconscious system*, thereby are revealed in ways that have not been possible through other means. Even as this work plumbs the extremes of the adaptive nether world, it illuminates features of our conscious resourcefulness — and its limitations. The result is, I believe, a new way of thinking about the emotion-processing psyche — and a new mode of therapy as well (Langs, 1992d, 1992f).

The present volume endeavours to make three broadly interrelated contributions:

1. *The presentation of a new and rather powerful technique of*

---

[1]Given the nature of the therapeutic/educational paradigm that is the subject of this book, I will use as synonyms the terms *patient* and *student*, as well as those of *therapist* and *teacher* or *instructor*.

*healing emotional ills which unfolds within a quasi-edu-
cational, quasi-therapeutic framework.* This paradigm is
an outgrowth of classical psychoanalysis and psychoanalytically oriented forms of psychotherapy. It is designed to
realize, in a most intense and thorough manner, the long-
standing goals of psychoanalysis and its variants to explore
the deepest and most compelling strata of the emotion-
processing mind—and to benefit from the profound
insights so derived. This particular treatment modality is
configured as a method of teaching individuals, singly or as
members of small groups, how to develop the skills needed
to engage in their own psychological healing via *self-
processing*—the distinctive form of self-analysis that has
been engineered through the communicative/adaptive
approach to human emotional life and psychotherapy on
which this work is founded (Smith, 1991; Langs, 1992a).

2. *The development of the means by which these same techniques of self-processing can be used privately by yourself
as a therapist.* Self-processing is an illuminating and
effective form of self-healing that has been devised to provide new forms of insight for psychotherapists into both the
realistic and deeply unconscious sources of the full range
of countertransference difficulties and personal emotional
issues with which they are so often concerned.

3. *The offer of perspectives on the architecture and evolution of
the emotion-processing mind, and in particular on the nature
of its adaptive resources and their constraints—especially
as they pertain to the therapeutic process and the nature of
psychopathology* (Langs, 1986, 1987, 1988, 1992a, 1992c,
1992e, 1993, in press).

Every new paradigm for the field of psychotherapy offers
both an innovative way of viewing the human psyche and its
means of adapting, and a novel way of observing and clarifying
how these coping efforts are achieved. This freshness sets a
path along which there are likely to be a fair number of unprecedented observations of and discernments into the adaptive
mind — its daily functioning, its dysfunctions and their alleviation, its search for optimal emotionally charged decisions and
choices, and its contributions to the transactions of a thera-

peutic encounter. In turn, these unprecedented realizations inevitably lead to revisions in theory and practice that foster a new round of uncommon perspectives, creating a never-ending cycle of discovery, revision, consolidation, and fresh discovery yet again. It is the hope of this book to be part of these evolving and illuminating cycles of generative creativity.

For the communicative approach, the field of observation in psychotherapy has always centred on the therapeutic interaction between patients and therapists, and its setting and ground rules — the unique set of conditions that distinguish and frame a psychotherapeutic experience. Within that framework and the interactions it defines and strives to support, stress is placed on what undoubtedly is the most significant emergent capacity of the hominid mind — *the use of language for representation, adaptation, and communication, both direct and indirect, conscious and unconscious.*

These evolutionary developments include the creation of a remarkable and uniquely human faculty for the construction of *multiple-meaning messages*, conveyed most commonly in the form of *narratives* that simultaneously express several layers of meaning in a single storied line. These rich tales have multiple connotations of which two are most vital — those that are *manifest* or directly stated, including their evident implications, and those that are *encoded* or indirectly stated in disguised form. Each level of meaning has its own features, yet each is embodied in the same communication. Furthermore, each level reflects the workings of a distinctive system of the emotion-processing mind and is an expression of the adaptations of that system.

The manifest level of meaning conveys the workings of the *conscious system* of the human mind and its coping responses to *consciously registered* stimuli (impingements or triggers). On the other hand, the encoded level of meaning stems from the workings of the *second or deep unconscious system* of the mind, which has been designed to cope with *unconsciously or subliminally registered (repressed)* stimuli or triggers and their ramifications. This distinctive two-layered form of human emotional expression is, then, a reflection of the distinctive two-system design of the emotion-processing psyche. Each system has its own particular adaptive preferences and modes, but consistently it has been found that deep unconscious adaptations are far superior to those that are made consciously. This implies a great need to access the operations and wisdom of this deep system — and doing so is a central goal of self-processing therapy.

* * *

Recent studies of the immaterial human *mind*, and the material human *brain* that is its substrate, have shown that evolution has fashioned a human psyche that is fundamentally adaptive, survival oriented, outer-directed, and structured primarily to deal far more with external rather than internal impingements (Calvin, 1990; Ornstein, 1991; Langs, 1992c, 1993, in press). Indeed, such inner mental events as affects, instinctual-drive needs and fantasies, whether conscious or unconscious and whatever conflicts they may secondarily arouse, essentially are part of our adaptive armamentarium and are themselves largely responses to external inputs that range from nurturing and supportive to dangerous and traumatic.

These evolutionary contingencies have generated a human mind that is quite limited in inner-directedness for reasons of basic design as well as dynamic defensiveness. The human capacity for self-observation and self-understanding are fundamental capacities that are vital both for dealing with emotional issues and for carrying out successful efforts at *self-processing*. However, even though these capacities are far more advanced in humans than in other animal species, they nonetheless are quite rudimentary and poorly developed. As we will see, in comparison with unconscious capabilities, our conscious efforts at self-exploration, self-awareness, and the like are remarkably constricted, easily abandoned, and all too readily blinded, falsified, and biased. Efforts to enhance these faculties stand as another of the searching goals of this book.

But beyond this sense that self-awareness is a mental capacity in need of further evolutionary development, there lies an even more basic problem. The human psyche is called on continually to deal with a staggering array of enormously complex and often powerful multilevelled emotionally charged stimuli fraught with varieties of information and meaning, much of it potentially disruptive; our evolved gifted minds are forever at risk of system overload.

To handle this rather relentless onslaught, evolution has fashioned an emotion-processing mind that is, as Freud (1900) so brilliantly suggested, a two-system, parallel-processing, adaptive structure. However, where Freud essentially envisioned a single, integrated emotion-processing psyche with conscious and unconscious components, studies of the mind's adaptations reveal a critically different picture — the existence of two distinctive adaptive systems of the mind that, in most respects, operate very differently and quite independently of each other.

One system — *the conscious system*, which has a *superficial unconscious subsystem*, is attached to direct perception and immediate awareness and is known to us via the direct or manifest meanings in experience and messages. The other processing system — *the deep or second unconscious system* — is attached to subliminal or unconscious perception and operates entirely outside of awareness; it lacks direct contact with consciousness and is known to us only via the indirect or latent (in the sense of being *encoded or derivative*) contents of many of the same surface messages that express and reveal conscious system functioning (Langs, 1992a, 1992e).

Each of these rather independent systems of the mind has its own distinctive adaptive resources and intelligence, as well as its own range of vision and focus, modes of experience, needs, viewpoints, self-observing functions, attitudes, ground-rule or frame preferences, and means of processing and adapting to incoming information and meaning. In a sense, then, each system has its own ego, superego, and id — which, as we will see, surprisingly tend to be quite at odds with each other. Most important, however, is the realization that the second unconscious system is not simply a blind, seething cauldron of needs and drives, but the locale of our most incisive adaptive resources *vis à vis* emotionally charged inputs — a point that will find extensive elaboration in the substance of this book.

The conscious system essentially is designed for short- and long-term *survival* and has little available energy or capacity to deal with social relationships and emotional issues. This task has been relegated primarily to the *deep or second unconscious system*, which has evolved to safeguard the functioning of the conscious mind by being the receptor subliminally of many emotionally charged impingements which thereby are spared conscious registration and processing — a gating mechanism that assures smooth conscious system functioning. And because this second system of the mind itself is safeguarded by being entirely divorced from awareness, it is able to process the information and meaning with which it deals non-defensively and relatively incisively. The second unconscious system, then, embodies an exquisitely sensitive and brilliant intelligence as it pertains to emotional impingements.

Assigned very different adaptive tasks by natural selection, each system of the emotion-processing psyche has its own purview and realm of experience, creating two distinctive realms of human experience that tend to be worlds apart and often in conflict. In this context, we can think of still another goal of self-processing therapy as facilitating emotional adaptation and cure by fostering a better integration between the two disparate systems of the mind.

This quest touches on what is arguably the most unexpected feature of the architecture of the human mind. As I indicated, the deep unconscious system and its superb unconscious intelligence have no direct link to awareness. As a result, the system's highly adaptive solutions to emotional issues *do not obtain direct or undisguised access to conscious experience*. This means that our most compelling insights into emotional conflicts and problems cannot be recruited for daily coping — for conscious adaptation. Indeed, while unconscious experience has a most telling influence on our emotional lives, we have no way directly of knowing and modifying these effects. This leads us to another goal of self-processing therapy, which is to render this deeply unconscious adaptive wisdom available as a conscious resource.

The communicated reflections of the operations of the second unconscious system are available to us consciously only through *displaced and disguised or encoded (derivative) messages*. These messages therefore must be *properly decoded* for their contents to be usable for conscious coping. In essence, the encoded meanings of messages reflect the adaptive activities of the deep unconscious system as it responds to contemporaneous incoming emotionally charged stimuli. As we will see, like vision, the second unconscious system responds primarily to here-and-now stimuli; unlike the conscious system, the deep unconscious system cannot be deflected into dealing with past or future issues except as they are linked to current situations and impingements.

This implies that an encoded communication can meaningfully be deciphered only in light of the immediate adaptation-evoking inputs or triggers to which they are a response. Indeed, because communication is an adaptive response, the essential meanings so contained are definable only in light of their stimuli — responses make sense only when their stimuli or triggers are known.

In respect to adapting to emotionally charged triggers, however, the situation is a bit complicated because there are both manifest, consciously known triggers and latent, unconsciously experienced triggers. Thus, at the same moment that the conscious system is reacting to one set of impingements, the deep unconscious system is reacting to a very different set of stimuli. Sorting out the world of human emotions and interactions requires a full appreciation of these distinctions, and self-processing is designed to make them abundantly clear — and relevant to emotional coping.

From this viewpoint, it can be seen too that *trigger decoding* — deciphering disguised thematic contents in light of their currently evocative stimuli — is the key to grasping deep unconscious experience and processing and to making use of the deep system's many unique and gifted capacities. This adaptationally oriented method of decoding is, as far as I know, the only means through which we can bring into awareness and benefit directly from the deep wisdom and perspectives of this marvellous unconscious part of the mind. Decoded narrative messages are a window into the depths of the human psyche and its adaptive resources.

Promoting the development of the disguised narrative material through which this deep unconscious system communicates with the surface of the mind, and identifying the triggers to which these narratives are camouflaged responses, is at the heart of the self-processing effort. Along with the establishment of a secured, holding frame, these pursuits account for both the educational and the healing powers of self-processing therapy. Nevertheless, this search for trigger-decoded meaning proves to be an arduous task because the conscious mind — again, for reasons of both psychodynamic defence and fundamental design — is configured to resist and interfere with the development and realization of trigger-decoded insights. The insights that such efforts produce are remarkably anxiety provoking and disquieting for the conscious mind, and a great threat to its stability — yet they are vital to emotional health and adaptive functioning.

We are, then, human beings with a basically divided emotion-processing mind in respect to its adaptive preferences. In essence, the conscious system's preference for defence and falsification tends to be pitted against the second unconscious system's incisive openness to emotional truths. Given that, by and large, the conscious system is the victor in this mental struggle, we may also state another goal of self-processing therapy: an endeavour to afford the second unconscious system a greater voice in the emotional life of the individual. This can be accomplished only by repairing nature's evolved schism so as to afford the student (and, secondarily, ourselves as teachers) an integrated wholeness and optimization of functioning that is not as yet characteristic of our adaptive minds.

* * *

To conclude this introduction, I offer a list of the more practical offerings of this book:

1. A new form of therapy — a mode of healing others and helping them to heal themselves.

2. A new method for expanding your own self-awareness as a psychotherapist, whomever you may be and however you do therapy or counselling.

3. A method of "cure" that is both educational and therapeutic in design and outcome, one with deep and lasting positive effects.

4. A technique that may be offered on a one-to-one basis as a tutorial or in large or small groups.

5. A way of teaching students how to access their own deep unconscious wisdom and benefit from an unused uncon-

scious intelligence and resource of supreme value in the emotional realm.

6. The means of offering the same opportunity to yourself as a therapist and individual.

7. A method of trigger decoding that will widen your client's and your own understanding of emotional coping and emotional life.

8. A way to broaden your perspectives on the evolution and design of the human mind, and its full range of adaptive resources — and their limitations.

9. The opportunity to live a fuller life with an awareness not only of conscious experience, but also of deep unconscious experience — two distinctive modes of being, seeing, reacting, and adapting.

10. A new healing process that, based on formal scientific evidence, appears to be the most powerful means of resolving emotional dysfunctions available today (Langs & Badalamenti, 1992a, in press; Langs, 1992a).

11. A means of engaging in *preventive psychotherapy* — a way of working with students who are not suffering from notable emotional disturbance in order to enhance their personal functioning, enlightenment, and maturation. This learning experience is configured to diminish the possibility of later emotional difficulties.

These are, of course, rather extravagant claims, but they will be carefully documented and supported on the pages that follow. Building on a hundred years of psychoanalysis, we are now in a position to extend the psychodynamic approach of Freud and his followers into deeper and more fundamental realms through a more incisive appreciation of both conscious and unconscious communication and adaptation. Because deep unconscious experience is so very different from the conscious experience of our daily lives, mastering the therapeutic and personal use of self-processing is an awesome and wonderful experience that, while often distressing to endure, is full of surprising hope and promise. It is the overriding goal of this book to help you to realize the fullness of this promise for both your patients or clients and yourself.

PART ONE

BACKGROUND PERSPECTIVES

CHAPTER ONE

The goals
of self-processing therapy

We are about to explore a technique of psychotherapy that is likely to seem both familiar and unfamiliar, old yet new. On the familiar side there will be the quest for unconscious processes and meaning, the allusions to unconscious systems of the mind, the importance of ground rules, frames, and boundaries, and the search for cure through insight. Less familiar — and perhaps more difficult to grasp — will be the redefinition of many of these basic concepts and a series of techniques and ideas that arise from the distinctive features of the method of therapy that is the subject of this book. A comparison of certain aspects of psychotherapy and self-processing therapy will introduce us to some of these issues (see also Langs, 1992d).

THE ADAPTIVE TASKS OF PSYCHOTHERAPY

There are, of course, many forms of psychotherapy, but it seems fair to say that, as a rule, they are relatively unstructured in respect to the unfolding of each session. In dynamic forms of therapy, there is a rather broad goal — namely, to resolve a patient's emotionally founded symptoms, whether subjective, psychosomatic, or interpersonal in nature, and to do so in an insightful manner that includes the illumination of unconscious factors. However, the goal or task of a particular session tends to be open-ended: the patient simply is asked to free-associate, and whatever unfolds from there is subject to the patient's selection of material or inclination to fall silent and the decision of the therapist as to when and how to intervene — if at all.

In all forms of psychotherapy, there is, however, an ever-present, generally unstated, and usually *unconscious* adaptive task that is a major factor in every session. In both patient and therapist there exists a psychobiologically established adaptive need that quite naturally is activated in each of them which compels them to cope with the behaviours and communications from each other — a reflection of the evolved, basic adaptive orientation of the human psyche.

More often than not, however, this adaptive effort is carried out by the deep unconscious rather than the conscious system. On the *conscious* level this task often goes unappreciated and unnoticed, though not because it is of little importance but mainly because it involves the kind of interpersonal, psychodynamically charged overload of inputs that leads the psyche automatically to repress and deny the relevant impingements. Thus, this rather immediate and compelling adaptive task is generally put aside unless a crisis arises in the therapy or a patient or therapist decides for some reason to focus directly on some aspect of their interaction.

The relative neglect of this compelling issue has many sources. Unless there is an overriding problem within a therapy or therapeutic relationship, this adaptive need is not experienced consciously and therefore its existence can be ascertained only through engaging in the adaptation-oriented trigger decoding of a patient's material — failing that, the need remains real but undetected. By and large, *the conscious system* tends defensively and by design to avoid many of the more anxiety-provoking aspects of the inputs derived from the immediate therapeutic interaction; instead, it favours manifestly addressing relationships outside of therapy — past, present, and future.

Oddly enough, however, a large portion of the communications from patients that overtly are concerned with experiences outside of therapy allude *latently* to the therapeutic interaction as well. Thus, a given manifest message from the conscious system typically will pertain *directly* to a relationship outside of therapy while simultaneously *encoding* the patient's unconscious perceptions of his or her therapist in light of the latter's interventions within the ongoing therapeutic experience. Access to these encoded meanings is made possible by means of a process called *trigger decoding* — a method of deciphering the themes extracted from a patient's narrative images in light of the adaptation-evoking stimuli or *triggers* to which they are a disguised coping response.

Trigger decoding reveals the surprising finding that the deep unconscious system is *at all times* primarily focused on and engaged in processing the implications of the immediate (and most recent) communicative exchanges within the therapeutic interaction. While a patient's conscious system can and often does look elsewhere, the second unconscious system is always centred on the present situation and especially the therapist's efforts therein.

For every patient, then, there is a continuous pressure to adapt to the ramifications of his or her therapist's behaviours and interventions. While, consciously, this appears to be an intermittent and often seemingly minor task, unconsciously these interventions — especially those related to the ground rules of the therapy — are a primary adaptive issue. The coping response is, however, usually made by the deep unconscious rather than the conscious system — it therefore is reflected in encoded rather than direct or manifest form. Much the same is true of a therapist's experience of the behaviours and communications of his or her patients, although this is more difficult to ascertain because the therapist generally does not and should not free-associate or narrate and encode. In psychotherapy sessions, he or she is constrained to the use of direct, conscious system communicating and functioning.

Because most therapies are geared to deal with *manifest contents* and their *conscious and superficial unconscious implications* — i.e., to work essentially in the realm of the conscious system and its superficial unconscious subsystem — the powerful unconscious interpersonal adaptive task of which I write is either neglected entirely or viewed in general rather than specific terms (Langs, 1992a, 1992e, 1993, in press). Because conscious system functioning tends to be global and vague, the well-defined meanings of the moment-to-moment therapeutic interaction and of the ramifications of the *specific* silences and interventions of a therapist are disregarded in favour of a broader and more naive and uncertain view. Conscious system operations automatically cover up a great deal and lack the attention to detail and nuance that is characteristic of most living systems — including the other system of the emotion-processing mind, the second unconscious system.

In therapy constituted as teaching patients to do self-processing, there are two crucial features that run counter to usual clinical practice. First, with the exception of the communicative approach on which it is founded, self-processing therapy tends to differ from virtually all forms of psychotherapy in that the formulations and interpretations of the instructor consistently are based on considerations of the immediate interaction between student and teacher as it is experienced by the former — consciously but especially unconsciously. Where the existing forms of dynamic psychotherapy are *conscious system oriented*, communicative and self-processing therapy are *deep unconscious system oriented*.

The second departure from the usual therapy paradigm involves the most singular feature of this new form of treatment. It entails the previously noted assignment to the student in each session of an explicit, conscious adaptive task — a responsibility that is absent in all forms of psychotherapy including the communicative version. Built into the format of the self-processing class or tutorial is the requirement that the student independently attempt to carry out his or her own self-processing exercise during the first part of each session. This implies that the student is asked to find the means of accessing the perceptions and adaptive processings of his or her own deep unconscious system and arrive at trigger-decoded insights — i.e., to undo the conscious system disguises and defences that prevent these meanings from reaching awareness.

This requisite can be met only by invoking the relatively well-defined structure and constraints of what is termed the *self-processing exercise*— the procedure that is designed to afford access to an individual's deep unconscious experience. In brief — and of course, this process will be fully elaborated in the chapters that follow — the student is obligated to begin each therapy class with what is called an *origination narrative*— a recent dream or dream-equivalent (a story that is composed spontaneously at the opening of a class and then treated as if it were a dream). The origination narrative is then used as a point of departure for what are termed *guided associations*; ideally, they are unrehearsed narrative associations to the specific elements of the initial dream or story. As I will argue from clinical and research experiences, *free associations* are not as powerful as *guided associations* and are not an element of the self-processing exercise (see chapter thirteen).

The personal emotional problems (so-called *self-indicators*) of the student are identified next, including all of his or her impingements on the ground rules or frame of the self-processing class. There follows a careful search for *triggers*— essentially, the adaptation-evoking, emotionally charged stimuli that have activated the adaptive efforts of the conscious and deep unconscious systems of the student's psyche. By and large, clinical experience has shown unmistakably that a self-processing teacher's recent interventions — especially those related to the ground rules and frame of the self-processing class — are the most powerful evocative triggers *for the second unconscious system* and its responsive (encoded) insights and directives.

Finally, the exercise culminates in the *transposing or linking process*— a method of extracting the themes in the *dream-associational network or narrative pool* and connecting them to the most compelling triggers on hand as valid, adaptive encoded responses. The linking of themes to triggers yields a deep grasp and understanding of the student's unconscious experience and processing of these triggers as they illuminate his or her emotional issues. The linking experience produces a genuinely unforeseen moment of insight that, upon reflection and in retrospect, proves to be remarkably self-evident — only the highly defensive conscious system could have missed it.

In practice, the two adaptive tasks — *consciously*, to produce a trigger-decoded insight, and *unconsciously*, to explore the interaction with the teacher — unite into a single effort in that the former is always constituted in terms of the latter. That is, as noted, the evolved design of the human psyche is such that in the deep unconscious realm, the emotion-processing mind is always working over its immediate interactions — other deep unconscious responses fan out from that central core. Thus, genuine insight as defined in terms of the deep unconscious experience of the student is *always* related to the specific interventions of the teacher. In particular, the second or deep unconscious system of the patient (though not his conscious system) is exquisitely focused on the therapist's management of the basic structure and framework of the self-processing class and is deeply affected by how the ground rules are handled.

Guided by consideration of the limited capabilities and intense defensiveness characteristic of conscious system functioning and by the encoded messages from the second or deep unconscious system, the activities of the self-processing teacher also are different from those of the usual therapist. Where the latter works in terms of the surface, the former is focused on the encoded depths. And where the latter has a variety of ill-defined guides for intervening, the teacher's activities are more precisely prescribed. Because the path to a trigger-decoded insight is remarkably narrow and the defences of the conscious system so pervasive and geared to avoid access to deep meaning, the self-processing class is, of utter necessity, exceedingly well structured and focused on issues of resistance — the conscious system requires an enormous amount of guidance and insight to achieve the goal of fresh deep understanding as defined in terms of deep unconscious system processing.

For example, the self-processing teacher is mandated to refrain from speaking for the first forty minutes of a class or tutorial, during which time the student attempts to carry out the assigned exercise entirely on his or her own. The balance of the teacher's time is then spent in helping the student to resolve the inevitable resistances that materialize in opposition to completing the process, and in developing the necessary components for the linking of triggers to encoded themes (the source of deep insight); both teaching and interpretive activities are utilized in these pursuits.

There is overwhelming empirical evidence for the proposition that there exists a definitive set of procedures that allow for maximal access to the domain of deep unconscious processing and experience. This accounts for the unusually precise demarcation of the procedures of the self-processing class, a framework within which both student and teacher can work quite creatively. Left to its own natural tendencies and resources, the conscious system — i.e., spontaneous conscious efforts — will achieve either a modicum of trigger-decoded insight or fail entirely in this respect. That is, the human mind has evolved an architecture that either precludes access to deep meaning or allows for only brief and incomplete moments of such understanding. This configuration arises principally because of the high energy requirements of the vital survival tasks assigned to the conscious system. Except in very small doses, emotional inputs tend to disturb that system's functioning and emotionally charged impingements are therefore either entirely screened out or greatly reduced though perceptual defences and denial and repression.

The stated requisite that the student pursue trigger-decoded insights creates an unusual opportunity for the self-processing teacher to study his or her client's adaptive mind in action. The effort discloses how the two systems of the emotion-processing mind function when asked to seek out deeper, unconscious perceptions, processes, and meanings. The situation is comparable to the shift from investigating a human organ in a cadaver to observing the same organ functioning *in vivo*. The result is a new level of understanding of the structure and functioning of the emotion-processing mind — and each of its two remarkable adaptive systems.

Because this approach maximizes encoded expression and facilitates the identification of repressed adaptation-evoking triggers, it is especially able to disclose a great deal about the adaptive operations of the second unconscious system. In self-processing therapy, great stress is placed on the production of narrative material because the voice of the deep unconscious system is largely narrative in nature. Indeed, formal research and clinical study have shown that the richness and power of the *derivative or encoded imagery* in self-processing therapy far exceeds that in the average psychotherapy session (Langs, 1992a, 1992b [1978], 1992c, 1992d, 1992e, 1992f; Langs & Badalamenti, 1992a, 1992b, in press). In the latter setting, the defensive operations of the conscious system tend to move free associations away from strong thematic contents and narratives, and towards unencoded speculations, formulations, analyses, and similar single-meaning intellectualized pursuits. This press towards narrative-guided associations is a major factor in the revelatory and clinical powers of the self-processing paradigm.

THE EFFICACY OF SELF-PROCESSING THERAPY

In its most basic sense, self-processing therapy is an effort to forge a path to the deepest level of unconscious experience and processing—the locale of our most effective intelligence and influence in the emotional realm.

There are, as we will see, at least five levels of human expression and meaning. Efforts at self-understanding can be confined to any one of these strata—ranging from manifest contents and their implications to symbolic decoding without consideration of triggers. Every form of legitimate insight has something to offer, but many of these realizations actually cover over or falsify other more essential truths. The problem is that currently there is no verified means of gauging the importance, strength, or healing powers of the knowledge accumulated in any given way. For most methods of formulating, there also are virtually no safeguards against misrepresentation and error. The development of truly efficacious healing methods needs to be fortified with reliable measures of both validation and relevance to the vicissitudes of emotional life—and the process of cure.

In this context, the present book attempts to meet the challenge of convincingly documenting the claim that self-processing therapy affords access to the deepest and most repressed and defended level of human experience, and that it is a compelling means of bringing into awareness the most crucial unconscious processes and meanings that pertain to emotional issues and their optimal adaptive solutions. The claim also will be made that this method of healing has an optimal help/hurt ratio — its degree of help is high and the cost or hurt is remarkably low. Empowered psychotherapy has much to offer at a very small price.

THE FORMS OF SELF-PROCESSING

There are three forms of self-processing: *personal* (an individual effort made without an instructor), *tutorial* (a single student with a single instructor), and *class* (two or more students and an instructor). Personal self-processing is arduous and difficult to bring to a moment of deep insight, whereas the self-processing tutorial is a very powerful experience capable of producing excellent educational and therapeutic results; it is ideal for those students who can tolerate its relatively secured frame and rather extensive expressions of deep meaning. The self-processing class, with its somewhat modified frame, is an intermediary form that provides a constructive setting in which effective self-understanding and healing can be developed quite well.

For the most part, this book will unfold through explorations of the self-processing class. Once that paradigm has been clearly established, I will, in the final chapter, offer a discussion of the distinctive issues raised by the other two forms of self-processing — personal and tutorial. In essence, however, the fundamental procedures of self-processing are identical in all of the contexts in which it is carried out — even when it is used in large classes or seminars for purposes of demonstration.

THE GOALS OF SELF-PROCESSING

The goals of a self-processing tutorial share much in common with most forms of psychotherapy, but also include some quests that are rather unusual for this kind of healing endeavour. To add further to our sense of the process, I will list them and briefly discuss each.

1. *To heal all manner of emotional dysfunctions*

The healing qualities of self-processing therapy are inherent to its design. They stem from the teacher's frame-securing inter-ventions (managements of — adherence to — the ground rules of the class) and from his or her unconsciously validated interactional interpretations, constituted as efforts at *linking or transposing* — connecting encoded themes to their adaptation-evoking triggers. These endeavours, when confirmed through encoded images, offer sound holding, deep insight, and the opportunity for a student's positive unconscious introjective identifications with a teacher who is able effectively to carry out such work — the deep unconscious system knows how difficult a task this is.

The healing goal of self-processing is, then, to enable stu-dents in some constructive and insightful fashion, consciously and unconsciously, to modify their emotional dysfunctions — whatever their form. In addition, the self-processing class pro-vides opportunities for emotional maturation and growth, and opens up new vistas in the lives of its students. The work is also designed to promote the development of better methods of daily coping in the emotional domain and to help students under-stand the unconscious basis of emotionally charged choices and decisions so they can be fashioned more effectively with the help of deep enlightenment.

2. *To provide a new means of learning about the emotion-processing mind, personally and in general*

The structures and functions of the emotion-processing mind cannot be appreciated or truly understood in the absence of observable active efforts at adaptation. Thus, the self-process-ing tutorial is a living teaching/learning situation *par excel-lence.*

The educational aims of the process, which give the work its particular cast, create two interrelated goals. The first is to train students in the techniques of self-processing so that they can, after extended tutorial or classroom experience, carry out personal self-processing with some degree of efficiency and success. Inherent to this goal is the effort to afford the student a familiarity with his or her own preferred conscious system defences and resistances, many of them characterological, and an understanding of his or her basic emotional issues and their current and biologically and psychologically genetic determinants.

The second educational goal is to offer the student intellectual knowledge of the basic architecture of the emotion-processing mind and its historical evolution, including a grasp of what these realizations imply for daily functioning — everyday adaptations and maladaptations.

3. *To prevent later symptom formation or decompensation*

Self-processing therapy is unique among healing methods in allowing for both the resolution of existing emotional difficulties and the strengthening of the relatively well-functioning, non-symptomatic individual as a protection against future disturbance. In general medicine, there are established and effective preventative efforts — well-baby clinics, nutritional advisors, annual check-ups, and the like. With the exception of recent efforts towards preventative care for mother/infant dyads, psychotherapy has had little to offer along these lines. The self-processing tutorial is a first step towards filling this void, because it is open to anyone interested in learning about the human mind; it is not limited to individuals with emotional disorders.

THE DISADVANTAGES AND LIMITATIONS OF SELF-PROCESSING THERAPY

I have been emphasizing the many advantages of the self-processing class. I therefore will conclude this chapter by discussing the limitations and mitigating factors that accrue to this paradigm. They stem mainly from the inherently deviant frame aspects of the self-processing class (which need not be the case with the tutorial) and, paradoxically, from the great power of the experience.

The self-processing class of two or more students is usually arranged through some type of frame-deviant recruiting process, and the classes themselves inherently lack total privacy and confidentiality because of the presence of other class members. The effects of these basic departures from the ideal frame — and frame deviations are always harmful in some way — can be counterbalanced, first, by a teacher's maintenance throughout the life of a class of a secured frame for the remaining sectors of the ground rules; second, by interpreting, at suitable moments, the unconscious meanings of any unrectifiable frame alteration; and third, by affording students the experience of *secured-frame moments* — incidents in which a teacher holds the frame in response to efforts by a student to have a ground rule modified and situations in which a frame break is repaired and corrected under the guidance of a student's derivative material (see chapter eight).

These frame-securing interludes provide unusual opportunities to explore and resolve *secured-frame anxieties* and the persecutory aspects of frame modifications — experiences that are crucial to an effective and lasting healing process. The key here lies in the principle that *the self-processing teacher strives to maintain a maximally frame-securing position throughout the duration of a class*. However hurtful, the deviant aspects of the classroom frame also provide salutary healing opportunities because these triggers evoke derivative (encoded) material that would otherwise probably never surface and render them available for interpretive efforts and deep insight.

Frame alterations are much like a double-edged sword — they may evoke regression, acting out, and pathological responses that reinforce a student's pathology, but they also prove to be a powerful stimulus for creative and growth-promoting self-processing exercises and trigger-decoded insights. The critical point is that the self-processing instructor must be aware of a frame modification when it is activated and see to it that it is used as one of the main triggers and organizers of the thematic material in the classroom exercise — and rectified if possible.

Beyond these frame-related considerations, the main limitations and disadvantages of this healing/teaching paradigm are:

1. *Some psychotic individuals will not tolerate self-processing therapy because the derivatives of unconscious meaning that emerge in the class are so primitive and intense that they are experienced as psychologically overwhelming and annihilating.*

These self-processing students also react to the secured frame with inordinate terror, even though it holds them best and most effectively — their sense of danger and entrapment is inordinate. On the other hand, the self-processing class is the most likely setting in which these individuals may be able to tolerate and work over the derivative material and frame issues that dynamically empower their psychopathology.

As yet, there have been no reports of emotional decompensation as the result of a self-processing class. The emotion-processing mind has sufficient resources to cope with the situation — remarkably, the deep unconscious system of the psychotic individual is relatively intact (as it is also with intellectually impaired individuals). Psychotic individuals therefore deserve an opportunity to engage in self-processing therapy to determine whether they can tolerate the procedures and their power; if they can handle their secured-frame anxieties and not run away in dread of the meanings contained within their encoded derivatives, they will benefit greatly from the classroom work.

2. *With rare exceptions, an individual in need of psychotropic medication — and in general, this pertains primarily to psychotic dysfunctions — does not work well in a self-processing class.*

The use of medication is a departure from the ideal frame — cure should be achieved by talk/insight and frame management alone. Still, a student who enters such a class while on medication is in a position to explore deeply the implications and meanings of the use of the drug. On the basis of trigger-decoded understanding, he or she then can choose a suitable course of action. This usually comes down to giving up either the medication or the self-processing classes. Trigger decoding — linking themes to triggers — guides such decisions quite well.

3. *Some individuals with a history of over-intense exposure to death-related experiences and high levels of death anxiety also show a striking dread of the secured elements of the classroom frame and the related encoded expressions of unconscious meaning* (Langs, 1984–85).

Nevertheless, they tolerate the self-processing class far better than communicative therapy or a self-processing tutorial. They are best seen initially in a classroom setting and later, when possible, shifted at the behest of their own corrective derivatives to individual self-processing work.

4. *While self-processing is designed to illuminate the unconscious sources of emotional symptoms, it is not a symptom-focused procedure.*

Therefore, individuals who are overly concerned with a symptomatic dysfunction are, in general, likely to prefer psychotherapy rather than self-processing. On the other hand, there are indications that self-processing therapy is more effective than the usual forms of dynamic psychotherapy, so there is reason to attempt to direct these individuals to a self-processing situation despite their stated preference for the more usual form of treatment.

5. *Because they are defined as students, there is no screening consultation or interview of potential self-processing class members.*

As a result, students with psychotic difficulties or severe affective disorders, and those with psychopathic and dishonest leanings, are not seen in advance of a class, to determine their capacity to carry out and not to interfere with the process. This poses some risk to the overall classroom experience. On the other hand, the prospect of self-processing therapy is sufficiently awesome and fearful to exclude most potentially disruptive members — they are extremely rare.

6.   *As noted, the self-processing class usually is beset with at least two fundamental departures from the ideal frame — the recruitment process, and the presence of other students as third-party figures.*

While much effective healing occurs despite these deviations, detrimental effects do exist and they remain to be fully defined. As noted, the potential harm can be kept to a minimum when a teacher does not deviate further as the seminars unfold and maintains a secured-frame position throughout.

The balance between the negative effects of frame alterations and the positive effects of subsequent frame-securing and interpretive efforts varies from one student to the next. The outcome can range from a highly positive net result, to the destruction of the process and some residual harm to the student. In this light, the ideal termination of a self-processing class would see the students move separately into self-processing tutorials — when possible, with a different teacher, but if necessary with the same one who taught the class.

* * *

Overall, the advantages of self-processing therapy far outweigh their minor drawbacks. Furthermore, the self-processing tutorial has few of these problems and offers a relatively ideal therapy situation for individuals capable of tolerating its secured-frame anxieties and powerful unconscious meanings. With this in mind, let us turn now to the story of how the self-processing paradigm was created.

CHAPTER TWO

The evolution to self-processing

The creation of self-processing therapy followed a tortuous and unplanned path. It was by no means the product of a deliberate search for a new and stronger mode of therapy and self-analysis, though such a need certainly was in the background of these efforts. Instead, it emerged as part of an evolutionary unfolding that began fortuitously with classes offered to both lay people and professionals on "Decoding Your Dreams". These seminars were devoted mainly to studies of the nature of dreams and what they reveal about human coping capacities, the architecture of the mind, and especially its unconscious operations. It was the shift from a university to a private setting for these seminars that set the stage for the gradual changes that led to the relatively well-defined structure and techniques of self-processing therapy and its therapeutic effects.

Because of the strong adaptational position of the communicative approach, there is an unyielding principle that all of its teaching efforts must be based on living exercises. As a result, each of these classes was developed around a dream presented by a student. Given that these were working exercises, the presentation might include additional material that facilitated the processing and our understanding of the dream — associations, triggers, etc. Nevertheless, the dream was centre stage and was used to illustrate general teaching points far more than to illuminate the emotional life of the presenting dreamer.

At first, then, the primary focus was on the dream *per se* and what working with a dream could reveal about its own structure, sources, and functions — and the intricacies of the emotion-processing mind. Not surprisingly, there were occasions when these efforts brought forth a notable deep, trigger-decoded insight into the conflicts and emotional life of the dreamer, but at first this was merely a coincidental happening. Yet as the work continued, there was a slow shift from an overriding focus on the dream *qua* dream towards attention to what the dream explorations were revealing about the presenting students.

With this movement towards greater consideration of the student himself or herself, there was a gradual formalization of the dream-processing effort into what eventually became the tried and true, rather standard, self-processing exercise. As noted earlier, this process came to include not only associations to the dream elements, but also the identification of both the student's self-indicators (emotional issues and classroom frame impingements) and the critical adaptation-evoking triggers for the dream and its evoked associations — the repressed stimuli that had activated the deep unconscious system of the emotion-processing mind and had led to both the self-indicators and the encoded communicative response. Linking the dream-associational network to their triggers emerged as the key source of deep understanding.

Given that the situation was defined as educational, only minimal attention was paid to issues of healing or to classroom conditions. The stress was on a rather naive search for deep unconscious meaning, primarily in the context of the everyday life of the dreamer. Indeed, only persistent attention to the derivative images and to issues of *encoded validation* eventually led to the gradual shift to an appreciation of the overwhelming centrality of the interaction between student and teacher.

A teaching frame was established and maintained in keeping with the usual loosely defined but seemingly appropriate practices for such a situation. With considerable reluctance, interpretive work was slowly and gingerly introduced, although an adaptational/interactional orientation and the use of trigger decoding were characteristic of these efforts from the outset. Included too were attempts to make the teaching and interpretations related to these dreams anything but arbitrary; the use of *encoded* narrative responses to these efforts as a means of testing their validity was borrowed from communicative psychotherapy and seemed to work quite well. These safeguards guided the slow reshaping of the structure of the original class and its teaching methods.

As this all began to fall into place, gradually we confirmed that the disguised themes in the dream-associational complex primarily tend to organize around the teacher's interventions — mainly those related to his or her management of the ground rules of the class. Because we were not engaged in doing therapy, the unsophisticated initial search for triggers had involved probes of the daily life of the presenting dreamer. But this group of evocative stimuli did not work well in eliciting trigger-decoded meanings and they did not obtain encoded (unconscious) validation. The seeming insights generated in this fashion were simplistic, flat, and transparent; they revealed little that was new or surprising — or especially helpful. The work with outside triggers seemed to be based on the relatively easily decoded images that stem from the superficial unconscious rather than the deep unconscious system.

On the other hand, the triggers relating to the teacher's management of the structure and framework of the class organized the thematic material in unexpectedly complex yet, once seen, readily grasped and surprisingly meaningful ways. Indeed, we were quite taken aback to discover the power of frame-related triggers to integrate the material from a dream-processing exercise and we were even more shocked to see the emergence of directives from the second unconscious system to clean up — *rectify* — previously unrecognized contaminated or deviant aspects of the frame of the self-processing class. Social contacts and teaching policies that are taken for granted in all kinds of teaching situations were revealed consistently as dysfunctionally frame deviant and hurtful in the eyes of the deep unconscious mind. Such simple matters as not collecting a fee at the appointed time or a teacher's talking to a student after a class — these and many other generally accepted class-room practices sanctioned by the conscious mind were shown to be disruptive disturbances in the frame of these seminars. In time, the students' derivative messages as triggered by their teacher's evidently lax frame approach and frame-management efforts led to a thorough reassessment of the ground rules of the self-processing class. Using the encoded material from the second unconscious system of the students as our guide, a set of broadly applicable and consistent, unconsciously validated or ideal ground rules emerged — the *optimal secured frame* of the self-processing class was identified (though some aspects literally took years to determine). We confirmed, too, the great power of frame-related triggers to activate unconscious experience and processes, and to influence the emotional lives of all concerned. Frame-related interventions not only led to encoded communicative responses but also unconsciously affected the behaviours and lives of both students and teacher.

The adaptive directives from the second unconscious system unmistakably called for the establishment of a *secured or ideal frame* for the self-processing class. But in addition to helping to create an enhanced frame, the experiences of these classes pointed to a definitive structure for the self-processing exercise itself. Without this structure, conscious system defences and resistances were such that the self-processing efforts repeatedly failed to reach the goal of trigger-decoded insight and suitable frame-management responses. It was becoming clear that the conscious system was designed to preclude such eventualities and was in general unable on its own, despite full resolve, to overcome these basic defensive needs.

While the details of the teaching methodology were being clarified through trial and error, several developments fostered the transition from dream decoding to self-processing therapy. For one, there was a growing realization, mainly through coincidental comments, that the lives of the participants in these seminars were changing in significant ways for the better. There had been no therapeutic intention to these endeavours, but genuine therapeutic effects were occurring nonetheless — regardless of our conscious intentions, nature was having its say.

We also confirmed that the self-processing exercise had an optimal frame and an ideal form — structures that facilitated the possibility of reaching trigger-decoded insights. The need to build the process around the initial report of a dream found considerable support, because it was discovered that this approach greatly facilitated the associational effort and optimized the possibility of generating strong and cogent encoded images and themes. Additional elements were added to the process as necessity dictated. But the main factor in these further developments was the burgeoning realization that, as is true of psychotherapy, a patient's narrative, encoded material does indeed reflect the responsiveness of the deep unconscious system to the teacher's frame-related efforts — the ground rules, frames, and boundaries of the teaching situation were firmly established as a crucial factor in the learning experience and its therapeutic potential.

THE TWO SYSTEMS OF THE EMOTION-PROCESSING MIND

Drawing on insights derived from self-processing itself, we began to understand some of the reasons why the ground rules of the self-processing class play such a crucial role in the teaching and learning experience. There are, as noted, two systems of the emotion-processing mind. The first is a *conscious system that has its own superficial unconscious subsystem*—a subsystem of preconscious and repressed unconscious processes and images that are relatively easily accessed by the conscious mind, directly or via the undoing of rather simple disguise. In essence, the conscious system operates via conscious feelings and thoughts — essentially through direct or manifest representations.

The situation is somewhat complicated in that the superficial unconscious subsystem is capable of sending forth sudden and unexpected insights and intuitions that are mistaken for deep unconscious wisdom. These direct realizations do not require trigger decoding to be comprehended — they are manifest rather than encoded insights; they are, however, in their naiveté very appealing to the well-defended conscious system. In addition, the superficial unconscious subsystem imparts minimally encoded images that reflect its silent workings, but these disguised messages are relatively simple to decipher; they lack the twists and intricacies, and the element of astonishment that is typical of deep unconscious insight.

For example, the superficial unconscious subsystem will encode a self-processing teacher's lateness by alluding in a dream or an association to a dream to the lateness of a parent or another teacher. Or a self-processing teacher's increasing his or her fee will be encoded in an image of a merchant who suddenly increases his prices. The relevant trigger-decoding efforts are based on adaptation-evoking triggers that are conscious and deal with meanings of these triggers that are self-evident. In addition, the linking of triggers to themes is relatively straightforward and unremarkable, and the decoded message is commonplace and hardly revealing.

The conscious system has evolved primarily to insure and enhance chances of personal survival. As such, the system optimizes capabilities related to the perception of real danger, and the development of modes of physical and psychological self-protection and defence, as well as survival skills such as the means of finding suitable food, protection, shelter, companionship, and the like. In general, while low levels of emotional impingement may enhance the conscious system's survival efforts and adaptations, the system is so delicate and easily unbalanced that most emotional encroachments threaten to disturb its equilibrium and functioning.

Because of this vulnerability and the massiveness of the inputs to which the conscious system is called on to adapt, evolution has favoured the creation of a second processing system for coping with emotionally charged impingements — a deep unconscious system that operates without awareness and thereby safeguards the conscious system from energy drainage and the danger of system overload. At the receptive end, this second unconscious system automatically receives a wide range of overcharged incoming stimuli that never register consciously; it also takes in via unconscious or subliminal perception many disturbing implications and meanings of manifestly noticed inputs that readily would disturb conscious system functioning.

Once unconsciously registered, this information and meaning is processed via a deep unconscious system of great intelligence and adaptive capabilities — *the deep unconscious wisdom system*. And because this system deals with information and meaning whose manifest realization would render the conscious system dysfunctional, evolution has provided *no access to direct awareness* for these adaptive efforts.

The deep wisdom system is, nonetheless, under evident pressure to communicate the nature of its experiences and adaptive solutions *in some form* to its own conscious system and that of others. To do this, the human mind has been designed by evolution to disguise or encode this information in narratives that pertain to situations other than the one that is being adapted to. *Displacement and disguise* are the key means through which we *bring into awareness in encoded form* the workings of the deep unconscious part of our minds. In essence, the deeply unconscious reactions to *situation (trigger) A* are encoded in a story about *situation (trigger) B*.

Because it is encoded, this information and insight cannot be recruited by the conscious system for adaptive responses. Trigger decoding alone — giving undisguised meaning to disguised themes in light of their adaptation-evoking stimuli — can bring this much-needed resource into awareness and render it available for coping responses. Indeed, because displacement and disguise play such a significant role in how the deep unconscious system operates and affects our lives, many emotionally charged behaviours and symptoms arise because an adaptive response has been displaced from its proper stimulus and mistakenly applied elsewhere — defensive adaptation leads to maladaptation. We therefore pay a great price for protecting and insuring conscious system survival-oriented functioning.

The expanding comprehension of the architecture of the emotion-processing mind had a significant role in the emerging design of the self-processing work and in the interpretative and frame-management efforts of its teachers. We discovered that the conscious system is allied with a *deeply unconscious fear/*

guilt system that speaks for morbid forms of death anxiety and for deep needs for punishment for crimes and misdeeds — real, fantasied, and borrowed from key family figures — that exist in all humans. Death is, of course, the existential frame of life; as a result, secured frames, however enhancing they may be, always arouse personal death anxiety and the need to cope with its ramifications. On the other hand, modifying frames allows for grandiose illusions of being able to defy the inevitability of death — though they do so at considerable (usually denied) cost because deviant frames also are persecutory and disruptive in nature.

As a result of these various factors, the conscious system tends to ignore or be cavalier about rules, frames, and boundaries — it is *frame insensitive* (which accounts for the seemingly alien qualities for many readers of discussions of this aspect of psychotherapy and self-processing — and life in general). In addition, the conscious system tends to favour defensiveness in the emotional realm and therefore will in general advocate and rationalize in favour of frame modifications rather than frame-securing efforts.

But matters are very different in the second unconscious system. There, the remarkably valuable attributes of secured frames are deeply appreciated. It is well understood that such frames are ego-enhancing, the basis for effective learning and for emotional health, essential for sound family and other social structures, promoters of peace and growth — and far more. Thus, the encoded messages from the deep unconscious system, as they reflect the adaptive preferences of that system, will always stand opposed to deviant conscious system choices and speak for secured frames. Derivative material will always confirm frame-securing interventions — be they by a therapist, teacher, parent, or whomever. They also will always fail to validate frame alterations and will speak to the pathological unconscious needs reflected in such efforts.

There is strong evidence that deep rather than superficial unconscious processing is the most powerful influence on our emotional lives. It follows, then, that encoded material, rather than manifest contents, is the best guide to how a frame should be established and managed. In time, trigger-decoded derivative expressions served this role admirably for dream-decoding classes, and the result was that the deviant aspects of the classroom frame eventually were secured to the greatest extent possible. This placed us on the threshold of self-processing efforts and the therapy it would sustain.

A DISTINGUISHING FEATURE
OF THE TWO SYSTEMS OF THE MIND

As I have indicated, the adaptive positions of the two systems of the emotion-processing mind — conscious and deeply unconscious — are often diametrically opposed. This arises in large measure because in the emotional domain, the conscious system is primarily defensive and fearful of encoded meaning and secured frames, while the deep unconscious system essentially is non-defended, open to meaning, and strongly in favour of non-deviant frames. It is important to understand, as noted earlier, that the emotion-processing mind is *not* organized as a single system with conscious and unconscious components, but instead is constituted as two surprisingly separate and disparate systems with little integration.

This brings us to another important realization that emerged in the course of the developing self-processing efforts. As suggested earlier, the remarkable adaptive design of the conscious system is such that this system can meaningfully and consciously not only deal with immediate situations, but also can turn to and work over past experiences and anticipate future events and probabilities. It is not fixed in its operations to the concrete images drawn from its present perceptions, but may conjure up, imagine, and move about among images related to the past, present, and future and may seek to resolve conflicts and dilemmas related to any of these time frames.

This ability to anticipate, remember, and imagine is entirely lacking or minimally developed in non-humans and appears to be a very favourable evolutionary development in that it frees the human organism from enslavement to the immediate present. In times of emergency, of course, the functioning of the conscious system collapses entirely onto the present moment (and deep unconscious system processing largely is abated to maximize conscious system responsiveness and coping), though automatically the conscious system will draw upon past experiences stored in the superficial unconscious subsystem as an aid in responding to an acutely stressful situation.

Matters again are very different for the second unconscious system. This system is like vision: it sees only the present and when it draws upon the past or future, the images are more vaguely registered, not capable of evoking a primary adaptive reaction and mainly conjured up in response to and connection with an immediate emotional adaptive task. In addition, a student's deep unconscious system does not respond to the intended surface meanings of a teacher's interventions, but is focused instead exclusively on the *unconscious implications* of these efforts — especially those that are frame-related and that affect the level of addressed meaning (unencoded or encoded). *Frame and meaning in the here and now* are the domains of the second unconscious system.

This insight has important clinical ramifications. If you work in therapy in terms of the operations of the conscious system and its superficial unconscious subsystem, you can justify explorations that pertain to relationships outside of therapy and arrive at superficial insights — a common approach in today's therapeutic work. But you will never influence the deep unconscious system, nor will you obtain encoded validation of your interventions.

A therapist may ask a patient to understand consciously a happening outside of therapy, and the conscious system will do so. But all the while, the deep unconscious system will be processing the unconscious implications of the therapist's request that the patient work over the outside relationship in terms of manifest rather than encoded contents (the issue of level of addressed meaning), and also will be processing the meanings of the therapist's avoidance of the immediate interaction within the therapy and activities related to its ground rules and frame. As a result, even as the patient consciously cooperates with the therapist and tells a *manifest* story of an incident outside of the therapy, he or she is simultaneously *encoding* a story about the immediate interaction with that same therapist within the treatment setting.

As indicated, the deep unconscious system monitors two facets of a therapist's interventions seldom addressed by the conscious system. The first is the therapist's preferences regarding the expression of encoded material — essentially whether or not a therapist avoids manifest-content interventions and consistently trigger-decodes the patient's material or, in contrast, treats the material in terms of its manifest contents and their implications. The second is the already noted management of the ground rules of the treatment experience. Both of these areas pertain to the immediate situation.

Clearly, the work you do in therapy and your understanding of the emotion-processing mind is entirely different depending on which system you work and observe with — the conscious system alone, or conscious functioning in light of deep unconscious processing. In practical terms, this difference is based on formulating direct meanings and their implications in a patient's communications versus consistently trigger decoding the same manifest themes as the bearers of encoded messages. These unfolding insights guided the negotiation of the path to self-processing therapy.

THE CONTRIBUTION FROM FORMAL SCIENCE

There was one other major factor in the early development of this new paradigm. It operated almost entirely outside of awareness and was recognized only in retrospect. It involved efforts to develop a formal science of psychoanalysis — a mathematically based quantitative science replete with laws and deep effects. This pursuit was unfolding at the same time that the transition to self-processing therapy was taking place (for summaries of this work, see Langs, 1992e; Langs & Badalamenti, 1992a, 1992b, in press).

It proved possible to identify several stochastic or probabilistic and three deterministic deep laws of emotionally charged communication — laws of entropy, work, and temperature. The research also was able quantitatively to define the degree of deep stability in therapeutic dialogues and to measure the extent of deep influence between patients and therapists. Considerable insight was garnered into the naturally lawful work-ings of the emotion-processing mind and the properties of its communications — and of the therapeutic interaction as well. This work was conceptualized as tapping into a level of experi-ence deeper than that of unconscious processing — we called it *deeper nature* (Langs & Badalamenti, 1992a, 1992b).

Among the many facets of this work that affected self-processing, the first came from a comparative study of six different psychoanalysts who carried out psychotherapy con-sultations with five different women patients whose therapies were stalemated. The results of this sub-study revealed that the therapists who worked in keeping with communicative principles produced the sessions that measurably were most stable, most powerful, showed by far the greatest interactive influence, allowed for the greatest complexity in how patients expressed themselves, and left the patient at the end of the consultation with the greatest amount of available inner en-ergy — energy that may well be the basis for inner structural change (Badalamenti & Langs, 1992a, 1992b).

The key factor in these results appeared to be the *relative silence* of the communicative therapist. That is, silent listening greatly facilitated the extent to which patients utilized commu-nicative vehicles that were likely to be carriers of powerful unconscious meanings. In contrast, the relatively active inter-ventions of the other analysts significantly reduced their patient's use of such material. *Silence on the part of a therapist emerged as a critical facilitator of unconscious expression.*

These studies also clarified the kind of material that carries encoded meaning. The five dimensions of therapeutic dialogues that were quantified for this research were measures of *commu-nicative vehicle* and *not* measures of contents or meaning. The *mode or form of expression* — *how* things were said, *not what* it was about — was the key to this research and its quantita-tive findings. That is, the vicissitudes of the means by which humans express themselves in emotionally charged dialogues (we later studied non-therapy couples and monologues as well) is deeply lawful and appears to be an inherent natural property of human language and the human mind.

On a line-by-line basis, we quantified the newness of themes, the extent of narrative (versus the use of intellectualizations), the degree of positive and of negative tone to the images, and the degree of continuity of the dialogue. It became clear that essentially we were quantifying *the vicissitudes of narrative versus non-narrative (intellectualized) expression*, and that this in turn was a measure of an individual's rotation in and out of communications rich in derivative or encoded meaning (narratives) or poor in such meaning (non-narrative speculations, analyses, and such). This postulate was validated through a correlational study with a second, independently arrived at measure of the degree of unconscious expression called *referential activity* (Langs et al., 1993). Indeed, this classification of communicative vehicles into *narrative (encoded)* and *non-narrative (unencoded)* forms is one of the most vital realizations to emerge from the research and from the clinical communicative approach and its self-processing paradigm.

The main effects of this insight on self-processing efforts were, first, that the dream, because it usually is narrative in form, was reaffirmed as an excellent communicative vehicle with which to initiate self-processing efforts. It became clear too that the dream functioned extremely well *as a source of associations* — of so-called *guided associations*, because they are not free to move about at will but are required to return again and again to elements of the dream. Indeed, the associations to dreams were found to embody themes that are, with few exceptions, far more compelling than those in a manifest dream *per se* and far stronger than those generated by free associating. The use of recent dreams as source narratives — *origination narratives* — for guided associations was thereby well established. The key insight was that in the search for deep meaning, *dreams are dreamt to be associated to rather than to be analysed.*

In addition, the research clarified and confirmed the communicative principle that any type of narrative material is likely to function as the carrier of encoded meaning. Thus, a story composed by a self-processing student could serve as well as a dream as an origination narrative — and as a source of guided associations. This meant that anyone could participate actively in self-processing classes, even people who did not remember their dreams. In all, these studies firmly established the importance of narrative communication for conveying unconscious meaning and for revealing the adaptive processes of the second unconscious system.

The research also contributed to the structure of the self-processing class by demonstrating mathematically the power of therapist's silence to enhance deep unconscious or encoded communication in patients. As a result, the first forty minutes of each class were turned over to the presenting student and the class, without comment from the instructor — the power of therapist silence was recruited for the self-processing class. This measure had the coincidental effect of providing a remarkable field of observation for both students and teacher — a study of the vicissitudes of how students go about pursuing the conscious realization of their own unconscious processes and trigger-decoded insights. We quickly learned that the conscious mind has been designed to do just about anything else — it would take a great deal of motivation and effort to alter its strong, if not somewhat fixed, defensive preferences.

In all, then, the research had a most salutary influence in helping us to find an optimal form for the self-processing class and its exercises. It was quite fortuitous that the two efforts — the formal research, and the development of self-processing therapy — coincided in time. Self-processing would have been much the poorer were it not for the formal science research findings.

AN EXCERPT FROM A SELF-PROCESSING CLASS

Having covered so much territory related to self-processing, let us pause to take a brief look at a consultation that bridges from formal psychotherapy to self-processing therapy. This will afford us a clinical sense of some of the ideas presented to this point in the book. The excerpt is taken from a self-processing consultation carried out by an inexperienced male self-processing teacher, Dr. Ball, who was a clinical psychologist.

Mrs. Cline called Dr. Ball and asked for a consultation, to which Dr. Ball acceded without investigating the source of the referral. Mrs. Cline began the consultation hour by describing the depression that had prompted her to seek help. Then, rather casually, she revealed that she was the cousin of one of Dr. Ball's current patients. Shifting to another subject, she went on to detail aspects of her early life history. She spoke of a vacation she had taken with several close family relatives. She and her cousin Sally had slept in the same room and they had engaged in sex play. Her uncle Frank had flirted with both her and Sally; family lore had it that he had committed incest with his daughter. Mrs. Cline's father, who is Frank's brother, had been openly seductive with her when she was an early adolescent and on one occasion had fondled her breasts.

Somehow, she continued, men had always come on to her — and they did it now even though she was married. There must be some way she gives off signals to these men, but she didn't know how. The time had come for her to figure all of this out so she could stop doing whatever she was doing and clean up her act.

To discuss this vignette briefly, the key adaptation-evoking *trigger* here is the therapist's departure from the ideal frame by seeing two cousins in any form of therapy. This situation violates the unconsciously defined, validated rules of the total privacy and confidentiality needed for psychotherapy and self-processing therapy, and modifies the restriction that therapy be carried out on a one-to-one basis (unconsciously, the cousin is experienced consistently as being in the room with the patient). The deviation arose because the therapist made the error of not asking his potential patient how she got his name — a query that should be made during all initial telephone calls. This frame-altering trigger had evoked Mrs. Cline's encoded narrative material — the story of the family trip is a dream equivalent.

In the session, *consciously* Mrs. Cline was attempting to tell Dr. Ball the nature and history of her symptoms — her conscious adaptive task was focused mainly on her personal life outside of the consultation, past and present. Simultaneously, her narrative tale *unconsciously* encoded her reactions to Dr. Ball's inadvertent departure from the ideal frame — the unconscious adaptive task was focused entirely on his deviant frame-related intervention.

For her part, manifestly and consciously, Mrs. Cline had sought this consultation knowing quite well that her cousin was in therapy with Dr. Ball. Her choice of therapist had, however, unknowingly and unconsciously been orchestrated by pathological unconscious needs related to death anxiety (loss is denied in threesomes by the survival of two of the members in face of the disappearance of the third member) and unconscious guilt (this particular frame is self-destructive and hurtful to all concerned). Nonetheless, *consciously* Mrs. Cline had ignored the frame-related aspects of her therapy except for the passing mention of her cousin and an expression of her gratitude that Dr. Ball had seen her so quickly. The typical use of defensive denial and repression by the conscious system in respect to frame alterations, and the system's preference for modified frames, were quite in evidence.

The situation was, as proposed earlier, very different for the second unconscious system as reflected in the same stories through which this patient presented her early history. To trigger-decode and interactionally interpret this material, the themes in these stories must be extracted from their manifest contexts and then transposed or linked to their latent evocative frame-deviant trigger — the repressed adaptation-evoking context. Thus, the therapist's unwitting decision to see two cousins in therapy had provoked unconscious perceptions of him as seductive and as creating an incestuous *ménage à trois*. He was in this symbolic but real way repeating a series of past pathogenic traumas that had involved the patient, her uncle and her father, and a different cousin. Indeed, although orchestrated by the patient, the therapist unwittingly had made the two cousins he was seeing into a homosexual couple — alterations in the frame are consistently experienced unconsciously as sexually tinged.

These are real but unconscious meanings that are inherent to this frame alteration that *selectively* have been perceived and processed by this patient's second unconscious system. That is, patients adaptive reactions are an amalgam of the implications of the actual stimulus on the one hand and, on the other, the patient's sensitivities and selective responsiveness.

The patient's inner needs and life history interact with the actual nature of the stimulus to produce a personally selective but valid unconscious perception of particular aspects of an evocative trigger. The responsive images are constituted as valid unconscious perceptions of the implications or meanings of the frame-breaking intervention — meanings that affect the emotional life of the patient (and therapist). Characteristically, a patient's conscious response to a frame modification is defensive and remarkably constricted, while the deep unconscious response is richly complex, expansive, and insightful — though conveyed in encoded fashion.

In addition to detailing the patient's encoded perceptions of her therapist in light of his frame deviation, it is critical secondarily to treat this material along the *me/not-me interface* (Langs, 1992a, 1992b [1978]) — i.e., as condensing into the same images the patient's encoded perceptions of herself as well those of her therapist. Mrs. Cline led the way in this respect by noting that somehow she set up inappropriately seductive liaisons — much as she did in choosing Dr. Ball as her therapist. The themes therefore also are linked to the patient's own frame-deviant behaviour (although consciously the patient had no idea she was breaking a frame, in her deep unconscious wisdom system she did know this was the case). Her frame break also reflects her own needs for incestuous, homosexual, and frame-violating liaisons — key unconscious factors in her choice of Dr. Ball.

Without awareness of the unconscious meanings of her own and Dr. Ball's frame-related behaviours, the patient, who was not seen again in light of her encoded frame-securing directive that it was time for her to stop acting like this, would only seek out another inappropriately frame-breaking therapist. Indeed, part of the adaptive processing of the second unconscious system involves developing and conveying the best available intervention under the circumstances. In this case, the choice was to forego therapy because the key frame deviation was unrectifiable — it could not be undone. This decision, which was based on the patient's own encoded material, is far more adaptive and healthy than Mrs. Cline's conscious inclination, which was to enter therapy with Dr. Ball — a move that would have had disastrous consequences for her emotional life.

A final note on the vignette. Dr. Ball interpreted Mrs. Cline's material along the lines indicated here and rectified the frame by using her disguised directive to not see her again — to stop his incestuously seductive behaviour and clean up his act. The patient responded by remembering a friend's father, a man who was very different from her own father. He was warm and yet respectful, and he allowed Mrs. Cline and his daughter to be together on their own without interfering. One time Mrs. Cline went on vacation with their family and the friend's father saw to it that the two girls had separate beds; nothing at all seductive went on.

This response is identified as *interpersonal unconscious or encoded validation* of the therapist's intervention through the emergence in a responsive narrative of a well-functioning individual who respected privacy and the frame. While many therapists, thinking only in terms of manifest contents and conscious experience, would believe that Mrs. Cline would feel rejected by Dr. Ball's decision not to see her again, under these frame-deviant circumstances, this is never the response of the deep unconscious system. As reflected in the narrative images, her second unconscious system saw this intervention in an exceedingly positive and caring light. Here, too, conscious and unconscious experience are radically different — a consciously felt dismissal is seen unconsciously as a sign of deep caring and respect.

We can conjecture too that Ms. Cline probably benefited from an inevitable positive introjective identification with a therapist who could utilize her narrative material to acknowledge, interpret, and rectify his frame break and error — something her uncle and father never did. She would also profit from experiencing a secured-frame moment. Securing the frame of this therapy was indeed, the most caring and healing intervention that Dr. Ball could make under the circumstances. To have done otherwise would have been to continue psychologically with a *ménage à trois* and to commit incest with his patient.

* * *

This excerpt affords a brief sense of the clinical observations that informed the development of the techniques and theory of self-processing therapy. The material illustrates the listening–

formulating–interpreting process; the concentration of the second unconscious system on the here-and-now with the therapist and especially on his or her handling of the ground rules and frame of therapy; the search for the indirect, encoded validation of all interventions; the very different conscious and unconscious reactions to frame alterations; the constructive role of frame-securing interventions — and more.

I hope too that this excerpt shows that although self-processing has a distinctly psychoanalytic heritage, it is not a theory-based effort at analysis nor does it embrace much of psychoanalytic jargon and mythology. The methods of self-processing are forthright and readily described; they are neither esoteric nor elitist. Many obstacles to effective self-processing are evident on the surface — there is a clear set of guidelines — and they can be modified and corrected through conscious effort. While some knowledge of psychodynamics is helpful for the interpretative comments of the teacher, there is a naturalistic and phenomenological quality to self-processing that makes it possible for any trained mental health professional to learn how to apply its techniques and reach deeply into the unconscious domain. With this as our introduction to the clinical worlds of psychotherapy and self-processing, let us turn now to the basic methodology of this ' .tter process.*

----

*With due respect for the privacy and confidentiality of the self-processing situation, the vignettes in this book are fictional narratives that nonetheless are faithful to reality. As is true of all clinical excerpts, they are offered solely as illustrations of the ideas presented in the book. Any reader who adopts the methods of listening and formulating of the communicative approach and its self-processing techniques will quickly discover for himself or herself the incredible world of the second unconscious system that is at the heart of this book.

PART TWO

COMMUNICATION:
LISTENING AND FORMULATING

CHAPTER THREE

The surface message

Thehere are many ways to think about and conceptualize the healing process. Psychodynamics, interaction, object relations, intersubjectivity, self and self-object, transference, countertransference, trauma, cognitive issues — these and many other concepts are used as leading edges into understanding psychotherapy and creating its methods.

Reflection shows, however, that fundamental to these diverse attempts to conceptualize the therapeutic process is *human communication*. All of the concepts brought to bear on the therapy situation are extractions and inferences made from examined behaviour — in substance, from observations of the conditions of therapy and the communicative exchanges, verbal and non-verbal, between patients and their therapists.

Given that all healing is transacted through communication, it behoves us to turn now to the fundamentals of human expression so they may serve as the clinical basis for the development of the self-processing methods to be offered in this book. This is a rather natural way to proceed because the process itself evolved through a deep understanding of human communication in its many intricacies and nuances.

Our goal, then, is to comprehend the therapeutic interaction in a manner that gives meaning, depth, explanation, prediction, insight, sensibility, and healing power to the therapeutic process. Our focus will be on the nature of human communication and the unique capacity of human language to embody simultaneously two basic levels of expression and meaning — one visible, the other so camouflaged as to render it almost invisible despite its many effects on our emotional lives.

The first level of meaning is *direct and manifest*, conveyed by means of surface messages that are fraught with *implications* — some consciously registered, some not. The second level is *indirect and encoded*; it is *disguised* within certain types of manifest contents, rather than *implied by the surface* — a distinction of great importance (see below).

In our pursuit of *unconscious meaning*, we will confine ourselves to exploring and formulating primarily the *verbal aspects* of communication. Because our ultimate search is for *identifiable unconscious meaning*, with few exceptions, we will leave aside the non-verbal elements of human expression such as intonation, body movement, facial expression, affects, seeming experiences of projective identification, and the like. Although each has a role in emotional life, they are all uncertain and secondary conveyors of *unconscious messages*.

This decision is strongly supported by both clinical experience and the formal research described in chapter two. The latter studies showed that the investigation of verbal communication alone — the use of narrative and non-narrative forms of expression — carries sufficient meaning and power to account lawfully and predictively for much of emotional experience (Langs, 1992e; Langs & Badalamenti, 1992a, 1992b, in press).

MANIFEST CONTENTS

All verbalized communications have a surface, *a manifest or directly stated meaning* (I leave aside gibberish and the like). This surface has considerable relevance to emotional issues, and, for reasons of evolved basic structure and psychodynamics, most people — including students and teachers — tend to confine themselves to this level of meaning when attempting to understand and respond to emotionally charged communications.

In general, however, individuals do not simply limit themselves to the cold direct message, shorn of all nuance. Instead, they inherently go beyond bare manifest contents and respond automatically to the *implications* of these surface contents as part of their essential experience of a message. The capacity to experience and extract the implications of surface messages developed quite early in the evolution of language (Bickerton, 1990) and is a basic component of how we consciously attend to incoming information and meaning.

Manifest messages *per se* carry considerable weight. They speak directly of and to emotional issues and stand squarely in the arena of *conscious* awareness, intention, and experience, as well as direct thought and decision making. Conscious messages are vital to how we adapt to consciously registered stimuli or triggers, emotional and otherwise. Someone tells us that, or behaves as if, they love us or are angry with us, and we listen to the surface of the comment or directly experience the behaviour; we try to understand its basis and logic; and then we decide — again manifestly and consciously — how to respond or adapt. Clearly, the immediate negotiation of social relationships, situations of threat and danger, life decisions, and many practical and emotional issues and choices — and far more — are all based on manifest contents and our assessment of their meanings and implications.

Attention to the surface of messages is a critical means of insuring personal safety, satisfactions, and survival (of the individual and the species) and is essential for dealing with immediate and long-term life problems and relationships. Self-awareness and self-reflection are grounded in analysing and comprehending manifest messages and in effecting surface realizations and responses. Manifest contents are responses to known triggers and fall into the domain of the conscious system; attention to surface messages promotes personal survival.

LIMITATIONS OF MANIFEST FORMULATIONS

There are, however, major limitations to negotiating life in terms of manifest contents alone. In the emotional domain, many maladaptive behaviours and disturbances cannot be anticipated or adequately explained on the basis of known triggers or surface messages and conscious thinking — i.e., through the direct processing of information and meaning. In addition, there are profound limitations to our abilities to self-observe, self-explore, and self-comprehend directly; these vital capabilities are subject to inner-directed perceptual and other unconscious defences that render them highly unreliable as a guide to self-knowledge and adaptive choices.

Still another problem with confining oneself to manifest contents stems from the basic limitations of conscious perception and the existence of major outer-directed perceptual defences, and the extensive use of denial and repression, found in every human being. Perceptual distortion and misperception of one's own and other people's surface communications — most of it based on conscious and unconscious conflict and anxiety, and the evolved design of the mind — are far more common than generally realized; they render conscious experience a rather unreliable observational base in the emotional domain. Conscious registrations and the readings of surface messages also are highly biased. Emotionally charged impingements and meanings are often denied or otherwise barred from awareness, narrowing the knowledge-base of surface communication and thereby restricting adaptive choices and responses.

Another constricting factor arises because the conscious system of the mind can process only very limited amounts of information and meaning in any given span of time without suffering from system overload and dysfunction. The conscious system must therefore limit incoming impingements with nonconscious gating mechanisms to insure smooth functioning, thereby reducing both the amount of input and the scope and range of conscious experience. These constraints are especially strong for emotionally charged information and meaning because of their high levels of conflict and energy requirements; the conscious system can work over emotionally charged messages in only small and very limited doses. Repeatedly, a conscious response to an emotionally charged trigger is constricted, minimal, and dense, while the deep unconscious reaction is elaborate and highly knowledgeable.

Finally, the roles of *unconscious* experience, meaning, needs, and motives are, by definition, excluded from surface formulations and direct responses. The demonstration of unnoticed or unconscious surface patterns and connections is a meagre resource, with little power to modify an emotional symptom or truly resolve an emotional issue. Nevertheless, this level of experience and of processing information and meaning does affect the quality of human life and the vicissitudes of direct emotional coping. While we must respect the importance of the realm of direct messages and conscious experience, we must also concede its limitations in enabling us to understand human emotional life and the psychological healing process.

THE ISSUE OF VALIDATION

In all, the surface or manifest contents of human communication are a limited and insufficient basis for predicting and understanding emotionally charged behaviours and both successful adaptations and psychological dysfunctions. While this need not imply that healing must extend beyond manifest expressions — conscious system work can within limits, though only at times, override unconscious experience — it does indicate that an in-depth and relatively thorough comprehension of human expression requires going well beyond the surface façade. It seems too that it is wise not to trust the conscious system as a confirming instrument for a therapist's formulations and interventions — it is far too defensively aligned and misleading to serve that purpose. This means that we cannot rely on direct and manifest responses to a teacher's interventions for indications of their validity — something less direct and in some sense deeper is required.

It is essential, then, to allow the deep unconscious system to be the arbitrator of the validity of an intervention. This means that we must use a non-manifest or unconscious means of confirming self-processing interventions and the theory on which they are based. The listening–formulating–intervening–validating process that we will develop certainly must take notice of conscious responses, but the final word has to come from the second unconscious system via indirect or encoded confirmation or non-confirmation. Without this kind of safeguard — however vulnerable to error and coloured by human judgement it too may be — arbitrary formulations are likely to dominate the picture and, with them, confusion in both theory and practice. *Unconscious or encoded validation* is the best tool we have to guide us through the confusing maze of human communication and its meanings.

A CLINICAL VIGNETTE

It will be helpful to sample a brief vignette from a self-processing session to illustrate and develop our discussion of the various levels of listening and formulating that can be applied to the data of human communication.

> Ms. Gold was a single woman of thirty in a self-processing class with Mr. Dean, a social worker. As the presenting student, she began one session by saying that she had had a dream the previous night in which her cousin Arthur had cornered her in his house and had tried to touch her breasts. She went on to say that Arthur always had been aggressive with women, including herself, and that she thought that it was partly because of him that she has had such mistrust of and problems with men. The evening before the dream an attractive man she had met at a party had come on to her and she had immediately felt cornered and rejected him even though she realized afterwards that she had acted precipitously and actually had found him quite attractive.
>
> Continuing, Ms. Gold remembered a time when another cousin, James, had tried to get her, as a teenager, to go to bed with him. She had been visiting him and he wouldn't

let her go home. Only when she had begun to cry and got hysterical had he allowed her to leave. The odd thing about the experience was that she has fixed in her mind an image of a miniature replica of the Eiffel Tower that he had on the top of his dresser.

Shifting topics, Ms. Gold said that she thought that the self-processing class had run over the previous week. She liked that because it meant that Mr. Dean had been so absorbed in the class that he had lost track of time.

It requires little effort to identify and formulate the manifest contents of this excerpt. They begin with a dream of seduction by a cousin that leads to a formulation by Ms. Gold herself that his seductiveness was a factor in her problems with men. Next, Ms. Gold, following a logical surface path, speaks of the man she rejected because she felt cornered — illustrating her difficulties in letting men get close to her. She then recalls an incident with another cousin in which a sexual overture actually had been made; it involved an attempt at, and escape from, seduction and entrapment by the cousin. Finally, there is a shift to an allusion to the self-processing class and its extension the previous week — which Ms. Gold saw consciously in a positive light.

Notice that in defining manifest contents we simply reiterate, summarize, or essentially restate the surface of an extended communication. We may make note of the trigger for the sequence and of the selection and sequence of images and themes, and of evident patterns, but the surface is, of course, the surface. A dream of seduction leads to a memory of entrapment and seduction, which is connected to the dreamer's mistrust of men and a specific instance in which that mistrust was activated. This incident appears to be the *conscious trigger* for the dream and Ms. Gold's associations. The pattern of feeling entrapped by men and needing to put them off is also evident on the surface. It is, however, a problem that Ms. Gold had long been aware of. Even if this were not the case, pointing out this pattern to her would imply an entirely intrapsychic conflict and would not involve anything more than a broad issue of adapting to relationships with men. The interpretation would lack the specificity and interactive responsiveness that characterize the functioning of the emotion-processing mind and would fail to identify the *repressed triggers* that lay beneath this relatively transparent surface.

Finally, the reference to the instructor's extending the class seems disconnected from the earlier material in that it is not manifestly seductive, nor is it in any way directly connected to the prior images. It is, on the surface, a *non sequitur*.

On the manifest level of formulation, we seldom consider hidden or disguised connections. In particular, the idea that there may be a concealed link between the two sets of disparate images or themes — one related to the cousins and the man, the other to the teacher — involves a connection that is unobservable on the surface. This implies that there is a severe limitation to listening and formulating when they are restricted to direct, surface contents. In any case, the effort seems to be rather naive, self-evident, and incomplete — genuine understanding calls for something more.

It is difficult to confine oneself to pristine surface themes and images in analysing a communication. As noted, the human mind tends naturally to complete and embellish images, and it is inclined to immediately experience or sense the implications of these images. Nonetheless, the surface of a message is an important marker. It tells us where a person is at, so to speak, including the nature of his or her emotional problems and solutions — and a lot more.

For example, the surface of Ms. Gold's material indicates that she is concerned with seduction and entrapment, that she has been subjected to seductive pressures from two of her cousins, that she has problems relating to men, and that she was pleased when her teacher extended the previous self-processing class.

These are mostly weighty concerns, and many people would be content to have unearthed these manifest issues, feeling that now at last Ms. Gold knows what her problems are. But the difficulty is that she already knew this information before alluding to it in class, and she even had some ideas about why she was suffering — but nothing had changed and no new solutions had materialized.

Technically, surface material generally alludes to consciously known, emotionally charged triggers — here, the man's come on at the party — and the evident dynamic and genetic issues that they arouse. The response often includes directly proposed solutions, most of them relatively simplistic. In this case, the self-indicator — the student's emotional problem — is loosely defined as difficulties with men and then specifically as impulsively rejecting the interest of an attractive man. The manifest, known trigger is the man's advances, and Ms. Gold's seemingly maladaptive response was withdrawal. All this is rather direct and uncomplicated, hardly the stuff of unconscious communication and meaning. Yet it does describe an adaptive sequence, so we are forewarned that while the conscious system tends to be vague about triggers, when it does recognize an adaptation-evoking stimulus it deals with that trigger in a straightforward manner. By definition and design, the conscious system has no awareness or direct response to repressed triggers, which, as we will see, are registered and experienced unconsciously and processed without awareness playing a role.

The healer who confines himself or herself to these surface images would be obligated simply to discuss these problems with Ms. Gold and to suggest directly ways that she could try to modify her present difficulties with men. The likelihood that this approach would have only limited effects is suggested by the fact that Ms. Gold herself is quite conscious of almost everything that could be said to her on this level — e.g., that her difficulties with men are connected to the earlier sexual overtures of her cousins. There is little more that a manifest-content healer could add to that formulation, even though this seeming insight had not enabled Ms. Gold to modify her difficulties in that area.

The manifest-content teacher would also have no substantial explanation as to why Mr. Dean's extension of the class appeared in this sequence of material — on a manifest level, it does not fit with the prior images. One would be compelled to see this allusion merely as a trivial shift in focus and contents. At best, one might notice that there is at least one theme that this allusion shares with some of the other themes — that of Ms. Gold being kept too long in some situation. Nevertheless, the teacher's behaviour was in no way manifestly seductive or explicitly entrapping, so something seems to be missing.

It seems evident again that it is necessary here to go beyond these direct messages to find a link between the earlier stories about Ms. Gold's cousins and the teacher's behaviour. We need to tap into other levels of meaning to grasp fully the implications of the entire segment of material as an integrated entity. It is experiences of this kind that speak for non-manifest, unconscious factors of some importance.

We might dwell a moment on Ms. Gold's reference to her cousin Arthur's aggressiveness sexually and her formulation that it is a factor in her mistrust of men. This is, of course a psychodynamic interpretation, but what level of listening and formulation does it embody?

Clearly, what is involved is the manifest contents of a dream and a manifest recollection, along with a direct proposal that these surface contents are connected to another manifest issue — Ms. Gold's problem with men. The student herself proposed this link, so it cannot be thought of as dynamically repressed and unconscious. It is a preconscious idea that is located in *the superficial unconscious subsystem* because it is thinly disguised and readily conjured up when needed. The argument that, despite this awareness, the deeper connections between the past and present are unconscious for Ms. Gold simply begs the question.

We are reminded again that almost all manifest contents are within the realm of awareness and that working with this level of meaning in a message calls for straightforward formulations and for direct responses from a therapist or self-processing teacher. Unconscious processes are entirely excluded from such efforts. This is a critical omission as far as depth of meaning is concerned.

THE COST OF EMOTIONAL RELIEF

In this context, I will reiterate the point that every form of healing has a help/hurt ratio — it gives something to its clients and it extracts a cost; no form of therapy is entirely without

pain or negative consequence. Manifest-content efforts at healing tend to have low help/hurt ratios — that is, they tend to
involve a great deal of defensive denial and abuse of a patient,
almost all of it operating without awareness or consciously
denied or ignored. Nevertheless, some people are quite willing
to pay this rather high price for ignorance of the unconscious
aspects of a symptom or emotional issue.

This preference arises from a variety of causes. In general,
surface efforts may provide immediate relief from suffering
despite the repression and denial involved. But in addition,
manifest work and its hurtful attributes satisfy deeply unconscious self-punitive needs that exist in all patients and in
people in general — the patient is often blamed, criticized, pun-
ished, and made to feel that his or her impressions of the
therapist are wrong and bad.

It seems likely that more effective and less costly methods
of healing either exist or can be fashioned; they are certain to
deal with the unconscious side of communication — and of
emotionality. By this means alone, both personal and general
knowledge can be expanded. Manifest clinical observations and
therapies, and the theories that they spawn, tend to be unin-
spiring, clichéd, flawed, lacking in predictive value, self-limit-
ing, and self-deceptive — however popular.

In contrast, theories that include a full consideration of the
nature of unconscious communication have the potential to
generate a wide range of insights that can expand our knowledge of human emotional functioning. Manifest observations of
human nature are too limited to be the basis of a comprehensive and enduring theory of the human mind or of a therapy for
humankind's emotional ills. Let us turn now to the implications
of these directly stated contents to see what they can add to the
picture.

CHAPTER FOUR

The implications
of manifest contents

The surface of emotionally charged human communication is straightforward and, in general, readily defined. But these same manifest contents serve other communicative functions that are less easily formulated. The simplest of these capacities involves *implications that are embodied in, and inherent to, the direct message* — the connotations added to the denotations of surface material. Human communication is an intricately woven fabric of expression with considerable extension even on the surface.

Every message we send and receive has a host of unstated, implied meanings. Even a simple message, like "Yes" or "No", can be overloaded with implicit intimations. Some of these meanings are consciously intended by the sender, others are conveyed entirely without awareness. Much the same applies to the listener who will consciously register some of the intended or evident implications of a message, miss others, and even read into a message meanings that are not intended by the sender. Once we move beyond raw manifest meaning we are faced with highly complicated and uncertain facets of human expression.

IMPLICATIONS
VERSUS ENCODED MEANING

Before entering this rather maze-like domain, we should be clear on one key point that has many ramifications for self-processing therapy — and for understanding the human psyche and its communications. Surface messages not only *connote or imply*, they also *encode or disguise*, meaning. These are two very different functions, and they reflect and access very different systems of the emotion-processing mind.

Implications are extracted directly from the surface of a message. They exist because manifest contents carry a load of meaning on their bare backs, so to speak, and this load is called *implied or inherent but non-stated meaning*. I will call this function of manifest contents the *capacity to convey surface implications*.

It is critical to contrast this property of messages with another, very different, and *simultaneous* function that involves conveying *disguised or camouflaged meaning*. I will call this function of manifest contents the *capacity to convey encoding meanings*.

The same message, then, can embody a surface meaning with multiple implications on the one hand and, on the other, a very different set of meanings that are not detectable through direct inspection of the message because they are encoded or camouflaged within these same contents; these latter meanings can be ascertained only through *a decoding process rather than via extraction from the surface*. Further, the decoding method must be adaptationally oriented and therefore a form of *trigger decoding* because the disguised message is a response to a *non-manifest* emotional stimulus or trigger, one that is repressed either entirely or in respect to its most vital meanings or implications. Many messages, especially those that are narrative in nature, are multilayered, and *each layer has its own distinctive adaptation-evoking triggers and meanings*.

While all messages have surface *implications*, a given message may or may not notably serve the *encoding function* of human communication. In general, however, virtually every *narrative message* does so with exquisite sensitivity and often in rich detail. Stories of all kinds, real and imaginary, dream and non-dream, are the fundamental means of conveying multiple-function/multiple-meaning messages with a strong encoded component. This realization helps to account for the existence of myths and narratives from time immemorial. More rarely, an intellectual comment may be structured to serve this basic dual purpose as well, but the resultant encoded message is usually relatively weak (Langs, 1992a).

There are several other complications to this situation. For one, implications may be read off from a message through simple conscious assessment — I will call these inferences *conscious implications* because they are arrived at by direct, conscious deliberation.

However, many implications, especially those that are anxiety provoking, are not noticed consciously; they register unconsciously through subliminal perception and are processed outside of awareness, primarily by the deep wisdom subsystem of the second unconscious system. Almost all of the critical frame-related behaviours, interventions, and messages from both students and their self-processing teachers are processed in this manner. The resultant *unconscious assessment* is then given access to awareness non-manifestly — indirectly — through encoded narratives whose themes reflect this deep evaluation and the processing of the unnoticed implied meanings. Decoding these themes in light of the message or trigger that has evoked them is the only means of realizing directly the nature of this deeply unconscious appraisal and of utilizing this rich adaptive response.

Trigger decoding an unconscious reaction to the implications of a communicated message affords access to what I will term the *unconscious implications* of a message, because they are perceived outside of awareness and alluded to in encoded fashion. The evolved adaptive design of the emotion-processing psyche is such that *encoded messages are a response to entirely repressed triggers or to the repressed, unconscious implications of consciously noticed triggers*. Work with this level of deep meaning is far different from that done with manifest contents and their evident implications; it touches on the substance of self-processing techniques.

THE CONSCIOUS ASSESSMENT
OF IMPLIED MEANINGS

Although they are selective both personally and as a result of the evolved general sensitivities of the deep unconscious system, *unconscious* assessments of implied meanings are exceedingly accurate and have the power to explain much of human emotional experience and behaviour. On the other hand, *conscious* assessments of the implications of communicated messages are personally biased and highly unreliable and are not part of the essential methods of self-processing therapy.

In self-processing classes, conscious system dialogues are, as a rule, more defensive than illuminating and often quite self-serving, inflexible, and deceptive. They serve also as a way of avoiding critical repressed triggers and encoded meanings — diversions that depart from the central issues and methods of the self-processing class. Manifest-content discussions — even when they address conscious implications — tend to be highly intellectualized and often prove to be ways of evading far more critical repressed triggers that pertain to the frame of the class and its management by the teacher — and the powerful dynamic issues aroused by these frame-related transactions.

In principle, a self-processing teacher should never participate in this type of exclusively conscious exchange. Instead, he or she should always work solely with encoded themes and their ties to evocative triggers. This prevents the class from getting stuck in the relatively inconsequential realm of the conscious system and its first unconscious subsystem which trade in the rather obvious and in unimportant meanings — including conscious assessments of the implications of manifest contents. Trigger decoding brings the process under the aegis of the second unconscious system, where emotional power resides and deep change is possible. Indeed, students are monitored as to whether they are operating within or outside of the self-processing domain — the realm of deeply encoded meaning. When outside of it, no significant unconscious meaning can be developed and no significant insight or deep healing will occur.

The conscious system is strongly inclined towards the direct reading off of supposed implications of manifest contents without resorting to trigger decoding. When formulations of this kind come to mind, a student is obligated to report them in class. But this rule does not apply to the teacher, who must safeguard the process and the class against taking up these impressions and exploring or discussing them directly, without trigger-decoded material. If a self-processing teacher has a lapse and engages in this kind of response, he or she should pick up this trigger at some point — the earlier, the better — and both rectify the error by disengaging from the manifest discussion and using this (addressed level of meaning) lapse as an organizing stimulus for the encoded material that is certain to follow.

Every person engaged in a self-processing class is under natural pressures to shift out of the deep unconscious domain into conscious system efforts and meanings. The self-processing teacher must be committed to identifying and rectifying these resistances and counterresistances. Adhering to this principle distinguishes the self-processing instructor from almost all of today's practitioners of psychotherapy.

DISCERNING IMPLIED MEANINGS

Virtually all prior efforts to deal with the implications of manifest contents — whether by patients or therapists — have involved the *conscious* detection or formulation of these connotations. A woman patient tells a story of a disappointing love affair in which she alienated her lover by forgetting a dinner date with him. The therapist suggests that the story implies hostility towards men or a castrating attitude, and most certainly a fear of intimacy.

The therapist directly and consciously has extracted implications from the surface of the story and has proposed ramifications of the patient's narrative and her behaviours of which she seems to have been unaware. In response, she acknowledges fears of intimacy but denies being a castrating woman. The therapist sees her denial as a resistance, and the battle is joined — a struggle that is typical of manifest readings of surface implications.

Let us briefly contrast this interpretation of the material with the formulation that the therapist would have made had he attempted to treat the surface message as an encoded narrative conjured up in response to a specific non-manifest trigger — an intervention that he had made in the previous session. It turns out that the *repressed* adaptation-evoking stimulus for this material was the fact that the therapist had been thirty minutes late for the patient's previous session. With this as the trigger, we can see that the material disguises the patient's unconscious perception of the teacher's lapse by invoking displacement and disguise — the typically indirect means by which unconscious responses to disturbing triggers are worked over and conveyed. The patient encodes or represents the therapist as herself and camouflages his lateness as her own failure to keep an engagement. The encoded — displaced and disguised — implication of this lapse, as reflected in the disguised story, is that the therapist wishes to get rid of his patient.

Ironically, at the very moment when the therapist is, on the basis of conscious implications, interpreting to the patient that *she* is afraid of intimacy, through his lateness, *he* himself has behaved in a way that indicates that he is suffering from exactly that form of anxiety. The latter is, of course, the interpretation arrived at through trigger decoding alone. Formulating the surface implications of a message takes you to a very different place from where you get to if you trigger-decode the same material — and leads to very different interventions.

At the very least, then, all conscious assessments of implications must be re-evaluated in light of the unconscious assessment of the same trigger (an intervention of the teacher) as reflected in the disguised narrative material of a presenting student. *Unconscious assessments* of surface implications — which are almost always very different from the conscious appraisal — tend to be quite unerring. Implied meanings are real and have their impact; the problem lies not with their existence, but with finding a dependable means of determining what they truly are.

IMPLICATIONS FOR STUDENTS AND TEACHERS

In a self-processing class we have a skewed situation which constrains the work that can reliably be done with implied surface meanings. I have argued that direct, conscious assessments are in general fruitless, and that encoded material — available for trigger decoding — must be used to ascertain the far more sensitive evaluation of these implications that is made by the second unconscious system. But to do this, *narrative material must be available in class.* The self-processing student reports dreams and associations and therefore fulfils this requisite — which then forms the basis for the teacher's various interventions.

In contrast, the instructor does *not* report his or her dreams and associations to the class, and therefore does not impart narrative material suitable for decoding — to do so would be a reflection of countertransference and an abandonment of his or her assigned role and functions. Indeed, the instructor's job is consciously to process the material from the student into direct understanding by removing the impediments to the process — the instructor is confined to using his or her conscious system and wits alone. However, because the behaviours and communications of the instructor's students are, of necessity, impinging on his or her own second unconscious system, the self-processing instructor is well advised to engage in his or her own *personal (private)* self-processing from time to time. Except for brief, silent efforts of this kind in response to acute countertransference expressions, the teacher's self-processing does not belong in the classroom (see chapter sixteen).

Returning to the self-processing student, let us recall that narratives primarily encode unconscious perceptions of others and secondarily of oneself, and that the self-processing teacher is a central figure in, and source of repressed triggers for, a student's world of unconscious experience. This means that a student's material essentially encodes unconscious perceptions of the implications of the teacher's interventions; as noted earlier, this is the consistent and unswerving focus of the second unconscious system . It follows from this that encoded assessments of these instructional, interpretive, and frame-management efforts are available in the self-processing class — and that they can be trigger-decoded and interpreted with respect to *the implications of the instructor's interventional efforts*, with special emphasis on those that are frame-related.

The presenting student's material also encodes unconscious perceptions of the implications of his or her own behaviours and messages and those of the other students. This kind of meaning is only minimally available in a self-processing exercise, and in principle it is addressed only after the available material has been trigger-decoded to obtain unconscious perceptions of the instructor. Oddly enough, students' conscious systems prefer self-assessments and self-interpretations and tend to protect the teacher from critical appraisal unless matters reach an extreme. But the deep unconscious system prefers and works with assessments of others — and of the teacher in particular. Here, too, the conscious and deep unconscious systems are radically different.

An important exception to these principles occurs when a student carries out a frame impingement of his or her own by either securing or modifying one or another ground rule of the class. At such times, encoded self-perceptions of the unconscious implications of this frame-related behaviour will be a prominent aspect of the dream-associational network — the thematic material at hand — and will need to be interpreted. Nevertheless, this must not preclude the interpretation of encoded perceptions of the instructor as well.

RETURNING TO THE VIGNETTE

In the vignette with Ms. Gold reported in the previous chapter, the dream of her cousin touching her breast manifestly is simply the dream as stated. This surface image has, of course, many possible implications. For example, it may be proposed that the manifest dream implies a view of men as failing to respect interpersonal and physical boundaries, as incestuously seductive, as behaving inappropriately, and/or as being overly aggressive or out of control.

In these formulations, the surface image of the cousin is taken to embody these latent connotations. The material is *not* being treated in terms of its encoding function — the cousin is seen as representing himself; there is no consideration or undoing of displacement and disguise, as would be necessary in decoding the same message. These purported implied meanings are latent to the manifest message in the sense of their being constellated in the direct communication and not as camouflaged secrets.

Unfortunately, Freud (1900) used the term *latent contents* to allude to both the unconscious implications contained in manifest contents and the transformed or disguised meanings that are accessible only through some kind of decoding procedure. The problem is compounded by the use of at least three different formats for decoding — symbolic, fantasy-based, and trigger-based. However, only trigger decoding is consistently cast in terms of immediate adaptive responsiveness and is the essential and most viable approach to a student's unconscious processes.

PROBLEMS
WITH CONSCIOUS IMPLICATIONS

Most of the psychodynamic writings on a therapist's listening and formulating efforts are centred on the free associations and behaviours of patients in therapy. *Inference making* is the most frequent basis for defining non-manifest (latent) meaning in a patient's material and for therapists' interventions. Patients are told that their associations imply anger or incestuous desires or a wish to seduce their therapists, or that they indicate a poor self-image or an intrapsychic or interpersonal conflict. Inference making almost never deals with ground rules or frames, and thereby misses a critical aspect of human experience — and of psychotherapy and self-processing.

Work with consciously proposed implications tends to be more confrontative than interpretive. The extracted meanings range from summary statements to theory-driven comments; indeed, implied meanings are typically selected on the basis of a therapist's theoretical preferences. As soon as an implied meaning of which a patient is supposedly unaware is pointed out by a therapist, an issue is joined with the patient who, because the work is on the manifest level, must choose consciously to agree or disagree — little else is available for response.

Criteria for the validity of an intervention based on consciously extracting implications are all but non-existent. In general, therapists believe in what they formulate and impart to their patients, and it takes a lot to change their minds. This hardly seems to be the basis for effective forms of therapy — or self-processing — but beyond the arbitrariness of this kind of work, there are clear findings that ferreting out implied meanings of manifest messages tends to be used by therapists as a way of inadvertently abusing patients and avoiding far more vital unconscious material and its ramifications.

Patients often disagree with the implications of manifest contents proposed by their therapists. Because there is no fair arbitrator in the realm of conscious assessments of the connotations of surface messages, the patient usually must chose between submission to the therapist's authority or rebellion. The latter is almost always labelled a resistance, and further conflict is likely to ensue.

The unwittingly defensiveness and the inconsistencies to which inference making lends itself are very damaging to the patient. The latter will accept this kind of intervention largely because of unresolved self-punitive (masochistic) needs. The patient's unconscious sensitivities are ignored and offended, and his or her unconscious indictment of the therapist — or affirmation when it is merited — is denied. Instead of a therapist's confirming a telling encoded perception, the patient is attacked as misperceiving and as ill or dysfunctional. By both denying the patient's unconscious perceptions and incorrectly formulating his or her material so that it is used to imply something other than the most compelling truth of the moment, the therapist undermines the functioning and reality testing and reality contact of the patient. Trigger decoding safeguards against this kind of injustice, and it also addresses the stronger aspects of the implications of messages by tapping into their unconsciously experienced meanings.

CONSCIOUS EFFORTS
AT EXTRACTING SURFACE IMPLICATIONS

Let us return again to the vignette with Ms. Gold. As an exercise, you might try to spell out all of the possible implications of the material in her vignette that you can formulate. This is, of course, an attempt to identify directly and consciously the connotations of her surface material — its conscious implications. For my part, I will cite a few of the implications that seem most compelling to me (*power* is important in the emotional domain where too much conscious attention is paid to relatively minor issues; see chapter thirteen). No doubt you will agree with some of my formulations and disagree with others. Further, you will probably detect some important implications that I have overlooked. This is similar to the way in which patients and therapists agree and disagree about the implications of a patient's free associations and behaviours in almost random fashion.

As for Ms. Gold, I will begin with her dream and suggest, as I did earlier, that it implies an incestuous experience with a cousin and a view of men as inappropriately seductive, hostile, uncontrolled, manipulative, and insensitive. I will assign a few additional psychodynamic formulations to this material — possible implications are seemingly endless — by proposing that the dream also implies a conscious or unconscious fantasy-wish to have incest with the cousin or some other male relative, perhaps a brother or Ms. Gold's father. Beyond that, by invoking the concept of transference (a type of formulation that is based on inference making rather than decoding — and seldom called for through trigger decoding), I could argue that the dream also implies a transference-based wish to touch or be touched sexually by the teacher.

However, these latter formulations actually involve some isolated, fantasy-based decoding (without identifying an activating trigger, the cousin is seen as an intrapsychically *disguised* representation of the teacher; see chapter five). It is easy to slip from implications of manifest contents to this kind of symbolic decoding — they are of similar ilk.

The implications of surface messages can be formulated directly in free-wheeling ways that are developed not only in

terms of naive possibilities, but also in keeping with a therapist's preferred theoretical position. On the other hand, because it is so basically descriptive, it is difficult to impose
theory-driven images on trigger decoding (though of course, no
human activity is devoid of such bias). And as I have emphasized, there is no reliable means of validating implication-
related interpretations and therefore no way to confirm or refute
the theories on which they are based.

The obviously arbitrary and personally selective nature of
the conscious formulations of the implications of a surface
message that are supposedly unconscious for a patient should
warn us that science cannot be served in this way, nor prediction (relief may nonetheless occur, for paradoxical reasons;
Langs, 1985). A therapy based on extracting implications from
surface messages is so authoritarian, subjective, and capri-
cious that it must have a low help/hurt ratio — i.e., it tends to
be more deeply hurtful than helpful.

Returning again to Ms. Gold, her holding her cousin accountable in part for her problems with men implies that early
life experiences can affect present personal difficulties and that
this student may be inclined to blame others more than herself
for her problems. The incident with James reinforces Ms.
Gold's view of men as incestuous, hostile, insensitive to her
needs, forceful, seductive, and rapacious. This story may also
imply that somehow Ms. Gold sets herself up for these attempts
at seduction. It also suggests that the only way to deal with
men is to take to flight and that escape is possible only through
hysterics, not through reasoning.

To move on to the final segment of her material, Ms. Gold's
thoughts of Mr. Dean, her teacher, imply that she likes him,
looks on him favourably, and enjoys his lapses. Of all of the
implications that I have suggested for these manifest contents,
it is well to keep this last formulation in mind so we can
contrast it with the student's unconscious (trigger-decoded)
view of her instructor (see chapter six). This will, as you might
suspect, be dramatically different from her direct and manifest
response and its implications.

Finally, it is to be noted that self-processing teachers do
engage in *silent* conscious system formulations of the implica-

tions of his or her interventions and the material from their self-processing students. This is done *not* for purposes of direct intervention, but as a way of organizing the encoded themes in a dream-associational network and extracting the most likely ramifications of his or her own efforts. The student's second unconscious system *encodes the unconscious implications* of a self-processing teacher's interventions, behaviours, and silences. Working over detectable implications from any source is a helpful way of orienting the instructor to the issues and meanings that the student unconsciously is dealing with.

In the situation with Ms. Gold, the themes of seductiveness, boundary infringements, and entrapment imply communicatively that Mr. Dean has modified the frame of the class in a manner that has called forth encoded perceptions along these lines. Thus, the teacher's conscious assessment of implications serves primarily to develop ideas about encoded themes and their repressed triggers.

STUDENTS' UNCONSCIOUS ASSESSMENTS

In principle, then, the bulk of self-processing involves working with the narrative material from students as it reflects their *unconscious assessment of the implications of their teacher's (mainly ground-rule) interventions*. As we saw, the only way to access these meanings, and the processing and coping efforts that they reflect, is to decode the available narrative images in light of the trigger experiences — the recent interventions of the teacher — whose unconscious aspects (unconsciously perceived implications) are being worked over and adapted to by the second unconscious system.

Technically, the themes of a presenting student's narratives are decoded as personally selected, *valid* encoded perceptions of the implied meanings embodied in the teacher's interventions. The selective factor is not a distorting influence (i.e., not a matter of transference), but a reflection of the student's mental structures, sensitivities, and his or her unconscious choices; the student automatically chooses from the universal meanings of a trigger those that are most pertinent to his or her emotional ills and health.

The remarkable value of these encoded assessments arises, however, primarily because unconscious processing tends to be highly incisive and accurate in its picture of the world and its happenings — far more so than the conscious system. Furthermore, these are the same implied meanings to which students unconsciously are reacting most strongly. These triggers and their implications deeply affect a student's daily emotional life — and attitudes towards and reactions to the self-processing class. Both teaching and healing are served by defining the unconscious implications of a teacher's efforts by decoding the encoded material from a presenting student. This work is at the heart of the self-processing experience and its cures.

POWERFUL IMPLICATIONS: FURTHER CASE MATERIAL

Therapists and self-processing teachers have been rather slow to comprehend the wide range of implications inherent to their interventions and too lax in defining which aspects of their efforts have the greatest effects on their patients or students. Conscious self-scrutiny and appraisals are strongly prejudiced — both personally and by the theory a therapist adheres to — and they are an unreliable guide. These attributes can be discovered only by trigger decoding the thematic material from students in response to the ongoing interventions of the treating person — only the deep unconscious system knows the true nature and effects of a therapist's or teacher's interventions.

On the whole, there are two key dimensions of human emotional experience that hold the greatest power over our emotional lives — and over our work as psychotherapists. As noted earlier, the first is the *level of meaning* that is being expressed by the patient and, most importantly, being formulated by his or her therapist. On the patient's side of this issue is the question of whether he or she is expressing *en-*

coded narratives or *unencoded intellectualizations* — single- or double-meaning messages. This pertains to the patient's basic communicative mode of adaptation, which is either through unconscious communication or by means of manifest messages essentially devoid of deeper, encoded meaning. On the therapist's side, the question lies with the type of formulation and intervention that he or she is making — whether it is restricted to manifest contents and their evident implications or extends from there into trigger-decoded meanings. Patients consistently but unconsciously monitor their therapists' choices in this regard and adaptively respond accordingly.

The second key dimension pertains to the status of the *ground rules and frame* of the class, and the polarities are *secured frame* versus *modified frame*. At all times, both students and self-processing teachers are either in a secured- or a deviant-frame mode (mixtures may occur as well). Each frame has its adaptive aspects and its cost of adapting, and each is the source of a distinctive set of psychodynamics. Here, too, a student continuously and unconsciously monitors the state of the frame of the class and the teacher's frame-management efforts — and again responds accordingly.

Mode of expression and the nature of the frame — each is the kind of disarmingly simple, ever-present yet critical dimension that is likely to be deeply lawful and to account powerfully for the vicissitudes of human nature. Our formal research has shown the lawful power of mode of expression; I have no doubt that future research will also reveal deeply lawful features to the vicissitudes of frame-related behaviours and experiences.

SUMMING UP

To conclude this chapter, the main points to keep in mind are the following:

1. *Therapists and self-processing teachers can learn a great deal about the unconscious implications of their own comments, interventions, and frame-management efforts from*

the narrative material of their students. They can do this best by taking their interventions — verbal and frame-managing — as the immediate triggers for their students' displaced narrative material. The themes contained in the emergent images are treated as valid encoded unconscious perceptions and assessments of the implications of the interventions at hand. The encoded material also contains recommendations for change and optimal adaptations — correctives for errant interventions, interpretations that have been missed by the teacher, limited interpretations of the sources of the teacher's errors, and models of rectification or frame-securing correctives when the frame is deviant. Clearly, the second unconscious system embodies a remarkable and unfamiliar intelligence of great scope and power.

2. *The most disturbing direct and implied meanings of a self-processing teacher's interventions are perceived unconsciously by his or her students, processed outside of awareness, and then reported through camouflaged or encoded narratives.* This is, of course, the rationale for the exclusive use of trigger decoding in dealing with the material from students. *Meaning in a self-processing class is accessed only when triggers are linked to displaced and disguised themes* to render conscious a transposed adaptational story of the student's unconscious experience of and response to his or her teacher's efforts.

3. *Communication and frame are the dimensions of human expression and interaction to which the second unconscious system — and the individual — is most sensitive.* They also are the two aspects of emotionally charged experience that carry the most power to affect our emotional lives.

4. *Explorations in self-processing classes have shown that the capacities for self-awareness, direct self-understanding, and the conscious processing of the implications of the teacher's interventions are crude and rudimentary functions, and often in error.* In the emotional domain, conscious system functions related to perception, memory, learning, evaluating, self-analysis, and the like are all impaired by the natural defensiveness of this system.

5. *The self-processing teacher must work with his or her conscious system alone and reserve the rest for personal self-processing.* The teacher should be on the alert for signs of countertransference and dysfunction — e.g., unneeded frame modifications, conscious system discussions in class, the use of conscious implications, missed triggers and themes, failure to obtain encoded validation after linking triggers to theses (the problem usually involves a missed trigger), flight from encoded meaning or secured frames (a universal tendency that often is difficult to identify), and any departure from the communicative principles of self-processing therapy. Once a countertransference issue is identified, it is essential that the instructor, in the course of carrying out personal self-processing, discover the *triggers* from the students' material and the classroom frame that have prompted the errant response. Private self-processing is then used to discover the unconscious implications of these triggers which are the external, activating cause of the teacher's dysfunction (see chapter sixteen).

6. *At bottom, the self-processing student is deeply affected by and responds unconsciously to the implications of a teacher's interventions — far more than to his or her own inner experiences and needs, the comments from and behaviours of other students, or impingements from life outside of the class.* The self-processing instructor is invested in and experienced unconsciously as a descendant of the shamans and priests — he or she has a most compelling mantle for the self-processing student. However casual a student may be consciously about the teacher and the classroom work, the second unconscious system is strongly and deeply invested in the teacher's interventions.

To know his or her students in the deepest sense possible, the self-processing teacher must know himself or herself in terms of his or her deep unconscious experience. This is a well-known maxim. Communicative understanding has given it new and vital meaning.

CHAPTER FIVE

Symbols
and isolated encoded meanings

We shift now from the realm of direct, manifest expression to meanings that are disguised or *encoded* in the same surface message. It is well to recognize at the outset of this discussion that methods of decoding are created by therapists — by listeners. They are not inherent to messages *per se*. They are human inventions, techniques designed to formulate and access levels of non-manifest meaning that are theorized to be cogent to human emotional experience. While these translations should possess both explanatory and predictive powers, and should touch on meanings of great import emotionally rather than on trivialities, their validity and cogency remain unmeasured and uncertain to this day.

Given the enormous defensiveness of the conscious system, we should be prepared to find that relatively inconsequential decoding methods will be attractive to the conscious systems of both students and teachers, more so than those that are of more profound and disturbing significance. The unconscious forces that shape our preference for one or another mode of listening and formulating are relatively unappreciated. We are faced with a catch-22 situation: a self-processing teacher must overcome the inevitable resistances against accessing deep unconscious meaning and engage in effective trigger decoding in order to discover why trigger decoding is so often by-passed by psychotherapists as the formulating method of choice — manifest and other types of formulating cannot provide answers to this dilemma. Nevertheless, we can benefit from discussing the issues raised by various approaches to delineating supposed disguised latent contents and by attempting to bring some clarity to a situation that has long eluded resolution. In the final analysis, we will see that only trigger decoding reflects the specific adaptive functioning of the emotion-processing mind and is the only means of defining latent contents that obtains encoded or unconscious validation.

Decoding methods can be classified as *trigger-related* (interactional and specifically adaptive in nature) or *isolated and intrapsychic* (the invocation of symbols and fantasy formations). However, before examining these methods of isolated decoding, we should recognize that there is an important distinction between a *conscious fantasy* (a day dream) that is experienced manifestly and directly and an *unconscious fantasy*, which is experienced in *encoded form* and must be decoded if a therapist is to comprehend its meaning. On the whole, working solely on the basis of their own conscious system preferences, therapists tend to formulate *conscious* fantasies (manifest contents) and their evident (conscious) implications; they have little mind for unconscious fantasies.

It can be shown, however, that in most instances a *conscious fantasy and purported unconscious fantasy encodes an unconscious perception* of a self-processing teacher in light of a recent, compelling (usually frame-related) intervention that he or she has made. In general, the non-adaptive formulation or one that is broadly couched in adaptive terms, however correct, serves to obscure or exclude the development of more compelling deep unconscious meanings and the precise contemporaneous adaptations of the second unconscious system.

TWO METHODS
OF ISOLATED DECODING

Basically, there are two forms of decoding in current use in the field of psychotherapy. They are called *isolated symbolic decoding* and *isolated fantasy decoding*. Both methods are intrapsychically focused ways of deciphering messages; a narrative or image is treated as an entity unto itself — as an expression of the communicator's inner mental world and intrapsychic conflicts. Both methods essentially treat the human mind as a relatively closed system and are supported by *a weak adaptive position* — the principle that everything in the human psyche is in some way part of general efforts to cope (Slavin & Kriegman, 1992). The specific triggers and definitive adaptations that characterize *a strong adaptational position* are overlooked.

In the symbolic method, the stress is on universal symbols — on representations shared by individuals, cultures and humankind in general. In the second and more complex method, the material from a patient is believed to reflect *isolated (non-triggered), intrapsychic disguised or unconscious fantasies, wishes, and memories*. These fantasy-formations are theorized to arise primarily because of the instinctual drive make-up, intrapsychic conflicts, and self-object needs of the patient.

In some versions of this latter approach, the viewpoint is that these inner needs, and the distorted view of the therapist that they create, are aroused in some vague and general way in the interaction with the therapist (though not by his or her specific interventions or triggers). As result, a disguised image from a patient is *not* decoded as a specific unconscious perception of the therapist, but as an unconscious fantasy aroused in the intersubjective experience and projections of the patient *vis à vis* the therapist (Stolorow, Brandschaft, & Atwood, 1987).

Another version of this work is based on the mistaken idea that the patient's mind contains inner fantasies and potentials that simply are released in interacting with a therapist (Weiss & Sampson, 1986; Slavin & Kriegman, 1992). The latter in some way liberates the inner potential of the patient, who uses the therapist to project onto and enact his or her inner mental wishes and needs. Even though interaction is taken into account, the listening–formulating process deals with manifest contents and their implications, and the decoding method, if any, is concentrated on accessing the patient's inner mental state without full consideration of its evocative stimuli.

These broad formulations fail to be faithful to human nature, which responds to specific stimuli with exquisite detail and precision. Goodheart (1993) terms this ill-defined way of thinking a form of *folk psychology* in that it serves the common need for global understanding and mythology and, as such, is loosely constructed and without the means of linking to formal science. This way of thinking stands in contrast to the scientific mode, where the specific details of moment-to-moment interactions are taken into account — including the intricacies of emotional adaptations.

Examination of the interventions made by these therapists reveals that despite their attempts to give an interactional cast to their work, they nonetheless confront and interpret by formulating the *conscious implications* of manifest material — and less so by decoding images for isolated, disguised latent meanings. At times, the two methods of formulation — extracting conscious implications, and isolated fantasy decoding — are used together. However, both are means of accessing the operations of the first unconscious system and its rather transparent forms of disguise — they do not approach the specifically adaptive and unexpected qualities of deep unconscious processes as revealed by trigger decoding.

The stress on *inner mental life* and *projected fantasies* distinguishes this decoding method from trigger decoding, where the emphasis is on the *unconscious perception of others* — and only secondarily on the inner elaboration of those perceptions. In isolated fantasy decoding, then, the focus is on the mind of the patient (as influenced secondarily by the interaction with the therapist), while in trigger decoding the focus is on the inputs from the therapist (as experienced and elaborated upon within the mind of the patient). This is one of those differences that makes a great difference (Bateson, 1979).

Isolated symbolic decoding

Symbolic representations — or symbols, for short — are weakly meaningful aspects of the latent contents of human images and narratives. There is some evidence that coming out of water symbolically represents birth, or that an elongated knife represents a dangerous phallus. These are universal symbols, but symbols may also be highly personal. For example, a particular room may, for a woman who met her husband there, stand for or represent love even as that same room universally symbolizes the womb. Symbols are in principle relatively fixed encoded representations that tend to disguise body parts and functions, and major events, issues, and conflicts that are common to most lives. They strikingly lack an immediate adaptive and interactional cast.

Symbolic meanings are grafted upon those that are manifest. Both exist in a communicated message; the issue is one of formulation and recognition. Some therapists never think in terms of symbols, others do so most of the time. In general, most therapists who engage in isolated forms of decoding that stress inner mental configurations will envision the presence of a symbolic expression when a patient communicates an image that seems to reflect a universal concern in some readily palpable form.

It is evident, however, that the nature of a symbolic representation is open to multiple interpretations, and the meaning selected usually is a matter of personal choice. The validity of a particular formulation of the symbolic content of a given message is left unanswered. In addition, there is no clear evidence for the cogency of symbols *vis à vis* the vicissitudes of emotional life and for their impact on others as a form of unconscious expression. As we saw with the implications of manifest contents, much is left to belief and personal, unconsciously biased opinion.

There is as well a rather impersonal quality to the concept of universal meanings. Formulations of this kind tend to lack interpersonal considerations and mainly imply the existence of symbols in the mind of the symbolizer based on archetypical, intrapsychic, or inner personal reasons, isolated from relationships and interactions. To the extent that symbols are connected to events in the life of the symbolizer, their formulation stresses personal reactions and inner response and almost never includes a sense of the interactive unconscious perceptions of others.

* * *

Ms. Gold's material contains few universal symbols. Perhaps the most obvious are the Eiffel Tower with its phallic qualities and the seductive cousins who represent family, incest, and men in general. More speculative is the suggestion that the house and home are symbols of her own or her mother's body.

Announcing these possibilities tells us little about Ms. Gold and her emotional issues. Symbols are intriguing but far from definitive; they are fascinating entities that are ripe for speculation — but little else. In the self-processing class, a teacher will keep an ear open for the symbolic qualities of a presenting student's material but will use this knowledge mainly as a general guide that might lead him or her to a key trigger and an encoded responsive meaning that bears some resemblance to the purported symbolic content.

Self-processing instructors do not engage in the isolated decoding of symbols. Fundamentally, this type of formulation is interdicted because, as is true with interpretations of so-called unconscious fantasy formations, it is arbitrary and it does not result in encoded validation.

Isolated unconscious fantasies decoding

The decoding and formulation of communications as reflections of isolated or aroused unconscious fantasies and memories is an inventive, fascinating pursuit that at one time was frequently engaged in by psychoanalysts, but is quite rare today. To do so, the material from a patient is scrutinized for images that might disguise a theorized universal or personal fantasy or wish — especially one that is the source of conflict. Common examples include oedipal stories of seducing maternal or paternal figures and killing off the rival of the opposite sex, oral cannibalistic fantasies of devouring others, anal-sadistic fantasies of evacuating them, and images of phallic prowess or vaginal receptivity.

The theory on which this type of decoding is founded states that wishes of this kind are forbidden and create intrapsychic conflict that must be exposed — decoded in isolation — from the patient's material, and interpreted in terms of intrapsychic and interpersonal issues and resolved. Another version of this theory states that fantasies of merger and adoration of others are at play and need to be identified and resolved (often, however, the level of listening involved in this approach is starkly manifest — the allusions are to directly stated conscious fantasies). In these situations, the therapist is, as I have said, seen primarily as a facilitator and convenient object for projection and the like, and not as a *real force* who is responsible for rich and active inputs into the interaction with the patient from one moment to the next.

The study of patients' encoded responses to this kind of effort reveals, again, that it is, in general, an exercise in the relatively arbitrary attribution of meaning that is focused on the inner mental world of the fantasizer with little adaptive or systemic consideration. As I have discussed, this approach flies in the face of the massive evidence that the human mind primarily is an instrument of adaptation to the outer world and therefore is activated by immediate external stimuli. Its responses ultimately must be understood in terms of these living adaptations — indeed, representing, affording meaning (conscious and unconscious), and adapting are among the most fundamental functions of language and of all messages.

As for unconscious fantasies and memories, the vignette from Ms. Gold could, with some imagination, be decoded to reveal a postulated unconscious memory of being seduced by her brother or father (as represented by her cousins), or perhaps it disguises an early incident of entrapment and seduction by a different primary figure whom the cousins represent. Similarly, the material might be thought to encode an unconscious fantasy and wish to be seduced by any number of men — the cousins themselves, Ms. Gold's brother or father, or whomever. In this type of decoding, both imagination and wish are invoked as guiding concepts.

In general, supplementary associations are needed to formulate unconscious fantasies and memories more accurately. Nevertheless, this level of meaning has been found to be of secondary importance in emotional behaviour and symptoms. As I said, their formulation by a therapist or self-processing teacher often arises as a way of denying and by-passing a meaning embodied in the same material as an encoded critical unconscious *perception* of the therapist or teacher based on a recent intervention. Although it turns Freudian theory on its head, it is this latter level of meaning that empowers emotional life — incoming perceptions rather than inner fantasies and outgoing projections.

Encoded fantasies about the teacher

There is a special class of encoded fantasies and wishes that are postulated to refer, in disguise, to a treating therapist or analyst — or to a self-processing teacher. They are termed *transference fantasies* or, more precisely, *unconscious transference fantasies*, in that they are said to allude *unconsciously* to the therapist. With respect to listening and formulating, these encoded fantasies should be distinguished from *direct allusions* to a therapist in the form of a conscious fantasy or wish — or a direct comment of any kind. This distinction is seldom fully appreciated in the literature.

In a self-processing class, the so-called transference figure would, of course, be the instructor. The issue in listening would then be that of identifying likely encoded (unconscious) fantasies about and wishes towards the teacher in the communications from the students. In general, the guiding principle is to consider all allusions to authoritarian figures, especially educators and healers, as displaced and disguised representations of the instructor. The material is then treated in various ways — as conveying a disguised wish or impulse directed towards the teacher, as misperceptions of the instructor, or as encoded projections of some content — conflict or need — within the mind of the patient onto the teacher.

In Ms. Gold's material, one or both of her cousins might be thought to represent her teacher; the material would then be postulated to reflect her wishes to entrap and seduce him.

Here, too, we are dealing with a type of formulation that may have a grain of truth, though its importance in the emotional life of the communicator is not very great. The entire domain of theorized transference fantasies is confounded by the fact that most therapists use *manifest* references to themselves as the basis for their formulations — the assessment of the material involves the purported implications of surface meanings. There is no disguised unconscious component in this thinking.

The main problem again is that, as is true of all forms of isolated decoding, formulations of encoded wishes directed towards the teacher serve in a critical way to close off and deny another and more compelling level of meaning in the same material — namely, the way in which the narratives encode unconscious perceptions of the teacher based on an intervention that he or she has made. While a student's inner mental life and its history is a strong factor in the selection of meanings he or she attributes to an intervention by an instructor, the real and actual implications of the instructor's behaviour also play a forceful role in what the student works over and must cope with — and communicate about.

A valid means of decoding must account for both consensually validated reality and its subjective interpretation — for both triggers (the external stimulus) and themes (the inner, unconscious response). The key issue is the means of how reality is assessed. If the patient or therapist chooses to do so through direct, conscious appraisals, the degree of error is enormous — even when others agree. The best means of grasping reality, oddly enough, is by trigger decoding the patient's unconscious view of the outer world and others. While inner need plays a role in this assessment, it is sufficiently free of conflict, bias, and distortion to be quite reliable and validatable.

* * *

These are, then, the two ways in which manifest contents from patients are treated as disguised messages that primarily reflect the intrapsychic world of the patient or student. Because these decoding efforts and the interpretations they generate do not obtain encoded validation from those to whom they are imparted, the communicative approach has cast about for a decoding method that does find confirmation and support on the deep unconscious level. This procedure is, of course, called *trigger decoding*, and it is the subject of the next chapter.

CHAPTER SIX

Trigger decoding

As I have said, the human mind evolved primarily under both physical and interpersonal environmental influence and was designed to deal with external dangers and satisfactions, and only secondarily with the need systems and other responses that they arouse. This fundamental principle holds for processes both within and outside of awareness. This implies that *mental activity*, whether conscious or unconscious, is *inherently and specifically adaptive*. The emotion-processing mind is activated primarily by the immediate stimuli arising from one's environment — settings, incidents, people, etc. — and to a far lesser extent by internal happenings, which become important only when unusually intense or critical. An individual's genetic endowment, inner mental world, and past history play their most essential role as shapers of the psychic resources — and dysfunctions — that determine when and how an individual deals with external impingements.

It follows from this analysis that both direct and encoded contents in messages are part of the flow of human emotional experience and adaptation. Mentation and communication largely are responses to external triggers as experienced through conscious and unconscious perception—and then processed. The triggers themselves are constituted as emotionally significant events and interpersonal interactions that involve communications (inputs) from others that are themselves quite complex—fraught with manifest and latent meanings. Human emotional life is never simple.

We will leave aside moments of satisfaction and gratification, which create their own special issues, and focus instead on the more common forms of trauma. In that respect and in principle, among the various concatenations of incoming information and meaning, those inputs that cause the greatest amount of anxiety, threat, and damage (physically and psychologically) evoke the most intense emotional responses and take on the greatest psychical significance. There is a general hierarchy of traumas—e.g. death, incest, physical injury and abuse, abandonment, the loss of a job, losing a dollar bill, etc.—onto which personal sensitivities are selectively imposed. In general, the more traumatic the input, the larger the number of aspects of the experience that will register outside rather than within awareness.

Conscious intake is processed by the conscious system and its first unconscious subsystem. The responses that this system generates mainly involve consciously identified triggers and manifest contents—and their directly detectable implications. *Unconscious intake*—subliminally received—is processed by the second unconscious system and involves triggers that are either entirely repressed or those meanings of known triggers that are registered outside of awareness. This is the realm of *encoded latent contents*. Both direct and encoded meanings are activated by emotional stimuli or triggers, but *the nature of the triggers that arouse each system are very different*—conscious system triggers tend to involve survival issues and manifestly disturbing inputs, while deep unconscious triggers are basically anxiety provoking and frame-related.

Trigger decoding is the procedure for ascribing meaning to encoded manifest contents that reflect the workings of the deep unconscious system. The decoding operates by undoing the disguises embodied in a surface message in light of their evocative emotional stimuli. The effort is a strikingly interactional and adaptive, systemic, and systematic approach to ascertaining latent meaning.

TRIGGER DECODING:
AN INTRODUCTION

Ron attacks Tim verbally. Tim experiences the assaultive message consciously and responds with a manifest rejoinder — get off my back. Ron says that anger should be controlled; one of his friends was killed the other night in an argument. Tim responds that some people are civilized and know how to handle rage.

This brief exchange began when Tim called Ron into his office to fire him from his job. An argument ensued, as did the brief narrative comments just described. This is a microcosm of emotionally charged life — a conscious exchange of angry words, with triggers that are survival related and self-evident. For Ron, the trigger is being fired from his job; for Tim, it is Ron's angry words. Unexpectedly, Ron introduced a *marginally related narrative* — the story about the friend who was killed (Langs, 1991). This narrative signals a shift from essentially single-meaning, unencoded expressions to a multiple-meaning, encoded communication that *simultaneously serves a surface and non-surface (latent) purpose.*

The story from Ron encodes his unconscious perception that Tim is trying to murder him by letting him go; the same narrative encodes Ron's own murderous rage towards Tim. The latent meanings of this encoded message were not consciously registered in either Ron or Tim, but we can assume from Tim's response that they were accurately perceived by his second unconscious system. In reaction, Tim offered a model of rectification — civilized people control their rage. The directive was aimed at both himself and Ron.

Communicative interactions are circular mixtures of conscious and unconscious, direct and encoded, messages. A trigger is multilayered with meaning, and it therefore evokes a direct reaction as well as an indirect one. The former is a response to the conscious implications of the trigger, the latter a response to those that are unconscious. The encoded story in turn prompts a conscious and unconscious reaction in the listener — and so on.

Were this exchange left undecoded and unprocessed by Ron, the experience of being the victim of a frame break (being fired) and of Tim's and his own murderous rage, much of it processed outside of awareness, could lead to devastatingly destructive, displaced behaviours that could harm both himself and others. Gaining awareness of the second stream of (unconscious) experience via trigger decoding is the only way this possibility could be eliminated — doing so can be a highly adaptive and sometimes life-saving endeavour. Indeed, there are certain critical emotional issues — e.g., those that are related to frames and to death anxiety — that can be adaptively resolved only via trigger decoding, because the deep unconscious system alone processes the vital meanings and issues involved.

For example, under the pressure of these encoded perceptions, Tim might pick an argument with his girlfriend, Carol, and precipitately end their four-year relationship. His conscious feelings and understanding, and the reality of the situation with Carol, while intense, would not predict or account for his behaviour — but his deeply unconscious experience would.

There is, then, at times of emotional crisis, a great need to get in touch with deep unconscious reactions — both perceptions and responses. Deeply unconscious responses include valid perceptions of disturbing impingements from others and self that can derail emotional equilibrium and behaviour. But it is not simply a matter of incisive (unconscious) perception; the same deep wisdom system that monitors this level of emotional encounter also arrives at exceedingly wise solutions to emotional quandaries. Optimally adaptive solutions can be forged only by facing and dealing with the encoded and awful truth.

The problem, however, is that these compelling experiences and adaptive reactions are encoded in responsive stories and their *themes* — they never enter awareness directly. *Trigger decoding*, which in essence *links triggers to the displaced and disguised themes* in the narratives evoked by those triggers, is the means by which this deep wisdom can be brought into awareness, and then used by the conscious system for adaptation. Without trigger decoding, this great inner intelligence goes for little or naught — and our lives are unknowingly and unwittingly run by our deeper emotions. To be master of your own mind and life, this invisible and distinctive unconscious world must be made to materialize through trigger decoding.

Trigger decoding is the key that solves the Rosetta stone of unconscious communication. It is a listening and formulating process that undoes camouflage by taking a series of narrative images, extracting their main themes and lifting them from their manifest or conscious context, and *linking or transposing* them to their unconscious or latent context — the repressed triggers to which they are an encoded response. The themes of stories told in one context are placed into a second context — that of a repressed (in full or in part) trigger situation that is different from the one that is referred to in the surface message. Typically, a story about an event outside of class — past, present, or future — latently encodes a story about the student's response to something (usually frame-related) that a self-processing teacher has done. The themes are taken from *there and then* and connected to the *here and now* (or recently) in class.

Once identified, a trigger is assessed for its likely implications and encoded meanings, and these readings are used as organizers for the linking and decoding effort. The triggers for encoded messages are always contemporaneous — specific emotionally charged stimuli to which the person is currently adapting unconsciously. The second unconscious system operates in the present, but this present includes recent frame-related interventions by the self-processing teacher that are maintained in active, unconscious form as holdovers from the previous class or two — perhaps the only way the second unconscious system at all transcends the immediate moment.

For example, suppose we decide that along with the rest of its functions, Ms. Gold's story of the seductiveness of her cousin Arthur is an encoded message. We would then search for an immediate trigger to which that narrative was a *displaced and disguised* response. The story, told in the manifest context of an early childhood recollection and current emotional problems with men (the manifest or direct trigger), must be placed into a different, current, but repressed context (the latent or indirect trigger). Clinical experience has shown without question that for a person in psychotherapy and in a self-processing class, the repressed contemporaneous current context is with few exceptions drawn from the interventions of the therapist. Thus, the main evocator of *conscious* adaptive reactions varies from one moment to the next, while the main evocator of *unconscious* reactions mainly is the self-processing teacher.

One or two prior interventions by Mr. Dean, Ms. Gold's self-processing teacher, must in some way constitute the specific *latent triggers* for the encoded meanings of the *themes* contained in her direct, surface recollection. The manifest story about her cousin Arthur (the *conscious context*) must be taken as communicating an encoded perception of a meaning of some recent intervention made by Mr. Dean (the *unconscious context*). Triggers evoke disguised themes, so disguised themes are clues to latent triggers. The extraction of narrative themes — releasing themes from their surface contexts — and the identification of their immediate triggers reveals the disguised and encoded meanings of a message. This work is, of course, essential to effective self-processing therapy.

Trigger decoding captures the results of both unconscious perception and unconscious processing and adaptation, carried forward by means of a deep intelligence that operates in terms of its own unique and deeply unconscious store of memories, knowledge, viewpoints, adaptive preferences, and experiences. In all, trigger decoding reveals a distinctive and unfamiliar world of human experience and adaptation. *We are indeed of two minds: we experience and cope with the world and ourselves in two very different ways — one conscious and the other deeply unconscious.* One goal of trigger decoding is to unite these two worlds and their coping inclinations into a better integrated and more serviceable resource.

THE KEY TRIGGERS
IN SELF-PROCESSING CLASSES

Communicative studies have shown that healing figures are unconsciously perceived and responded to as if they are among the high priests of today's world. Interactions with psychotherapists and self-processing teachers therefore activate the human mind in very special ways. There is a strikingly powerful and incisive reaction to the conditions or frame of these contacts as they are created by the healer (and secondarily, his or her students), and this reaction occurs mainly in the second unconscious system. The ideal ground rules or boundary conditions of a self-processing class are precisely defined in the deep unconscious system. This is one of the great advantages of the self-processing class: the activating triggers — most of them frame related — can, with few exceptions, be clearly identified and their implications exceedingly well characterized.

The observation that the key triggers for a student's *unconscious* communications are the interventions of the self-processing teacher simply reflects the natural investments and inclinations of the human mind and its second unconscious system. This proposition can be validated empirically through encoded (unconscious) forms of confirmation of interventions that are made in keeping with this tenet and through the non-validation of efforts that are not so constructed.

In general, the proposition that the interventions of a self-processing teacher are overridingly central to the encoded meanings conveyed in a student's material offends conscious sensibility. In its efforts to defend against the ever-present threat of unconscious experience and meaning, and secured frames, the conscious mind will garner any number of arguments against this realization. Patients and therapists alike, most of whom have never used trigger decoding and unconscious validation as their tools, will argue that such an idea is absurd — that the teacher can't be that important to his or her students. Based on conscious experience alone, they will argue that this proposition reflects an extreme narcissism on the part of the communicative self-processing instructor. They also will claim that this idea denies the importance of a student's everyday life (which is, of course, important for his or her *conscious* experience and general life, but not for the *main workings of the second unconscious system*) and that it minimizes the relevance of early life experiences and trauma. Some disagreement also arises because the instructor is arguably, in most instances, not at the centre of a student's *manifest* (conscious) communications and experience.

These arguments are quite unfounded. Nature is nature, and conscious concern is not the same as unconscious concern and focus. The second unconscious system is genetically and environmentally engineered very much in the ways described here. Besides, these propositions do not in any way exclude or reduce the role played by external reality and early childhood factors. In actuality, they acknowledge the role of both biological genetics and experiential genetics in the basic configuration of the emotion-processing mind and its current coping responses.

Two key concepts dominate this part of the picture. First, that evolution and biological genetics is accountable for the basic architecture of the emotion-processing mind and for individual differences in how we cope and communicate unconsciously — e.g., some people express many encoded images, others very few. Second, that early childhood experiences play a crucial role in the development of the human psyche and its deep processing systems and mechanisms.

TRIGGER DECODING CLINICAL MATERIAL

With an eye towards trigger decoding and linking, let us look once more at Ms. Gold's material. We could begin either with her themes or with the triggers that have evoked them; I will select the latter course because it will make the decoding process easier to comprehend.

What, then, is the key contemporaneous trigger for Ms. Gold's encoded manifest associations? Clearly, the answer lies in Mr. Dean's extension of the class the previous week. This is a frame-related stimulus in that it modifies the agreed-upon and unconsciously validated structure of the class by giving the group more time than allotted by the ground rules. It is a significant frame-break.

We may initiate this fresh study of the classroom situation with Ms. Gold's manifest reaction to this frame alteration. This response appears in her surface associations. In essence, her conscious system saw Mr. Dean's error as a positive intervention — a sign of interest and nothing more.

But what then of the response of Ms. Gold's second unconscious system? That is, how can we trigger-decode her material to reveal her unconscious perceptions of this same trigger? This effort is the essence of the listening–formulating process that is used in self-processing classes — the extraction and transposition of the themes from a manifest narrative into a latent trigger situation.

There are three main stories in Ms. Gold's associations — one refers to her cousin Arthur, another to her cousin James, and the third to the man who came on to her. In her dream, Arthur corners Ms. Gold and touches her breasts, while the associations to the dream recalls that Arthur was aggressive with her as he was with women in general. The main *themes* are of physical contact with a relative (something akin to incest), entrapment, aggressiveness with women, and being the victim. We *extract* these themes from the manifest dream and the associated recollections (the dream-associational network) — lift them out, so to speak — and prepare to connect them to the trigger of Mr. Dean's frame-deviant lapse. This will then reveal the unconsciously perceived meanings of the trigger-intervention that Ms. Gold conveyed in disguised form in the manifest story about Arthur.

Before linking these themes to their trigger, let us abstract the themes of the other two stories. James is also remembered as entrapping and as wishing for sex with Ms. Gold. Here the themes become repetitive (an attribute that often signals important encoded thematic material) — they again are of sexual entrapment with incestuous overtones. In addition, there are themes of getting hysterical and escaping. The story of the man also reinforces these themes — there, too, there is a sense of entrapment and flight or escape. Themes in hand, we are now set to carry out the process of *linking or trigger decoding*.

There are four key aspects to trigger decoding: first, collating a set of powerful and diverse but integratable associations from the available narrative material; second, extracting the most powerful and relevant themes from this narrative material; third, selecting a critical trigger that is likely to have evoked these disguised images and developing a sense of its main implications; and fourth, linking these two components — *themes and triggers* — and treating the resultant story as reflecting valid encoded perceptions of the implications of the trigger and, secondarily, as conveying unconscious reactions to these perceptions.

The formulation or interpretation derived from trigger decoding is stated in narrative form, in terms of cause (trigger) and effect (themes) because the second unconscious system is a logical adaptive system. Its perceptions and processes must be stated as a story that begins with a given trigger and details the unconscious responses to that trigger.

The student's narrative material is, as noted, called a *dream-associational network* or a *narrative or thematic pool*. Its main function is to embody in disguised form the responses of the deep unconscious wisdom system to emotionally charged inputs — triggers. Trigger decoding proceeds by identifying and extracting the specific themes in the narrative material and by then linking these themes to the immediate trigger(s) that set them off in the first place. Themes and triggers, triggers and themes — they are the substance of trigger decoding.

For example, one key theme in Ms. Gold's material is that of a sexual (incestuous) entrapment. And the key trigger is the teacher's extension of the class. By linking the trigger to the themes, and treating the result as a valid encoded perception, we arrive at the following trigger-decoded formulation: *Mr. Dean's extension of the class was unconsciously perceived by Ms. Gold as an incestuous entrapment and seduction.*

Clearly, this formulation is far different from all of the previous conjectures about this material. It departs dramatically from our earlier assessments made on the basis of exploring these manifest contents and their implications or by invoking isolated forms of decoding (including a formulation of possible transference meanings). This new evaluation is also different from Ms. Gold's own conscious appraisal of the intervention; indeed, the conscious and unconscious assessments of the situation are, as is usually the case, diametrically opposite to each other.

Trigger decoding brings us to conceptions and conclusions — and to a world of emotions — that sharply differ from those we develop and reach on the basis of any other method of ascribing meaning to material from patients and students — and to human communication in general. All such approaches omit interactional/systemic considerations as embodied in specific triggers and definitive responsive themes. They fail to recognize the fundamentally and immediately adaptive aspects of human communication. Where other impressions of this material are entirely focused on Ms. Gold, the trigger-decoded statement is shared by her and her instructor. Fantasy is replaced by perception and subsequent inner response, and responsibility for experience and reaction are afforded to both student and teacher.

Strikingly, too, Ms. Gold's conscious reaction to the extended class is both limited and very positive, while her encoded perception is quite elaborate and negative. This is a critical point. It seems evident that the second unconscious system's assessment of Mr. Dean's frame break is fairer and more compelling than the one made by her conscious system. The latter experience is denial-based in seeing the intervention as reflecting care and concern; the former is non-defensive in seeing the harm that was done. Surprisingly, we find again and again that the conscious lives we lead in the emotional domain are narrow and relatively devoid of richness and strong meaning — at least in comparison to the abundance and complexity of the unconscious lives we simultaneously live as well.

Which assessment will more greatly influence Ms. Gold's emotional life and psychic state? Clinical evidence shows that the unconscious evaluation has the greater share of power, but it shows too that these effects are almost always *displaced onto situations with others* and virtually never consciously connected with their deep source. The consequences of the unconsciously processed part of the experience are real but misplaced and all too often quite detrimental.

On the other hand, the conscious assessment of the teacher — the source of the activating trigger — goes unmodified by its unconscious counterpart; the two systems of the emotion-processing mind are indeed substantially independent of each other (the mind is split). Thus, Ms. Gold will continue to praise her teacher and to work with him without criticism even though she is for the moment unconsciously feeling harmed by his extension of the class — and acting out aspects of that harm elsewhere.

Via displacement, then, Ms. Gold will react negatively to other seemingly innocuous or positive stimuli — as seen in her flight from the man at the party. In typical fashion, she flees an innocent person rather than the truly dangerous (for the moment) teacher. These generally unrecognized consequences of teachers' frame alterations involve unconsciously displaced responses that reflect something of the inherently maladaptive aspects of the evolved emotion-processing mind; they are the source of much that is emotionally dysfunctional.

Another disturbing likelihood is that had Mr. Dean's frame deviation been more blatant and traumatic — e.g., an attempt at actual seduction, a major personal self-revelation, an abrupt and sizeable increase in his fee — there would have been an initial *conscious* response abundant in its praise of the teacher and it would have been supported by *unconscious denial and over-idealization* as well. In time, the unconscious (but not the conscious) denial and reversal mechanisms generally will give way to severely negative encoded perceptions, but the first response is extremely paradoxical in its positive imagery — a reaction to extremes of trauma that cause deep unconscious system overload and shutdown and the desperately protective but costly unconscious use of denial.

There is, in addition, evidence that the conscious denial of hurt would gratify deeply unconscious, self-punitive needs in Ms. Gold. Her largely unconscious guilt over earlier incestuous experiences with her brother and an affair with a married man played a role in these self-hurtful needs — they are typical of psychotherapy patients and self-processing students. The emotion-processing mind is strangely configured and in great need of trigger-decoded insights to set it straight — until evolution moves forward with its job of creating a more efficient and integrated emotion-processing mind.

TWO POSTSCRIPTS TO THE VIGNETTE

Two postscripts to this excerpt will further support these ideas. First, in the course of her associations, Ms. Gold described how, on the day before the present class, she had been approached for a date by her gynaecologist. He had stood menacingly over her while she still lay on the examining table, as if he would block her way if she tried to leave. At first, she had consented to his proposal, but then she backed off after deciding that there was something inappropriate about his offer.

This revelation confirms the previously made trigger-decoded formulation of her material. We call support for initial formulations and intended interpretations that are not offered to a student the *silent cognitive validation of a silent hypothesis or planned intervention*. Clearly, the gynaecologist's behaviour again encodes an unconscious perception of Mr. Dean's intervention as inappropriate, seductive, and entrapping. But the story also contains another striking behavioural response to her encoded perceptions of Mr. Dean in light of his frame break. We are reminded again that the consequences of a teacher's (and therapist's) interventions are not only intrapsychic but also involve real actions and symptoms — and serious ones at that.

To clarify, Ms. Gold's gynaecologist had proposed a modification in the usual and ideal physician/patient frame — as had Mr. Dean in respect to the student/teacher frame, though not in overt seductive fashion. Ms. Gold's initial acquiescence had arisen in part because of her unconscious perceptions of Mr. Dean's intervention. Students typically unconsciously introject and exploit a teacher's frame alterations by acting out frame breaks of their own in their daily lives — the sanction of corrupt and other kinds of pathological behaviour is commonly sought unconsciously by self-processing students (and patients in therapy). A self-processing teacher must be on the alert for this kind of misappropriation of his or her errors and frame breaks; consequent hurtful acting out, which nevertheless is the responsibility of the student, should be interpreted as such in light of its triggers from the self-processing teacher.

On the other hand, Ms. Gold's change of mind was, as we have seen, *an unconscious model of rectification* — an encoded corrective. It was her way of saying, unconsciously, that she — and her teacher — should not participate in seductive frame alterations. Her eventual rejection of the date is much like her flight from her cousin James, but behaviourally it has somewhat different implications from her rejection of the more appropriate man who had shown an interest in her at the party.

Based on Ms. Gold's material, Mr. Dean was able to interpret his student's encoded perceptions of his frame break and to pledge to his students that he would be careful to adhere to the time frame of the class in the future (his offer of rectification based on the student's derivatives). Ms. Gold responded with a fresh narrative association to her dream. This narrative reaction is a crucial way of giving the second unconscious system a fresh opportunity to confirm or disconfirm a teacher's interpretation and frame-management responses. As discussed, the derivatives emanating from the second unconscious system are the ultimate arbitrator of the validity of all interventions.

Ms. Gold responded to Mr. Dean's request that she provide a fresh guided association to her dream by recalling that James had reformed some years after the entrapment incident. She also remembered an incident in which a man she had been dating and then broke up with had pushed his way into her apartment and had been physically abusive. James had shown up while the ex-boyfriend was there and had taken the man to task for his behaviour. The man apologized and never bothered her again.

Ms. Gold's new images encode a response to the fresh trigger of Mr. Dean's interpretation and his promise of rectification. The themes mainly are those of reform and resecuring a violated frame. They convey a confirmatory response via both forms of unconscious validation — *interpersonal* in the form of well-functioning people and *cognitive* via images with meanings that extend the teacher's intervention in unexpected ways. As I have said, emotionally cogent validation is not a matter of conscious agreement, but should occur on the encoded level where each responsive image is treated as an encoded reaction to the most immediate comments and behaviours of the instructor.

* * *

The richness of human communication is such that many levels of formulation and intervention are possible. But as I have repeatedly stressed, the most critical level of meaning and influence in the emotional realm lies with the second unconscious system as revealed through encoded narratives that embody immediate responses to current emotionally charged triggers. It is this compelling level of experience and adaptation that is captured most effectively and precisely through trigger decoding in a self-processing class. The design of the class maximizes the expression of encoded meaning and facilitates the recognition of active triggers. Therein lies the extraordinary power of the self-processing methodology and classroom experience. The greater the access to the second unconscious system, the stronger the therapeutic process — and, most certainly, its constructive and lasting effects.

Having completed our survey of how therapists ascribe meaning to the material from patients, and having outlined the preferred method for teaching self-processing to students, I turn now to the specific details of the self-processing class and the means by which it is structured and taught — the basis for its educational and healing powers.

PART THREE

THE TECHNIQUES
OF SELF-PROCESSING

CHAPTER SEVEN

The modes
of self-processing therapy

W e are now ready to explore the techniques and teaching principles of the various forms of self-processing therapy. We will begin by looking at the three modes in which these efforts are made — personal, tutorial, and in a class of two to six students. They have much in common, yet each has its own distinctive features — its own frame and consequent holding powers and issues.

THE SELF-PROCESSING TUTORIAL

The self-processing tutorial is designed as a one-to-one situation, usually but not necessarily once weekly, in which there is a teacher and a single student who engages in the process within a well-defined frame. Because this mode of self-processing can be carried out within an ideal secured frame or within a frame with the fewest possible departures from this unconsciously sought ideal (e.g., it can be arranged with full confidentiality and privacy, and with suitable anonymity for the instructor), it is the optimal form of self-processing. Indeed, the self-processing tutorial is quite extraordinary in its healing powers, and the day is awaited when it will be an important part of accepted clinical practice.

Because of its relatively well-secured frame, this particular form of self-processing therapy evokes intense secured-frame anxieties in a potential student (and in his or her instructor). These anxieties are based on unconscious fears of the privacy and intimacy of the tutorial, and of the strong derivatives — carriers of unconscious meaning — that are generated in this space. They also stem from the entrapping qualities inherent to the consistency of the structure of the one-to-one class and, as noted, the intense but natural death-related anxieties stirred up by the claustrum attributes of its frame.

Nonetheless, the intense activation of deep issues inherent to coping in the emotional domain provides the self-processing tutorial student — and his or her teacher — with an exceptional opportunity to experience and insightfully resolve the basic anxieties of life and living. This paradigm also offers an extremely rare type of curative holding and unmarred secured-frame moments that, properly managed and interpreted, have remarkable healing powers that can lead to symptom alleviation and change the course of a life.

The secured frame of the self-processing tutorial does, however, create rather unbearable anxieties for some potential students. In the main, these people suffer from a syndrome I call *the over-intense and premature exposure to death anxiety and related issues*. Characteristically, they have experienced one or more major life traumas or disruptive death-related experiences — a significant early loss; a major illness, especially early in life; the loss of a close relative through suicide or a fatal accident; a recent death of a loved one; and so forth.

A self-processing teacher who conducts a consultation with a person seeking therapy, and who offers self-processing therapy as part of his or her healing repertoire, should, in principle, recommend individual self-processing when that particular mode of help seems best suited to the consultee — which it often does. However, if there are clear indications of this kind of death-related sensitivity, the therapist seems well advised to recommend a self-processing *class* rather than individual (communicative) therapy or a self-processing tutorial. To do this, the therapist/teacher must have a waiting list of potential students; he or she should bring the consultee into a fresh class, not into an ongoing one.

The self-processing tutorial is best structured as a one-and-a-half-hour session, with the student afforded the first forty minutes entirely on his or her own and then interactive teaching for the remaining fifty minutes. The fee should be in keeping with the peculiarities of the modality, which is a mixture of education and therapy and of greater length than the average therapy session. The tutorial is best done in four session units — with renewal at the option of the student. In order to secure the frame, the teacher is obliged to set aside the agreed-upon time for the student for as long as he or she wishes to continue with the self-processing experience; the time should remain set throughout the life of the tutorial. As noted, for those students and teachers that can bear it, the self-processing tutorial is the ideal therapeutic modality (see chapter sixteen).

THE SELF-PROCESSING CLASS

The self-processing class is ideal for individuals with over-intense secured-frame anxieties and for those who cannot afford the fee of a self-processing tutorial. Although there is, in principle, no limit to the size of the class, experience has shown that it is best restricted to a small number of students — four seems ideal. However, the process will work well with up to six (and more rarely, eight) students and with as few as two. Once-weekly sessions at a fixed time is the rule.

The class should be two hours long, with the first forty minutes turned over to the presenting student and the class members. The balance of the time again is given over to inter-active teaching efforts, which are concentrated on reworking the student's exercise in order to identify and resolve resistances and to bring the class to the point where themes are linked to triggers and deep insight is achieved.

Six to twelve weekly seminar units seem to work well, and the fee should be set fairly and maintained without change for the life of the class (see chapter eight). Although the presence of others is a departure from the ideal one-to-one frame, this deviation lends itself to processing and interpretation in the course of the class's self-processing exercises. In time, the derivative material usually will propose that this basic frame alteration be rectified in the only way possible — the termination of the class, with the students either finishing with self-processing or shifting to a tutorial situation.

In all, though, the class modality is an effective way for students to learn the techniques of self-processing and to benefit from their healing properties. It is a process that generates rather exciting and absorbing work with considerable and generally positive impact on its students — and its teachers as well.

PERSONAL SELF-PROCESSING

Personal or individual, private self-processing is carried out on one's own without an instructor. It is without a doubt the most difficult form of emotional self-exploration in which a person can engage. To carry this process forward effectively, there must be a well-defined frame and the basic self-processing methodology must be adopted and maintained throughout. Indeed, resistances against adhering to the essential principles of self-processing are inevitable, and vigilance for their many guises is essential to the success of this effort. Self-observation must be maintained in an unfailing manner, and the principles of self-processing must be safeguarded — departures from the basic approach are certain to derail the effort. Nevertheless, this mode of self-processing is the only avenue into the second unconscious system and its vast storehouse of much needed knowledge. There is no better way to appreciate the design of the human mind and the unconscious struggle of your own patients and students than to find yourself, in the course of personal self-processing, caught up in this same battle within yourself.

It has been said that every surgeon should have at least one operation, every gynaecologist, one baby. Every therapist should spend one period of their professional lives attempting to do formal self-processing — it's good for our professional souls.

CHAPTER EIGHT

The frame
of the self-processing class

We begin our study of the self-processing class with its structure — the ground rules or framework that defines its setting and procedures. As is true of psychotherapy, this edifice is of critical importance to the self-processing experience and its outcome. The teacher's management of the frame is organized along *frame-securing* and *frame-modifying* lines. Whenever the ground rules of the class are considered, *this attribute must be identified because it is the primary organizer of deep emotional life* and the source of most unconscious psychodynamic conflicts and their resolution.

As is true of boundary conditions throughout nature, the status of the frame has an impact on every other aspect of the self-processing experience. Indeed, because it is a crucial and ubiquitous, ever-present dimension of life, it can be fairly said that within and outside of psychotherapy we are always dealing with one of the two forms of frame-related anxieties — deviant or secured — or a mixture of both.

While each type of frame offers a measure of gain, the deviant mode overall is more maladaptive than the secured-frame mode. Each type of frame also generates a degree of anxiety (much of it unconscious); deviant-frame anxieties reflect the actual persecutory attributes of that type of frame, while secured-frame anxieties are largely existential in nature, yet far more dreaded than those connected with altered frames. Much of this sounds unfamiliar largely because *evolution has assigned the monitoring of and adapting to frame conditions to the second unconscious system.*

Frame management is a contextual action or behaviour, and, as a result, ground rules, frames, and boundaries exert a strong influence on the entities within their confines — the students and teacher. The ways in which the class members and the instructor interact and express themselves, and the meanings and implications of those actions and communications, are continually affected by the conditions within which they engage each other. Further, the great sensitivity of the second unconscious system to the state of the frame, and the major influence that frames have on the students' emotional lives, insure a primary role for this aspect of the self-processing class. Indeed, as I will show, the work of the class, centred as it is on the processing efforts of the deep unconscious wisdom subsystem, is *organized around the state of its frame* and the frame impingements — securing or modifying — of both students and teacher. Frame-related interventions deal with the main class of triggers around which the encoded responses of students organize, and they exert great power over the lives of students and teachers alike.

A properly managed frame, moved consistently towards frame securing *at the behest of students' derivatives,* is a crucial part of the healing process. Unneeded frame alterations do damage to all concerned, while inadvertent frame lapses, while hurtful to some extent, are a propitious means through which issues and material are mobilized that might otherwise lie dormant. Given that these infractions of the ideal ground rules are inescapable, their careful processing — interpretation and rectification — is a vital part of effective classroom teaching and healing.

The frame configures the relationship among the students and between them and the teacher, and it shapes and defines their roles and interaction. The frame also influences the effects of the interventional and interpretative efforts of the teacher.

Interpretations and other kinds of comments that run counter to a teacher's frame-management efforts will be deeply doubted and experienced as self-contradictory signals designed to drive the student crazy (Searles, 1959). The contradiction between word and deed will, in general, have a very negative impact on the students (and on the teacher as well). In contrast, interpretations that are supported by the frame-securing efforts of the instructor are internally consistent and most salutary.

The frame establishes the physical, interpersonal, and psychological boundaries between each student and between the students and teacher. It also secures the relative impermeability of the boundary between the classroom and the outside world (Newton, 1971). The frame is a real entity, as is its management, and these powerful realities must be dealt with continually whenever frame issues are activated. As a special class of triggers, *frame impingements* (and these may be either *frame securing or frame altering*) always must be both *managed* (the frame must be either secured or modified — a choice must be made) and *interpreted* in light of the encoded material from the exercise at hand. Inaction with respect to a frame issue is as much a response as action — the failure to act leaves the frame either intact or altered.

Among the responsibilities of the teacher, none is more important than frame management. The deep unconscious wisdom systems of both students and instructor are sharply focused on the vicissitudes of the frame. *The most compelling activated, dynamic unconscious meanings experienced and communicated about by a student involve responses to the instructor's frame-managements efforts.* The frame itself (i.e., the therapist's management of the frame) can hold and heal, or disrupt and harm, depending on whether it is secured or modified, and on whether the anxieties attendant to either effort are interpreted in light of the available responsive derivatives.

SOME PRINCIPLES OF FRAME MANAGEMENT

We need some background information on the nature, functions, and effects of the ground rules or frames of a healing situation. *The ideal or secured frame is defined entirely through unconsciously validated frame-management interventions.* In contrast, the deviant or altered frame is any situation in which these unconsciously sought ideals are compromised through *interventions that are not derivatively validated.* It is the second unconscious system and not the conscious system that dictates the appropriate structure of a healing relationship. The conscious system is clearly self-defeating in this respect because, regardless of the cost, it favours defensiveness and immediate relief through inherently damaging frame modifications in lieu of more reasoned and healthy secured-frame alternatives.

There is, as I have argued, a *universal unconscious need for secured frames* in all types of relationships and settings — and healing situations are very much among them. While conscious frame attitudes vary greatly, and almost always lean towards some degree of deviation, the position of the second unconscious system is unmistakably and uncompromisingly in favour of frame securing. This means that both encoded validation and positive therapeutic effects will accrue as a result of frame-securing efforts by the self-processing teacher. In contrast, non-validation and harm, much of it unnoticed or denied, always follows upon frame alterations.

Frame modifications, then, are psychologically hurtful for all concerned. They can, however, stimulate paradoxical reactions in students subjected to them who, at times, independently secure frames in their daily lives when they have been modified in class — *an enacted model of rectification.* In addition, as I wish to stress, in a self-processing class these interludes can be turned to good stead by keeping them to a minimum, developing sound interpretative interventions, and securing an altered ground rule when possible.

In order to establish a reasonable perspective on this crucial aspect of self-processing therapy and life, once the value of the ideal frame is recognized, we must acknowledge the stark aspects of the human condition and the pressures of uncontrollable aspects of reality, the enormity of everyone's *silent secured-frame anxieties* and an instructor's own unavoidable frame-deviant needs. It is well to adopt a humble and realistic attitude towards frame alterations and maintain an alertness for the effects of inevitable lapses and for activated secured-frame anxieties, when they materialize. Being at peace in a secured frame is a rare event that soon gives way to secured-frame anxieties despite the enhancing qualities of the experience. As for technique, *the principle of avoiding unnecessary frame modifications and opting for frame-securing or frame-maintaining interventions holds in the self-processing class at all times.*

THE SECURED FRAME

The secured frame is that setting in which all of the unconsciously validated ground rules of a self-processing class or tutorial are intact. It offers an ideal hold with basic trust, safety for open expression and communication, clear and firm interpersonal boundaries, a sense of the teacher as sound and sane, and other inherently supportive and growth-promoting qualities. However, basic anxieties are also mobilized by the restrictive and frustrating aspects of the secured frame. These anxieties are persecutory (paranoid-evoking), entrapping (claustrophobic-inducing), depressive (imposed distance and separateness), and death-related (rule enforcing, in the sense that death as an ironclad rule must follow life).

The secured frame deprives both students and teacher of their usual but overly costly defences against and maladaptive responses to these fundamental anxieties and concerns. This kind of frame undermines the use of such mechanisms as denial, manic kinds of celebration and fusion, counterphobic manoeuvres, forms of grandiosity and omnipotence, and active aggression as a cover for persecutory feelings.

These underlying apprehensions are, of course, the inescapable anxieties of life and living, and they especially touch on the inevitability of personal death. Through a basically secured frame — or secured-frame moments — students are afforded a unique opportunity to experience, mobilize, explore, resolve, and recast issues and adaptations that are fundamental to emotional existence. Despite the fears that this experience raises, these are potential growth-promoting interludes of extraordinary uniqueness and power.

Perhaps the greatest failure of evolutionary design by natural selection in this area lies with the *absence of a conscious secured-frame anxiety signal* comparable to the anxiety we experience as a danger signal when endangered physically or psychologically. As a result, students and teachers suffering from acute secured-frame anxieties are almost never aware that this is the case — a situation that promotes considerable unconsciously motivated defensive acting out, sometimes to a point that jeopardizes the continuation of the self-processing experience. Secured-frame anxieties are a silent psychological plague that not only jeopardizes secured-frame therapies and self-processing efforts, but detrimentally affects the life of every living person.

Overall, the secured frame offers a tower of strength but mobilizes basic human anxieties, especially death-anxiety; it creates a fundamental existential threat that, on the one hand, fosters the self-processing work but, on the other, threatens its continuance. This latter prospect arises because most humans believe unconsciously that they cannot master or survive the anxieties raised by personal death and secured frames. Indeed, the human mind has evolved on the basis of that particular premise. The very anxieties that put self-processing at risk foster emotional health to the greatest known extent. In the final analysis there are, in principle, powerful therapeutic and anti-therapeutic forces activated solely through how a self-processing teacher manages the setting, ground rules, and frame of the class.

THE ALTERED FRAME

In an *altered frame*, one or more of the basic ground rules of the self-processing class are permanently or temporarily modified. Except for professionally referred students who are then seen in secured-frame self-processing tutorials, self-processing efforts are carried out in somewhat modified frames. Still, the activation of secured-frame moments when an aspect of the altered frame is rectified, together with the interpretation of activated derivatives pertaining to the modified frame conditions, serve well to counterbalance the injurious effects of these deviations.

Whatever the hurtful consequences of an altered frame, there are distinct advantages to dealing with this kind of frame in a self-processing class as compared to psychotherapy. When a frame alteration occurs in the latter situation, dreams and narrative material are, by and large, rather sparse and the frame issue itself may not be alluded to or well represented in the patient's encoded material. As a result, the working over and processing of the relevant dynamic issues and their consequences are difficult to carry forward.

In contrast, the self-processing method has been designed to generate a maximal degree of narrative material and to optimize the chances of identifying a given activating frame deviation; interpretation — and frame rectification if possible — are therefore facilitated. In this way, insight into the ramifications of a given frame modification can be developed and frame alterations kept to a minimum. The overall effect is far more in the direction of healing rather than harm. Whatever limitations frame modifications pose to the therapeutic process, the self-processing class provides an opportunity to work over the activated issues to great advantage.

As for the negative side of frame alterations, they always imply some compromise in a teacher's holding and containment of his or her students. In addition, all frame breaks are actively persecutory (rather than inevitably and paradoxically threatening, as with the secured frame), and they afford all concerned pathological forms of merger and fusion that foster dysfunctional relationships in everyday life. They also offer manic defences against depressive anxieties and counterphobic defences against the claustrophobic anxieties seen with the ideal frame — defences that are then sought after, often at great expense to self and others, in the outside world. Emotional learning is also impaired in the context of an altered frame — there is excessive use of denial and many unconsciously disorienting contradictions between the teacher's management of the frame and his or her verbal interventions. The illusory gains derived from a deviant frame are costly to human adaptation, and in the long run they are distinctly maladaptive.

Deviant frames are quite attractive to the conscious system. The price paid for these frame alterations is routinely denied or attributed to other causes. Nonetheless, an altered frame does not doom a self-processing class, in that the effects of a particular deviation can be limited, especially when the instructor maintains the remaining aspects of the frame in sound and secured fashion or, when possible, rectifies unneeded deviations — doing so always at the behest of the students' encoded material (which consistently offers this kind of frame-securing corrective and guidance).

A self-processing instructor who initiates a seminar series with a basic frame alteration must be on the alert not to invoke additional deviations unnecessarily as the class proceeds. A consistently frame-securing approach in the face of an initial frame alteration is an effective setting for self-processing work. In contrast, the instructor who continues to alter a basically modified frame is likely to have a chaotic class with little effective healing.

There is without let up a continuous struggle between the conscious system and the second unconscious system with respect to the framework of the self-processing class. Within every student (and instructor), a significant intrasystemic struggle ensues between the two systems of the mind. The conscious system, in alliance with the fear/guilt system, is driven (motivated) towards frame deviations by deep anxieties, including fears of death, and by needs for self-punishment. This combination of forces generally overwhelms the encoded and often unnoticed frame-securing voice of the second unconscious system which has little direct effect on a student's or teacher's frame-related behaviours and choices.

In class, this trigger-evoked internal battle typically is transformed into a struggle between the students and the self-processing teacher. This arises because characteristically students fall prey to their conscious system needs and naively seek frame alterations. They make little effort to decode their own images in light of frame-related triggers, and they seldom fully grasp and structuralize (sustain) the decoded insights arrived at with the help of the teacher as they speak for the salutary aspects of secured frames.

On the other hand, the effective self-processing teacher must be capable of overcoming and to some extent resolving his or her deviant-frame needs and secured-frame anxieties, and of truly appreciating and committing himself or herself to the constructive effects of a secured-frame moment or situation. He or she therefore consistently and quite legitimately draws from the students' exercises the unswerving preference of the deep unconscious system for secured frames. In the long run, successful self-processing will lead to changes in the position of the students from a preference for frame deviations to a greater appreciation of the value of secured frames.

It is essential, then, to be mindful of the natural — genetic and psychobiological — human conscious preference for frame modifications and to guard against ignoring their real negative consequences. Further, it is well to realize that while the secured frame offers the greatest amount of strength to those within its confines, secured-frame anxiety is a universal and exceedingly strong dread — a malevolent silent force of considerable power.

Every self-processing teacher learns quickly that he or she must guard against interventions motivated by his or her own secured-frame anxieties and deviant-frame needs. No one is exempt from lapses; they are inevitable because of the way the mind is configured. All one can do is be vigilant and alert to these needs, opt for frame-securing responses whenever deciding how to manage an ambiguous classroom frame issue, and be observant enough to recognize lapses.

AN OVERVIEW OF THE IDEAL FRAME

There is, as I have said, an unconsciously validated, universally ideal frame for the self-processing class. The following are its main components:

1. The physical setting — the classroom

Assuming that the instructor is a mental health professional, the setting should be his or her own office, properly sound-proofed and entirely private. The locale should be a professional building and should be a single suite for the teacher alone. The classroom should be of sufficient size to hold all of the students comfortably, without crowding or physical contact.

The teacher should work behind a desk, using it as a supportive physical boundary between himself or herself and the class members. Each student should have his or her own chair, and the coat closet or rack should be designed to avoid contact between the garments of the students (keep in mind that we are dealing primarily with a very sensitive unconscious system). Finally, the location of the classroom should not change during the duration of the class.

Common departures from this ideal, many of which constitute workable triggers for self-exploratory work, include a shared office suite or the use of a room in a school where the teacher works — or rents space. Far less workable are home/office and apartment/office arrangements which involve self-revealing and third-party contaminants that adversely affect the second unconscious system and the student. Finally, if the teacher moves his or her office, the locale of the class will, of necessity, need to be changed; this frame change is quite powerful and must be processed in class. Unconsciously, this kind of frame alteration is experienced as the loss and death of the teacher; persecutory forms of death anxiety are quite strong for all concerned.

2. *The selection of students*

The students accepted for a self-processing class ideally should have had no prior contact with the instructor, nor should any member of the class know any other student who is either in the class itself or has been taught, treated in therapy, or is now being seen in any other capacity by the instructor. This requisite insures one aspect of the necessary relative anonymity of the instructor, as well as the total confidentiality and relative privacy of the class. In essence then, ideally the student should be someone referred professionally to the teacher.

Given that as yet professional referrals for self-processing therapy are exceedingly rare, aspects of this particular ground rule are commonly modified. The most workable frame alterations in this area involves students who have taken an open course — say, on psychoanalysis — given by the teacher and who subsequently shift over to a private self-processing class.

It is to be stressed, however, that none of these students should have or have had an outside personal relationship with each other — or with the instructor. Attempting to do self-processing with individuals who are related, or who know each other socially or through business, involves frame modifications of privacy, anonymity, and the requisite that all contact between students and between the students and their teacher be confined to the self-processing classroom during the agreed-upon time period. This particular deviation is usually quite toxic, and its effects are difficult to limit and work through — it is a relatively malignant frame alteration. Often, when two students have had contact outside of class, both eventually are lost to the process and harmed.

Another more workable modification of this aspect of the frame involves enrolling students through a teacher's professional writings and lectures. In the case of a student who has read an article, professional paper, or book written by the instructor, frame rectification calls for the student to discard the material. As stated before, this is carried out as dictated by the student's own encoded directives. While this kind of frame modification may have a lesser effect in the context of self-processing therapy than it does in the usual forms of psychotherapy (Langs, 1992d), it is nonetheless a frame alteration. These extensions of the boundaries of the self-processing class and the student/teacher relationship are ever-present background triggers; when they are activated, they should be processed for unconscious meaning — and for rectification if possible.

Similarly, advertisements for self-processing classes have definite procuring qualities, yet they too prove in general to be quite workable if properly processed in class.

Nonetheless, there is a small group of students for whom these departures from the ideal frame create a setting in which they are unable to do effective therapeutic work. For them, both the deviation and the subsequent frame-securing efforts of the teacher pose unbearable threats. These students are in general subject to extremes of death anxiety and often have a history of being the victim of a significant early illness or loss, or extreme childhood assault or seduction. Often, they are individuals who are barely managing to manage. They are defending themselves against and covering over a deep psychotic process; their equilibrium is gravely threatened by the basically mixed and insecure frame of the self-processing effort.

Finally, there is the question of transferring a psychotherapy patient into a self-processing class. While I know of no instance in which this has been done, there is no established principle that precludes such a change. There is, however, an unconscious issue regarding this shift because the frames of the two situations differ in important ways, and the role of the psychotherapist is quite different from that of the self-processing teacher — one specializes in silent listening and holding, the other in listening silently at first and then becoming exceedingly active (Langs, 1992d). In general, the human mind is more flexible than we tend to appreciate. The main question is whether this particular shift, which is a frame break in the context of both healing modalities and yet a way of securing a new frame, constitutes a workable or unmanageable deviation. The final answer to this problem must await empirical study, though I suspect it is a viable and often advisable move.

3.   *A one-to-one relationship*

As noted, the ideal self-processing class is a tutorial. However, great benefit can be garnered from self-processing classes, as long as the work includes a processing by each individual student of the implications of the presence of the other students in the class — third parties — when this issue is activated. This is a basic deviation that serves the defensive needs of both the students and the teacher, and the financial needs of both as well. The self-processing instructor must be on the alert for *encoded representations* of this trigger (it almost never comes up directly) and for the derivative themes it evokes — expressions of the relevant unconscious perceptions and their consequences.

This particular issue often arises when a class is dealing with an immediate frame alteration or frame-securing moment, or when the students are deciding whether to renew their contract with the teacher — as well as during a termination period. Still, a frame modification is a frame modification, and the presence of third parties in a class otherwise geared towards frame securing eventually will activate themes of violent and murderous intruders, acts of madness, seduction, group sex, and brutal betrayal — among others. The self-processing teacher must have the openness and courage to deal with these incisively perceptive and valid derivatives or they will get lost among other themes and triggers, and leave damaging un-processed residuals in the students — and the teacher as well.

A supplementary aspect of this component of the frame requires that *the membership of the class be fixed.* That is, ideally, no one should be added to the class — or leave. Once the class is constituted and the fee is set, both should remain unchanged throughout the life of the group.

The most common modifications of these tenets arise when a student leaves the class. An especially difficult frame situation arises when a class is reduced to two members. In principle, whenever a student drops out, the related trigger is that the instructor is responsible for the loss — unconsciously and sometimes consciously, the instructor is seen as having driven the student away.

As students are lost, the fee may have to be increased — though always at the behest of the students' derivatives, which will consistently show the way. Too low a fee unconsciously is seen as seductive and a masochistic sacrifice by the teacher. Further, under these circumstances, a fee increase is justified to some extent by the fact that with fewer students in the class, each remaining member leads the exercise more often than before.

Another way of insuring a fair fee for the teacher for time spent with the class, and of doing so without a fee increase, is the addition of new members to the class. As with a fee increase, this deviation is best avoided if possible — it is a blatant viola-tion of the original contract between the students and the teacher, and it is overloaded with hurtful implications for the existing and prospective students. Nevertheless, the deviation may be necessary when the students in a reduced class express a wish not to pay a higher fee — even when, as would be expected, their own derivatives advise them to do so. If this step is taken, the addition of a new member to a class calls for intense processing — it is usually a workable deviation even though its effects never entirely disappear once invoked.

Finally, when two students are left in a class, some self-processing teachers maintain their existing fee per student, but reduce the duration of the class from two to one-and-a-half hours. This may in some instances be a reasonable compromise, but teachers are well advised to keep frame changes to a minimum — and of course, to process every frame alteration that they invoke. Experience will show each instructor which frame modifications tend to be relatively viable and benign, and which tend to be quite malignant and often unresolvable — and which may cause the demise of a class.

This type of situation involves a rather interesting group of frame-related issues that are difficult to resolve in that the teacher must either choose between two frame-deviant possibilities or between altering the frame or sustaining it in a fashion that is blatantly self-sacrificing. Another related class of problems arises when a teacher must *modify the frame to secure it*. Common examples of this last kind of problem occur when two friends or relatives have inadvertently entered a class; when a teacher has made a mistake regarding the basic fee, such as setting it too low or too high; when a third party has inadvertently and incorrectly been added to a class, etc.

In principle, the instructor uses the material from an exercise activated by these kinds of frame issues to *find the least deviant or single best frame-securing solution to these dilemmas*. For example, the derivatives will, as a rule, recommend that a friend or relative of a class member be asked to leave the class; that an erroneous fee be corrected; and that an unwarranted third party also be asked to leave the class. These decisions are encoded in the themes of the presenting student's material; the teacher has only to hear and formulate their meanings and implications, and connect them to the proper activating trigger. The course of action is then usually quite clear.

4. *Total privacy*

This rule implies all of the following tenets: that no sounds or voices move in or out of a classroom; the exclusion of all outside parties from the class; the complete acceptance of and adherence to a pledge not to reveal any aspect of the classroom experience to others (this applies equally to the students and instructor); and a prohibition against the use of insurance or other third-party payers for the fee of the class.

The pledge not to speak to outsiders about the happenings in class and, by implication, not to engage each other outside of the classroom must be taken seriously and obeyed to the letter by everyone. Any breach in this aspect of the frame is a deviation that will need to be processed immediately and rectified — i.e., it requires a sincere pledge that it will never recur.

Privacy is also supported by a professional setting for the classroom; a home setting risks exposure of class members to the family and friends of the instructor. Any violation of these frame-related principles by the instructor is a major breech of the frame and usually is of malignant proportions. Major efforts at rectification and interpretation are called for.

5. *Total confidentiality*

Privacy and confidentiality go together. The latter implies that there will be no written material related to the self-processing class — no notes written during or after (or before) class. The constraint against speaking to others about the transactions of the class is also relevant to this ground rule. Privacy and confidentiality ensure a safe and holding space for the work of self-processing. Indeed, it is for this reason that all of the vignettes in this book are informed fictions — illustrations rather than evidence.

6. *The face-to-face mode*

For the self-processing class, the students should sit in some kind of a circular arrangement, with the instructor behind a desk. This configuration provides a natural physical barrier between the class and the instructor that helps to establish and confirm the necessary psychological boundaries between them; it also accentuates the differences in role and functions between teacher and students. As might be expected, no one lies on a couch.

7.   A set fee, locale, and length of class

These are aspects of the so-called *fixed frame* (Langs, 1992a). The fee should be reasonable and fair to both sides; it should reflect the mixed nature of the class — educational and heal-ing — and the unusual length of each seminar. The cost per session should be set when the class is recruited and not modified for the life of the class. It is a form of tuition and therefore should be paid in advance for a specified number of sessions — the "semester unit" of the class. This usually is done sometime before the first meeting or at the time of the class' inception. A student's failure to comply in full should preclude entry into the class until the rule has been satisfied. On the other hand, this particular ground rule is an aid in dealing with seminar-threatening resistances and issues because implicitly it encourages students, who already have paid for the sessions, to continue to attend the self-processing class and to explore thoughts of termination before acting on them.

The class, which is two hours in length, should start at a fixed time, should begin and end on time, and should be continued through renewals of the class's contract with the teacher for as long as the students wish to do so. Units of six to twelve classes per contract work best; the unit size should allow each student to present the same number of times per semes-ter, and the unit itself should remain fixed for the duration of a group.

8.   Confinement of all interpersonal contacts to the classroom time and location

There should be no outside contact between the teacher and his or her students, or between the students themselves. This restriction includes travelling together to or from the class and talking in the waiting room. Accidental meetings should be treated with great reserve and limited as much as possible. For the second unconscious system these contacts are departures from the ideal frame and fraught with pathological unconscious meanings and consequences. There are no viable exceptions to this ground rule.

9. *Consistent adherence to the structure of the exercise*

All modifications in the ideal self-processing exercise — the substance of the classroom work — are frame alterations and should not knowingly be invoked. The class should at all times maintain its pursuit of an optimal frame and unconscious meaning and should not veer off into other kinds of discussions or activities. Departing from the essential process is a common resistance among students and is an important frame-modifying indicator that needs to be understood for its unconscious sources.

10. *The absence of physical contact*

Except for an initial handshake — and one at termination — there should, of course, be no physical contact of any kind between students and teacher or between students.

* * *

These, then, are the essential ground rules of self-processing therapy. Active adherence to these propositions creates secured-frame moments, while departures involve frame deviations. All such moments are potentially curative in that processing the responsive material from a presenting student will, in most instances, lead to insight — and with frame deviations, to the possible experience of a frame-securing intervention.

There is a unique frame issue that comes up in self-processing classes and tutorials, one that again reveals the extent of deep unconscious sensitivities. Let us approach the subject by asking this question: When a self-processing teacher takes a vacation and interrupts the consecutive sessions of the class, how should the situation be handled? For purposes of discussion, I will take a four-session unit tutorial as my self-processing model and walk us through the frame-management issues.

First, what of a one- or two-week vacation that falls during a particular sequence of sessions — say, after two of the four weeks? If the teacher arranges to be paid for just two classes before he or she leaves, the agreed-upon number of sessions in a unit is modified, but if the teacher accepts the full fee for all four sessions, the frame is held in respect to the number of sessions in the unit, but the patient is to some extent exploited financially. Clearly, a choice must be made between these two alternatives.

Self-processing exercises appear to offer a consistent solution to this dilemma in that the derivative material indicates that the second unconscious system tends to see the acceptance of the fee for the four sessions as the least deviant choice. Thus, the decision to accept the full fee limits the deviant qualities of the situation to the greatest extent feasible.

Note too that the teacher's vacation is a mixed intervention in respect to the frame: it is a modification of the frame within a secured frame. That is, the therapist's vacations, when announced well in advance and not excessive, are a part of the secure-frame contract in that a self-processing therapy without interruption is deviant. On the other hand, unconsciously, students appear to expect self-processing therapy to unfold without interruption even though that condition is not part of the established agreement — the break is therefore also viewed unconsciously as frame modifying. The vacation issue will always be worked over unconsciously as a trigger in its own right. Deep unconscious system reactions to each trigger will be condensed into the reactive encoded themes.

What then of a more extended vacation of three to five weeks? This is most problematic when the four-session unit ends at a time that precedes the self-processing teacher's vacation by one to three weeks. Should an extra one to three sessions be held, thus altering the agreed-upon number of sessions in each teaching unit, or should the four-unit frame be maintained and those hours cancelled?

The answer to this question requires an additional and rather interesting perspective. Self-processing is framed as an educational situation but functions as a form of therapy. While the two frames share most secured-frame attributes, in the situation under consideration they are in rare conflict: the self-processing frame speaks for a specific number of sessions per unit, no more, no less. On the other hand, the therapy frame speaks for holding sessions until a therapist goes on vacation. What now?

The answer again lies with the encoded images of each student in response to this *anticipated trigger* — i.e., an expected intervention by the therapist like a planned vacation or an intervention requested by a student or announced for the future by the teacher. Students respond to these expected interventions with encoded material that reveals the adaptive processing of the deep unconscious system — its perception of the implications of the planned intervention. With respect to the question just raised, it turns out that students actually produce images that point to both possible solutions. However, in all cases observed until now, the most compelling derivatives indicate that the unconscious preference ultimately is in favour of holding the odd number of sessions rather than cancelling them entirely. Evidently, *the second unconscious system sees self-processing more strongly in therapeutic rather than educational terms.*

* * *

In concluding this discussion, recall again that the conscious system is easy going and cavalier about ground rules and frames, while the deep wisdom system is insistent on a sound frame. In this light, any conscious feelings that the ground rules presented here seem overstated or excessively stringent must be understood as a defensive and an inappropriate conscious system protest. There is overwhelming clinical evidence and encoded support for the components of the ideal self-processing frame proposed here and for the proposition that secured frames hold and heal, and that altered frames disrupt and harm — whatever costly relief they also may bring. This is human nature and its surrounds — how things are. Trigger decoding frame-activated encoded messages will make this irrefutably clear.

TWO VIGNETTES

I will close this chapter with two vignettes, one involving a frame modification and the other a frame-securing moment. They will give us a sense of how the second unconscious system and we as human beings respond both directly and deeply to frame impingements — secured or deviant.

Mrs. Fine, a woman in her early fifties, was in a self-processing class with Dr. Dunn, a woman psychiatrist. The student had been in a class on psychoanalysis given by Dr. Dunn, and when she had suggested a self-processing group, Mrs. Fine and three other students had decided to accept her invitation. After the final meeting of the course, Dr. Dunn had held a party in her apartment for the class; Mrs. Fine and the other people in the pending self-processing class had attended.

In the first self-processing class, Mrs. Fine, as the presenter, remembered a dream from the previous night. In the dream she is with an old friend, Clara, who is embracing her sensuously.

In associating, Mrs. Fine recalled that Clara was a college room-mate who was homosexual and who had, on one occasion, tried to seduce her — an attempt Mrs. Fine had repudiated. It was not that she objected to lesbianism, it simply was not something she wanted for herself. After the incident, Mrs. Fine was afraid to fall asleep before Clara lest Clara touch her in her sleep. Mrs. Fine had changed room-mates as soon as she could. Their room at school had a copy of a Matisse drawing on the wall; this brought to mind the Matisse poster on the wall of Dr. Dunn's apartment.

To discuss this material, the main trigger is certainly the outside contact between this instructor and her class (it means little to the second unconscious system that this contact took place before the self-processing classes had actually started). This is a frame-modifying trigger because it violates the tenet that contact between teacher and students and between the students themselves is confined to the self-processing class-room and time. In addition, the party also violates the frame of the class on psychoanalysis, where a similar ground rule prevails.

The gathering also modified the relative anonymity of the instructor in that it revealed where and how she lived; it also modified the requisite that her offerings to her students be confined to the teaching process. In all, then, a gesture looked on with favour in most academic circles has strong frame-deviant attributes for the self-processing student (and for the *unconscious experience* of students in general).

Consciously, Mrs. Fine had taken pleasure in being invited to Dr. Dunn's apartment; she had seen the party as a warm and friendly gesture. But what then of her view of this same interlude in her second unconscious system? If we take the themes in this dream-associational network and transpose or link them to the frame-deviant trigger, what can we say of Mrs. Fine's unconscious perceptions of the intervention?

To answer, it appears that the invitation to the party was experienced in Mrs. Fine's deep unconscious wisdom subsystem as a homosexual seduction and a source of grave mistrust. Support for the connection between the derivative material and the identified trigger — the *bridging image* — is provided by the references to the art work by Matisse. Once again we find two dramatically different frame-related experiences in response to a single stimulus, one in the conscious system and the other deeply unconscious.

Notice too that the conscious response is relatively flat and devoid of psychodynamic meaning, while the reaction of the second unconscious system is highly charged — another typical difference between the two systems of the emotion-processing mind. And again, the conscious system once more favours deviation, while the deep unconscious system addresses its harmful effects and offers an adaptive model of rectification — Mrs. Fine's repudiation of the homosexual overture (i.e., we shouldn't be doing this) and her decision to leave her room-mate (she should leave such women).

Another telling realization arises when we examine which assessment empowers Mrs. Fine's behaviour *vis à vis* the teacher. Clearly it is the *conscious* system, in that her direct assessment of the party and her direct view of Dr. Dunn as a kind and giving psychotherapist leads Mrs. Fine to enter the self-processing class. This decision runs counter to her unconscious assessment and her own encoded directive to stay away from seductive women. We can see now why it is hypothesized that the deep unconscious wisdom system has essentially no effect on emotionally charged decisions.

However, the problem with this consciously guided decision is that, in some other part of her life, we can be certain that through displacement Mrs. Fine will act out hurtfully based on her unrecognized unconscious perceptions — especially if they go uninterpreted. Around this time, she actually quit her job because she had mistakenly thought that her boss, who was a woman, was trying to seduce her. These self-harmful behaviours are so removed from their repressed evocative triggers and so well rationalized by the conscious system that their very existence and deep unconscious sources are difficult to detect. Nevertheless, consistently they occur after a student experiences an uninterpreted and unrectified frame break in a self-processing class (or in a psychotherapy).

Yet another problem with the evolved design of the emotion-processing mind — and evolution had far too many trade-offs to deal with to have done better in the available time — is found in the discovery that, unconsciously, Mrs. Fine had chosen to be in the self-processing class with Dr. Dunn largely because the conditions were frame-deviant. The altered frame supported her unconscious view of women as inappropriately seductive and sanctioned her own homosexual leanings which she typically projected onto others. The seductive aspects of these frame modifications lessened her unconscious guilt, and, in addition, the frame-deviant situation served to defend against her own death anxieties — her mother had died in an automobile crash only a few months before she began the self-processing classes. Deviant-frame classes are almost always selected unconsciously by students for reasons of this kind; it is essential that the self-processing instructor find the appropriate material from the class's self-processing exercises through which these pathological needs can be exposed, processed, and modified.

* * *

The second vignette is of a different order.

> Ms. Young was a self-processing counsellor and teacher
> who had elected to initiate a self-processing class with
> several of her former college students. On the day of the
> first class, Mr. Kelly, a member of the group, indicated
> that he had forgotten his chequebook and would pay his
> tuition the following week. Ms. Young accepted his
> proposal and, with Mr. Kelly staying on, she proceeded
> with the class for which Ms. Baker was the presenter. The
> student began the classroom exercise by recalling a dream
> in which she was in a restaurant with her friend, Amy, an
> old college chum. They were drinking some champagne
> and seemed to be celebrating something.

> There were a series of initial guided associations to the
> dream that need not concern us here. As she went on, Ms.
> Baker eventually recalled that Amy looked like her
> younger sister, Dolores. During her childhood, their
> mother had indulged Dolores in countless ways, and as an
> adult Dolores had become an alcoholic. Amy had been
> involved in the 1960s in a campus rebellion. Ms. Baker
> remembered a time when Amy's picture had appeared in
> the local newspaper because she illegally had entered the
> Dean's office at college for a sit-in. She had been
> photographed as the police forcibly removed her from the
> office. Even Ms. Baker, who was her friend, thought that
> Amy had gone too far by disrupting campus life for
> everyone else instead of finding a legal means of
> expressing her objections to school policies.

> At the end of the forty-minute exercise conducted by the
> class, which reached no essential trigger-decoded insight,
> Ms. Young asked the class to identify the most compelling
> and active triggers for Ms. Baker's dream-associational
> network. It took some effort in the face of strong
> resistances, which the teacher kept working over through
> leading questions, before the students did so — it was Ms.
> Young's decision to allow Mr. Kelly to remain in class even
> though he had not paid his tuition. The group then
> realized that this intervention was frame-deviant in that
> the ground rules explicitly stated that tuition was to be

paid in advance of the beginning of the first class. The students also were quite surprised that this realization had eluded them — that they had forgotten to classify the frame attributes of the prevailing, active triggers. Nonetheless, because of conscious system defences this type of oversight is commonplace.

When a trigger has been identified, the key task is to extract the themes in the narrative material and to link them to their repressed triggers. This effort reveals the student's unconscious processing of the meanings of the activating frame-related intervention of the instructor. Taken as personally selected but valid unconscious readings of the actual implications of the target intervention by the teacher, the linking effort produces remarkable insights — many of them surprisingly self-evident, but only after they have been formulated. The problem lies with overlooking key triggers and failing to properly link derivative themes to their adaptation-evoking stimuli; the emotion-processing mind is designed to avoid such operations.

The class was now able to see that the themes in Ms. Baker's guided associations involved favouritism, spoiling someone, and then an illegal entry and sit-in — followed by a corrective in the form of removing the person involved in the illegal activity. Once the themes were stated this way, the link to the trigger leapt out at the class members.

The obvious stimulus for this encoded material had been overlooked by the class but was now transparent, as were the transposed disguised images and their meanings. To state them succinctly and in the essential *narrative-adaptive form* that they should take, the teacher's decision to allow Mr. Kelly to stay on in the class without his having paid his tuition had been unconsciously perceived by Ms. Baker as a destructive indulgence, a repetition of the hurtful behaviours of Ms. Baker's mother, and as the sanction of an illegal and disruptive presence. (In this instance, of course, the dream, which occurred prior to the class, was not affected by this frame-deviant trigger, but the recall of the dream and the associations to it were certainly under its influence.)

In Ms. Baker's last association, there also was a striking encoded directive regarding rectification of the frame break —

the enforced removal of the intruder by the arm of the law. Decoded, Ms. Baker's deep unconscious wisdom system had proposed adaptively that Mr. Kelly be asked to leave the class until he paid his tuition and conformed to the law/rules of the class.

In the class, Ms. Young interpreted this material essentially as stated above, and Ms. Baker was the first to articulate her own encoded corrective. Ms. Young then agreed with her student, acknowledged her error in allowing Mr. Kelly to stay on in the class, and, in keeping with her student's encoded directive, she asked Mr. Kelly to leave the class, suggesting that he return once he could pay his tuition. Mr. Kelly accepted the proposal, got up from his chair, and left the class.

At first the class reacted to his departure manifestly and consciously. The students remarked that they felt a bit uncomfortable about Mr. Kelly's leaving — even though they could see its logic and necessity. (The conscious system seldom is able to be consistent about frame rectifications even when their basis is unmistakably clear.)

It is, however, essential at these junctures to allow the second unconscious system to speak, and this can be done only through fresh narrative associations to the dream — which is what Ms. Young asked of Ms. Baker.

After a brief pause, the student reported that she was thinking again about Amy who had gone on in her life to become a district attorney. Much to everyone's surprise, the great rebel became a strong defender of the law. Ms. Baker thought of a case that Amy had handled that had received some notoriety. A man had posed as a beggar and had got into a house that he then robbed; he had beaten the couple who lived there and they had nearly died. Amy had got a conviction in the case.

These new associations encode an *indirect validation* of Ms. Young's frame-rectifying intervention. Disguised in the allusion to Amy's career and changed attitude is a form of unconscious *interpersonal validation* (an image of a well-functioning person — here, one who also stands for secured frames). Unconscious *cognitive confirmation* is also in evidence through the encoded material related to the shift in the teacher's position from being on the side of lawlessness to being on the side of the law — i.e., from breaking to adhering to the ground rules of the self-processing class.

This fresh association also encodes an additional and disturbing unconscious implication of the seemingly well-meaning deviation — it is not only a criminal act and an invasion of other's people's rightful space, it also is an assaultive attack on the class and its members. The same image, however, also encodes via condensation the teacher's prior, and the students' newly mobilized, secured-frame anxieties — within the confines of the closed space, there is a vulnerability to attack. Such are the ways of the human mind — in a single act, one issue is resolved and another is mobilized.

Overall, we see again that the values of the conscious and unconscious systems are strikingly different — the first seeks and accepts frame modifications, while the second experiences them as assaultive, overindulgent, and criminal. In this situation, only the second unconscious system appreciated that the students — and the teacher as well — had been violated and robbed of their right to a secured frame space. As is true of psychotherapy, attention to the second unconscious system shows that the self-processing class revolves around the frame-management efforts of the instructor and that virtually all critical psychodynamic issues and conflicts are stimulated by frame impingements and their management.

* * *

Since our appreciation of the frame of the self-processing class hopefully has been afforded a firm footing, we can turn now to an explication of the specific details of how this frame is created and managed — and of how the self-processing class is conducted. We should proceed mindful of a vital maxim for all healing endeavours: *frame issues come before dynamics and content, dynamics and content arise from frame issues.* This is a characteristic of the evolved functioning of the emotion-processing mind and its deep unconscious system, and it is therefore a guiding principle of self-processing therapy.

CHAPTER NINE

Initiating
the self-processing class

We have established a framework for self-processing therapy. It is time now to walk through the average self-processing class in order to develop the specifics of how the class is conducted. The procedures and techniques of self-processing are precisely demarcated, remarkably so. This regimentation is necessitated, as I have said, by the defences and architecture of the emotion-processing mind and its conscious system which is designed, for reasons of personal survival, to subtly and grossly oppose the search for secured frames and deep unconscious meaning.

In principle, a student (and self-processing teacher) either follows the relatively narrow path to the second unconscious system or he or she will fail to reach deeply encoded wisdom — it's as simple and as difficult as that. For the teacher, the goal is to integrate these procedures sufficiently into his or her way of doing self-processing therapy so they can be used as broad guides and safeguards within which he or she works intuitively, creatively, and effectively.

There are an infinite number of digressions along the path from the report of a dream or other origination narrative to a meaningful linking of triggers and themes. It is therefore essential for each instructor and student to build an *internal map or template* that precisely defines the five steps needed for a successful self-processing exercise. While this may seem unnecessarily complicated and somewhat rigid, experience has shown that these steps simply must be used properly or the exercise will fail. In practice, the model generally falls into place quite well and produces remarkable results.

THE STUDENT BODY

Let us assume that the self-processing teacher has a suitable, private, soundproofed office or room that will serve well as a classroom. How then does he or she go about getting students? To answer, I will extend the comments made in the previous chapter; the following are the most common means of developing a class:

1. *Through professional referrals.* This is the only truly frame-secured means of obtaining pupils. One way of conforming to this ideal is for the therapist/teacher frequently to recommend self-processing as the treatment of choice whenever he or she does a psychotherapy consultation. There are, as we saw, many reasons for favouring self-processing over psychotherapy. While the optimal recommendation is a self-processing tutorial, offering a referred patient the opportunity to become part of a new self-processing class is a suitable alternative — especially for consultees with notable levels of death anxiety or limited funds.

2. *Through teaching and other professional contacts with potential students.* There are a number of other means of obtaining students that are departures from the ideal frame but nonetheless have proven to be workable and viable. These include giving seminars and teaching courses on subjects like dreams, psychoanalytic topics, and self-processing itself and then recruiting students from these classes. It is also possible to advertise in professional news-

letters, newspapers, and the like — as long as it is done honestly and ethically.

There is, however, a tendency for teachers to minimize or rationalize away many of these frame-deviant recruitment practices, largely because they are self-serving and evoke in students rather devastating unconscious perceptions of the instructor. It therefore must be stressed that in every situation where a student has been solicited in a deviant fashion, the instructor must keep in mind that this frame alteration constitutes an important background trigger. While it is not the responsibility of the teacher to bring up the issue, he or she can be assured that the student will do so at some appropriate and necessary time. The main task for the teacher lies in being certain not to repress or deny the existence of the trigger and its impact on the student and to be certain to recognize evidence for its activation as reflected in the material from a self-processing exercise. It is essential too that the instructor see to it that the trigger is interpreted when it is activated and the derivative responses are in evidence — and rectified if at all possible.

In general, it is inadvisable to stretch the frame of the self-processing class beyond these kinds of recruiting efforts. Self-processing therapy does not go well with personal friends and people whom the teacher has met socially. There is clear evidence that referrals from current or past students for a self-processing class should not be accepted. To do so is to invoke what is called an *unrectifiable frame deviation* because the loss of privacy, confidentiality, and anonymity cannot be repaired. The damage to both students and teacher is considerable — and as frame-related realities, they cannot be analysed away. Excessively contaminated referrals are best avoided; they should immediately be processed *and rectified* if they inadvertently materialize.

ARRANGING THE FIRST MEETING
OF THE CLASS

There are a number of essential measures that should be taken in order to establish a self-processing class. They are:

1. *Arrange any necessary preliminary meeting as early as possible.*

The self-processing class is usually developed through telephone contacts or through a meeting with prospective students following a course that has been taught by the self-processing instructor. If students are being recruited from a course, it is essential that a meeting with all of the potential students be held in an available private space (e.g., the classroom in which the course is being taught — but after the rest of the course participants have left). This meeting is best held a week before the final class of the course in order to answer questions and give potential students time to think through their intentions. A second meeting is held after the final class, at which time definitive commitments are made on both sides. The planned private self-processing classes should begin as soon as possible after these assemblages. Delay in establishing the self-processing class will usually lead to the loss of potential students.

2. *Specify the closed nature of the self-processing class.*

Perhaps the most important frame-securing ground rule to be articulated when establishing a new self-processing class is that of limiting membership in the class to the initial class members as long as the class stays intact. Since most dream seminars are open to the coming and going of students, this secure aspect of the frame should be spelled out in advance to the prospective pupils. This gives them the opportunity to consider seriously the commitment that they are making to their fellow students and the instructor, and to take a long-range view of their responsibilities to themselves and the other participants.

Other ground rules that should be announced at this preliminary meeting pertain to the total privacy and confidentiality of the class, and the relative anonymity of the instructor (see also below). It should be stressed that the classroom will be a closed space from which there should be no leakage. Students also must be certain that they have had no prior contact with the teacher or with anyone who has worked with him or her.

3. *Approach the group with a specific two-hour period in mind for the class; change the intended time only if the students cannot make the hours you have chosen.*

The instructor has the primary responsibility of establishing the frame of the planned class. Thus, he or she should be the one to suggest the time for the class and to make alternative suggestions if the time does not suit the potential class members. Beyond that, a student may suggest a time if the instructor is at a loss. However, once a time has been agreed upon, it should stay fixed for the life of the class. It should be clear to the students that the commitment to do self-processing is renewable in fixed seminar units for as long as the class wishes to continue the work; the teacher sets aside the time as he or she would for a therapy patient.

4. *A single and fair fee should be stated for the initial contract, which usually is for six to twelve classes or for four tutorial sessions.*

The instructor should gauge the financial capabilities of the students and set a suitable fee and the number of classes per "semester" or self-processing unit on that basis. Once the pattern is set, it should not be changed — in principle, the teacher should strive to keep ground rules and frames as consistent and reliable as possible. Secured frames reduce the intensity of emotional impingements and help to stabilize conscious system functioning and foster the therapeutic work.

The fee should not be subjected to negotiation or bargaining. For example, in New York, for a class of four students, a fee of forty to sixty dollars per student seems about right. However, in stating this possible range of fees here, it should be understood that in actual practice the teacher should decide on a single, fair fee and state it to the class as his or her fee — period. The size of the fee should be determined by such factors as the teacher's level of expertise; the mixed goals of education and healing, which call for a fee that is intermediate between that charged for the usual college course and that charged for therapy; the length of the class; and the evident financial resources of the students.

The instructor should explain that the basic structure of the seminar is that of a classroom experience and that the ground rules and frame will be fashioned for an ideal learning situation — one that involves intense emotional feelings and deeply personal perceptions of self and others. The classroom model calls for the tuition to be paid in advance of the first class. As we saw in the vignette offered in the previous chapter, students who fail to meet this requirement should not be allowed to enter class until they do so.

Finally, there should be no provision for refunds for students who drop out once the tuition is paid and classes begin. This ground rule actually both insures the teacher's promised and deserved income and structures the situation in a way that favours a student's full participation even when severe resistances develop. On the other hand, the assurance of a student's attendance places a strong responsibility on the teacher to fulfil his or her part of the contract — i.e., to attend all scheduled classes, not to alter the frame of the class unnecessarily, and to do an effective job of teaching.

5. *Set a date for the first class that is as reasonably close to the day of the organizational meeting as possible.*

The date of the first class should not be left to later telephone calls, nor should the start of the self-processing work be unduly delayed. Prompt initiation of classes speaks to a clear and strong frame and increases the likelihood that students who have committed themselves to the self-processing classes will actually attend them.

6. *Indicate where the classes will be held.*

The instructor tells the new students where his or her office or classroom is located. He or she does not give the students anything in writing, such as a professional business card, but allows the students to make their own note of the address — and with their own pen or pencil. The teacher should also provide his or her office telephone number.

7. *Offer a very brief explanation of how the classes will be conducted.*

If the students know nothing about self-processing, the teacher may wish to clarify the basics of the self-processing class at this preliminary meeting. This should be done very briefly as a means of orientation and of preparing the first presenter for his or her task. In general, the description of the components of the specific steps in a self-processing exercise should be reserved for the first class and elaborated as needed in subsequent classes. Here, the purpose is to ready the students by simply informing them that the work of the class will be organized around dreams or their narrative equivalents, and that the details of the process will be spelled out at the first meeting.

Questions should either be answered briefly or deferred until the class convenes. In principle, this kind of orienting contact is entirely deviant (it occurs outside of the self-processing classroom) and should be kept to a minimum. This contact is an unavoidable frame modification that is required to secure the frame; it should be confined to providing the information needed to give the potential students an opportunity to enrol in the class based on some sense of the process. In principle, here, less is better.

Once the students have made their commitment to the class, the instructor should close the discussion by requesting that the students be prepared to pay their tuition at the opening moments of the first class. The teacher adds that when the students arrive for the first class, they should wait in the waiting room until he or she comes for them at the appointed time.

8. *Screen out frame-deviant students.*

In substance, there is *no* formal evaluation of a potential student for a self-processing class. As an educational process, anyone interested in taking the seminar is accepted as a student. The only restrictions apply to individuals for whom the frame is excessively and irreparably deviant (see above and chapter eight). Other issues, frame-related and otherwise, that arise in connection with a particular student should be dealt with in the course of a class so the answers that the student and instructor come up with will be derived from classroom exercises and the linking of triggers and themes — i.e., with full consideration of deep unconscious system processing and recommendations.

9. *Orient potential students who are in psychotherapy.*

It seems best *not* to exclude a student from a self-processing seminar because he or she is in psychotherapy. The encoded material from students in this position unmistakably indicates that the existence of two therapies for one individual constitutes a frame deviation for the self-processing class — and for the psychotherapy as well. The ground rule that a given individual should engage in one healing process at a time prevails in the second unconscious system. Nevertheless, the student who wishes to enrol in a self-processing class while he or she is in psychotherapy is, on some level, expressing a therapeutic need and registering an implied (or direct) complaint against his or her current therapist — one that usually is quite valid. The student is therefore entitled to discover as much as he or she can about the unconscious basis for this dissatisfaction, and this can best be done in a self-processing class.

Eventually, for most students, a choice must be made between the two modes of healing — the self-processing class or the psychotherapy. Nevertheless, giving the student the opportunity to do this on the basis of self-processing exercises provides the greatest possible range of encoded material and chance for deep insight available at present.

* * *

From the very beginning, adopting a secured-frame attitude and keeping deviations to an absolute minimum sets the ideal tone for a self-processing class. This kind of approach serves well the healing needs of both students and teacher and offers the best foundation for effective teaching.

CHAPTER TEN

The first class

We are about to pass through the gateway to a deep and mysterious world whose pathways are obstructed by and alien to the conscious mind. It is a journey no one takes without trepidation, yet it is a trip that no one should miss. We will, in this and subsequent chapters, mark it out full well.

THE FIRST MOMENTS

We have now reached the point at which a self-processing instructor has made arrangements for an initial class of self-processing students. The agreed-upon time has almost arrived. The instructor is in his or her office or classroom, and the students are in the waiting room. The hour strikes and the instructor goes into the waiting room to greet the new students. In general, handshaking is not in order because the teacher has already met the students; where this is not the case, a brief greeting — "Hello, I'm Dr. or Ms. So-and-so" — and handshake is called for. There are, however, no other introductions or comments made in the waiting room, which is outside of the secured classroom space. The teacher simply invites the students to enter the classroom and allows them to find their way to their seats. As a rule, their place is easily recognized because the instructor sits alone behind a desk.

The instructor closes the door(s), sits at the desk, and begins the class. If there is a missing member of the class, the doors are closed nonetheless (the physical or setting aspect of the frame is secured). The tardy student will, as a rule, find it necessary to knock on the classroom door and the teacher will let him or her in, even though this involves a minor frame break that disrupts the class and its closed boundaries (the secured-frame alternative — and it is not to be taken lightly — of not allowing the student into the class seems too punitive and radical).

Here again is a small example of the need to modify the classroom frame in order to resecure it. And although it is difficult for the conscious mind to fathom, even this seemingly minor frame-deviant trigger (opening the classroom door to let the student in) will evoke a response from the second unconscious system and must be kept in mind as a stimulus for the material that will come up in the very first exercise carried out by the class. The instructor must be alert to such triggers because thinking in terms of deep unconscious processes tends to collapse in the presence of acute, on-the-spot triggers — the more traumatic they are, the greater the shift to conscious system thinking and functioning (a typical emergency response).

We will turn now to the conduct of the first class. As is true of all of self-processing therapy, these initial moments are exquisitely prescribed. There is such an overabundance of conscious and unconscious meaning conveyed in every word and behaviour of a self-processing teacher, and such a natural tendency to operate via conscious system, countertransference-based interventions, that it is imperative to orchestrate as carefully as possible what is said and done — all the more so because some of the interventions in the first class come from the instructor without the usual derivation from encoded material from a student. Creative teaching within well-defined constraints is the ideal approach to doing self-processing therapy.

STARTING THE FIRST CLASS

Formal structure is introduced from the first moment of a self-processing class. Let us now trace how this holding edifice is imparted to the students as the initial seminar unfolds.

1.   *Payment of the fee*

The first ground rule to be enforced is the payment of the fee in advance of the start of the activities of the first class. Many students will spontaneously pay the fee as they enter the class-room, but the instructor must be prepared to request payment from students who have not done so. This is not a harsh or greedy act, but an invocation of a secured-frame structure that serves the needs of both students and teacher for steady hold-ing and a stable, reliable, low-intensity environment. Adhering to this ground rule moves the class towards its first secured-frame moment — a seemingly small, but important event.

Several issues may arise at this early juncture. As I present them, keep in mind the important principle that any effort by a student to modify the ideal frame is *provoked by some prior trigger from the teacher* — one that almost always is also frame-deviant in nature and only rarely frame securing. This adaptive–systemic way of thinking is basic to the self-process-ing teaching effort — there is accountability on both sides.

As for possible issues, a student may wish to pay for the course in cash. This poses an unusual and delicate problem in that cash payment is not *per se* a frame break. Nevertheless, it generates a sense of uncertainty regarding the frame in that it leaves open the question of whether the instructor will record and report the income. In many people, the second unconscious system perceives the teacher as dishonest when he or she accepts cash.

Cash payment creates one of those situations in which the teacher must make an uncertain frame-related choice and should *select that option that is least deviant and most frame secure*. It would seem, then, that the best intervention is for the instructor to ask the student to pay him or her with a cheque. This is, of course, a directive and a departure from the rules of intervention that state that *the instructor should intervene on the basis of the presenting student's encoded material as linked to triggers*. Nonetheless, in this situation there is a cause for action (here, again, inaction is an action) — which of course will then be processed unconsciously by the student's second unconscious system.

If the cash-paying student does not have a cheque or cannot pay in that manner at the moment, the instructor's evident choices are to accept the cash or to allow the student to pay by cheque next time. It is also possible for the teacher to accept the cash and indicate that he or she will not deposit the money and will return it to the student the following week when he or she brings in a cheque.

Holding the cash until a cheque is received entails a sacrifice by the teacher in that he or she cannot use the money for a week. Yet this may well be the best compromise available, one that is less deviant than accepting the cash outright. Whichever way the instructor decides to handle the situation, his or her responsive intervention is an important trigger for the class and its processing efforts. It is, as I said, also especially critical to find the *antecedent deviant trigger* that the student is exploiting by acting out in this fashion — the cause of this effect.

Another problem may arise if a student wishes to pay for only one session at a time — or anything less than the full seminar course. Here too the deviation may be dealt with in one of two ways. First, the student may be allowed to remain in class until the encoded material of the exercise generates themes that can be linked to the frame-deviant trigger of the teacher's decision to allow the student this privilege. As we saw in the vignette with Mr. Kelly and Ms. Young in chapter eight, allowing the student to stay in the class until the corrective appears in the material of the self-processing exercise means that the instructor has begun the series of seminars by accepting and participating in a blatant frame modification. This sets a deviant-frame tone for the class, creates a compromised hold, and generates a *conscious* image of kindness and leniency but an *unconscious* image of a teacher who is fearful of the secured frame and unable to stand up to adversity. Frame securing, although not based initially on a student's encoded derivatives and therefore somewhat arbitrary (but supported by clinical experience), seems to be the better choice. Indeed, processing a frame-secured moment tends to be more therapeutic than working over a frame-deviant interlude.

The second possibility (and experience indicates that this is usually the preferable course) is that the teacher simply reminds the delinquent student of the established ground rule — namely, that the class is a seminar that must be paid for in advance and that failure to comply with the ground rule calls for leaving the class until the rule can be adhered to by the student.

Note that the student's failure to pay the tuition is a frame-related *self-indicator — a resistance and sign of difficulty in the student*. For the student, it is not a *trigger;* the latter is constituted as an intervention of the instructor. The students' communicative and adaptive responses and material in class — the results of processing by his or her deep unconscious wisdom system — are stimulated primarily by the triggers created by the instructor and only secondarily by the students own frame impingements. Under these circumstances, given that the student has impinged on the frame by trying to modify it, both triggers and self-indicators would need to be interpreted interactionally.

Note again that there are two triggers to be dealt with in this case. The first is the teacher's handling of the frame *prior to* the student's deviant behaviour — this is marked as the first or *background trigger:* the stimulus that has evoked the student's resistance and frame-deviant behaviour. The second trigger is the teacher's contemporaneous interventions with respect to the resistance/frame break proposed by the student — the *immediate trigger*. Both triggers should be identified and used to organize the themes of the exercise and for the linking effort.

The student who modifies the frame of the self-processing class so early in the process — and he or she speaks for the class as well — usually has experienced a strong prior deviation from the teacher, often via the recruiting process. He or she also tends to have a strong personal investment in violating the secured frame and is likely to be extremely secured-frame sensitive as well.

Some students insist on multiple modifications of the frame as a condition for entering a self-processing class. They accept the class because of the initial frame deviations and expect — and even insist — that more deviations follow. When these frame alterations do not materialize, they may want to quit the class or challenge its basic structure. Other students are hypersensitive to shifts in a teacher's frame-management position when it vacillates between securing and modifying. Overall, however, the more a teacher maintains the frame as secured, the greater the likelihood of a stable class and the less the chance of losing a student.

2. *Introducing class members*

Once everyone is settled in, the instructor asks the class members to identify themselves by first name alone. In principle, students are referred to in this way, while the teacher will usually be called by his or her surname and title — if any.

3. *Introducing the self-processing class*

After the personal introductions are completed, probably for the only time in the history of the class the instructor will speak for an extended period of time without material available from a self-processing exercise. The overall goal is to outline the structure and procedures of the class, and to *do it as briefly as possible*. The route to trigger decoding is spelled out with only as much detail as is needed to get the first exercise going; if the students are familiar with the process from a prior class, then only a few words are necessary — teaching is always best done on the basis of the exercise itself.

The instructor initiates his or her remarks with a general overview of the nature of the class — beginning perhaps with its highly personal and revealing qualities and the need for total privacy and confidentiality. The class is told that the main pursuit is for insight of a unique kind that is derived from a deeply unconscious system of the mind that embodies the greatest known power to influence and drive their emotional choices and lives.

The goals of the seminars are next clarified. It is stressed that the self-processing class is designed to teach the student about the nature of the human mind as it copes with emotional issues and to acquaint each student with his or her own emotional concerns, adaptive capacities, and defences in this vast area. It is also explained that while the process is basically educational, it has profound healing qualities and is designed with therapeutic intentions and to enhance emotional coping. Mention also is made of the unique aspects of self-processing, including its ability to bring the student into the frightening but glorious and rewarding world of unconscious experience.

Little more need be said along these lines because the nature of the work will be clarified as the class proceeds. The main point is to stress the need to train the conscious system to modify its basic structure and unneeded defences in order to develop the means of accessing and benefiting from the wisdom of the deeply unconscious mind. A balanced presentation is called for, one that stresses the unique and powerful aspects of self-processing therapy while noting the inherent anxiety and opposition of the conscious mind to these most illuminating efforts.

a.   *Defining the remaining ground rules of the class.*

The instructor next defines the ground rules and frame of the self-processing class. Most important among these tenets is the requisite that all class members (and the instructor as well) pledge themselves fully and faithfully to keep everything that transpires in the class to themselves alone — the assurance of total confidentiality. The necessity of this stricture is presented as the essential means of creating an atmosphere of trust and safety within which openness of communication can take place. Note taking of any kind is interdicted; this rule also allows human nature to speak spontaneously and express itself on its own unimpeded terms as it copes unconsciously with the unfolding frame of the class. The remaining ground rules are touched on briefly as needed (see chapter eight).

b. *The self-processing exercise*

The instructor next turns to how the classes will be conducted. There is, as I have stressed, a basic route from a dream to a trigger-decoded insight, and, although it takes many forms and wends through many variations, its fundamental structure is quite specific.

   i. First, *the fundamental rule of saying whatever comes to mind* is established. This is a *not* a requisite to *free-associate* (*guided associations* are called for), but it advises students not to suppress any thought, feeling, or image. The stress is on the *absence of censorship.*

   ii. Next, the rule of *guided associations* is presented. It directs the presenting student to attempt to exercise two constraints on what comes to mind: first, that most of his or her associations should arise from elements of the dream — or dream equivalent — that is told at the beginning of each exercise; second, that he or she should endeavour to generate as much strong narrative material as possible.

4. *The specific procedures of the class*

The next task of the instructor is to define the sequence of procedures that are to be followed uniquely, but relatively unvaryingly, in carrying out a *self-processing exercise* — the necessary procedural frame. This too is an ideal to be sought after — however well or poorly it is achieved. Self-processing is designed to observe and understand the basis for resistances as much as to generate deep insights — beyond its primary therapeutic purposes, it is a remarkable means of investigating human nature.

The following are the basic components of the self-processing exercise:

a. *At the beginning of each class, the members are asked to express briefly anything important that is on their minds.*

In general, these introductory comments should refer to the seminar itself, but there is no restriction as to subject; it is asked only that the statements be brief. It is explained by the instructor that he or she will not respond to these remarks, but will keep them in mind for later reference.

Often, the comments allude either to a concern about the class or the instructor, or to an emotional problem a student is having (a *self-indicator* of student difficulty). As a rule, the self-processing exercise that follows should illuminate the unconscious factors beneath the issues raised by the students during these opening moments of the class.

In this regard an important teaching principle must be stressed again: a teacher's interventions and comments should always serve the pursuit of *unconscious experience*. This implies that he or she will never immediately answer a question directly or engage in a manifest-content, conscious system discussion. All of his or her teaching efforts, interpretations, and frame-management responses should be based on the encoded material from presenters — and on the ultimate linking of triggers and themes. The goal is to communicate and work consistently in the deep unconscious domain.

b. *Explaining the general framework of the self-processing exercise.*

Once their preliminary comments have been stated, the class turns to the *self-processing exercise*. It is explained that this exercise will occupy the balance of the first forty minutes of the seminar. This time is turned over to the students, and the work is led by a *presenting student*, an *origination narrator* — the person who will present a dream or its equivalent and, with the help of the other class members, attempt to develop the process so that it eventually reveals a measure of surprising, trigger-decoded insight. The instructor explains that he or she will be *completely silent* during these first forty minutes of the seminar. Even in the first class, once these procedures have been spelled out, the instructor should maintain silence during the exercise — no matter how much the students falter. The presenting student and class most certainly will not do the self-processing exercise properly — it is outside of the repertoire of the conscious system — but the working over of the resistances that emerge in the course of their efforts is an essential part of the teaching experience and process.

c. *Establishing the role of the presenter or origination narrator.*

It is the responsibility of the origination narrator to carry the self-processing exercise forward in keeping with the steps needed to complete an exercise. The other students may comment, ask questions, identify a gap or resistance, point something out, make a specific interpretation, suggest a frame rectification, or comment in any way thought to be helpful at any time during the exercise. However, students are advised to be on the lookout for their own and the presenter's resistances, manifested as departures from the specified configuration of the self-processing exercise and flight from meaningful material. Students unconsciously tend to share a deep need to defend against reaching trigger-decoded insights; resistance is both an individual and shared (social) phenomenon. Despite these warnings, students tend to search for and speak of meaning rather than resistance — a defensive conscious system proclivity that is very difficult to modify. The instructor should allow the class to arrange its own order of presenters. This is usually accomplished by having the students volunteer for a particular position in the sequence. Once established, the order of presenters is maintained without change throughout the life of a particular class with but one exception — a student is not allowed to present if he or she has been absent from the class prior to his or her turn. This restriction is necessary because meaningful self-processing exercises typically organize around triggers constituted by a teacher's most recent interventions. The absent student is unaware of these triggers and allowing him or her to present without that experience would deprive the class of the opportunity to work over the current issues that have been activated in their own deep unconscious systems. If a student misses a turn, he or she must wait until that turn comes around again before presenting.

d. Introducing the basic components of the self-processing exercise.

The instructor next defines each of the five steps or components of the self-processing exercise, including the general order in which they should be developed.

i. Component number one: the exercise must begin with a dream or a dream equivalent, an origination narrative.

Ideally, the dream should be a recent dream, but an older dream can be substituted if nothing more recent is available. In the absence of a recent dream, however, the best alternative is a brief fictional (dream-like) story that the origination narrator composes at the moment — at the start of the exercise.

The dream or story is called an *origination narrative*. It is the basis for most of the presenter's associations. This particular dream is an extraordinary human creation; it serves as a most remarkable power source, and it is the potential fountainhead for the development of a strong *narrative or thematic pool, the dream-associational network* — the collection of encoded material and themes that later will be extracted and linked to the active triggers.

ii. Component number two: the origination narrator's guided associations to the dream.

For ease of presentation, in much of what follows I will use the term *dream* as an equivalent of the term *origination narrative* because the dream is the most common form taken by this initial story. Once the dream is told in its entirety, the dreamer associates to its various elements. This process, as noted, is called *guided associating* and it is different from, and more powerful than, the free associating of dynamic therapies. Indeed, where the latter tends to become increasingly non-narrative and imbued with defence, the former tends to become increasingly narrative and derivatively meaningful. Each element of a dream is a potential source of one or more associations. *Narrative associations to dream elements are by far the most weighty carriers of encoded meaning.*

In principle, it is permissible for an origination narrator to allow each association to a dream to move out from a dream element to other associations if they come to mind, but he or she should be cautioned not to allow this chain of associations to wander too far from the dream. It is advisable to return to the power source before too long for a fresh start and to repeat this process as often as possible.

Ideal associations — the best carriers of encoded meaning — start with a given dream image and develop a narrative line that is different from that in the dream image itself. That is, the strongest guided associations take a dream element as a point of departure and spontaneously *move to a fresh narrative in which the time, place, and persons differ from the original dream image.* Furthermore, the associated narrative ideally involves a *specific incident* and not a general description; the latter should be taken as a marker that calls for additional associations in the form of a specific recollection. A great deal of encoded communication is carried by the *fine details of a definitive story.*

Most cogent guided associations involve prior events in the life of the origination narrator, but they may take the form of a newspaper story, an incident in a movie or novel, or anything else that details a happening. *The second unconscious system speaks only through specific stories.* In contrast, the conscious system prefers generalizations, broad and non-specific recollections, and intellectualizations — anything that lessens the narrative voice of the deep wisdom system.

Guided associations are generated spontaneously and naively *without thought of possible triggers.* As noted, dreams are dreamt to be associated to, not to be analysed. They are powerful condensed creations of the human mind, exquisitely wrought to condense a variety of unconscious perceptions and responses to these perceptions into remarkably honed manifest elements that carry in tightly packed form the unconscious meanings that empower our emotional lives. Dreams are the power source for self-processing, and that power is realized through guided associations that tell fresh and dramatic stories. Indeed, *the associations to a dream are virtually always far more powerful than the manifest dream itself.*

The self-processing teacher should make a mental note of all dream images and general stories that are alluded to but not pursued for their specifics. During the teaching time, he or she will help the presenting student to discover and fill in these voids. While the teacher's first job is to identify resistances to the process, his or her second job is to modify those resistances by enabling the presenter to fill in the inevitable gaps — the undoing or by-passing of a resistance.

> iii. *Component three: the student's self-indicators — signs of his or her emotional issues and impingements on the framework of the self-processing class.*

Self-indicators or markers are the students' side of the equation in a self-processing interaction. These are *indications* of the students' status with respect to their emotional issues and impingements on the frame of the class. Both emotional dysfunctions and modifications of the frame are signs of emotional distress and therefore constitute the immediate basis and need for therapeutic and educational interventions, including the teacher's interpretations and frame-management efforts. Self-indicators therefore are the usually dysfunctional targets (but sometimes signs of progress) whose *unconscious* structure should be illuminated when themes are linked to triggers.

There are, then, two classes of self-indicators: the first touches on the emotional issues, symptoms, or concerns of the students — *symptomatic indicators*. They are reflections of current emotional problems and states. As a rule, this subcategory pertains mainly to the origination narrator.

The second, and far more important, category of self-indicators involves the students' impingements on the frame of the class — *frame-related self-indicators*. These behaviours are termed *frame impingements* because they may be either *frame securing or frame altering*; further, they may arise from the origination narrator or anyone else in the class. Frame alterations are *gross behavioural resistances* (Langs, 1981) whose unconscious functions and structure will be revealed through the linking process.

After creating a full and powerful *thematic or narrative pool*, the presenting student should carefully review his or her current emotional concerns and list all of the known class-related frame impingements that he or she and the other class members have engaged in; frame incidents outside of class should also be noted. The other students should add to this list any classroom frame-related behaviour of which they are aware, including those that they themselves have created — e.g., not talking about the class when asked by someone (frame securing) or telling someone about the class (frame modifying).

The full list of frame impingements should be gathered together and summarized. Every frame issue on the list should be *marked as frame securing or frame altering*, depending on its nature. The sum total of this listing affords the group *a sense of their current position with respect to and their attitude towards the frame* — whether they are inclined towards frame securing, frame modifying, or a mixture of both. *The single most important classification of emotionally charged behaviours is that of frame-securing and frame-modifying actions or requests — it touches upon a fundamental driving force and issue in all emotional adaptations and in human life.* Again — frame impingements are the single most critical organizers of emotionally charged behaviours and communications.

In all, then, listing all of the *self-indicators* identifies signs of either pathology/regression or healing/maturation that become the immediate, psychically active targets for deep understanding — an essential aspect of the cogency and curative powers of the self-processing exercise. Upon completion, *the link between triggers and themes should reveal the unconscious basis of the major self-indicators in a self-processing exercise.* Manifest speculations about these resistances are no substitute for trigger-decoded insight.

> iv. *Component four: the identification of the prevailing triggers.*

Triggers are the emotionally charged stimuli and experiences to which a student is reacting and adapting consciously and unconsciously. As was true of self-indicators, there are two types of triggers: the first and less important group involves the *outside life* of the presenter, while the second involves *the interactions with, and interventions of, the self-processing teacher* — and, secondarily, the other class members. This latter class of triggers has, in turn, two subclasses: first, the always critical *frame-related triggers*, most often invoked by the instructor; second, those triggers that are constituted by all of the instructor's other interventions — teaching comments, interpretations, timing, vocal tone, side remarks (if any), manifest comments, and the like. The latter group of interventions and their attributes are called *impression triggers* because they are often difficult to define validly and are open to distortion on all sides.

Although generally less important than frame-related triggers, all of the student's notable impressions of the teacher, including overt criticisms, belong on the list of potentially active triggers. They must, however, be assessed subsequently in light of unfolding the encoded material in the self-processing exercise; only those impressions that are confirmed through derivative material can be accepted as valid.

The search for frame-related triggers is conducted in two ways: first, by attempting simply to list all of the known frame impingements by the teacher — *the method of direct recall*; second, by turning to the themes and using them as a guide to the identification process — *the themes-to-triggers method* (see chapter fourteen). As encoded responses to triggers, themes give clues to the identity of their evocative stimuli.

> v. *Component five: the final step in the process is the linking of the triggers with the extracted themes to reveal the unconscious experience and adaptive responses provoked by the triggers.*

When the trigger list is seemingly completed (and the class must remain on the alert for repressed triggers that have been missed), the students select the one or two strongest and most compelling triggers. It is these stimuli that then are linked to extractions taken from the narrative pool of encoded themes in order to generate deep insight.

Linking is a way of *transposing* themes from their manifest context and placing them into the context of the latent triggers to which they are an encoded response. It is a far different process from *analysing*, and it is the culmination of a self-

processing exercise. It is an effort that should yield an unexpected deep insight because the themes are not known to
connect to the repressed triggers, and, once the tie is established, it reveals remarkable and unforeseen encoded perceptions of the instructor in light of his or her (usually
frame-related) interventions. An effective trigger decoder is surprised again and again by how easily his or her conscious
system has missed what turns out to be an obvious but crucial,
usually frame-related, issue — and its implied meanings.

Linking is accomplished by lifting the strongest themes in
the *dream-associational network* — the manifest dream and the
guided associations to the specific dream elements — and connecting them with an identified trigger and its implications. The
resultant picture is configured as *selected, but valid, encoded
perceptions* of the teacher in view of the implications of his or
her behaviours and comments. Those images that do not fit well
and logically as disguised perceptions usually are *correctives or
models of rectification* — directives to the teacher as to how to
intervene properly, usually in the form of advice to secure a
particular ground rule.

Linking is articulated by means of a narrative statement
that begins with the stimulus and then defines the student's
unconsciously perceptive and processing responses to that
stimulus — *it is a sensible and logical story of adaptation*. In
addition to connecting with a teacher's triggers, the themes will
also, secondarily, reflect a student's unconscious perceptions of
his or her own frame impingements and those of other class
members.

In principle, every powerful image in a derivative network —
and every self-indicator of note — has been stimulated by a
strong trigger; a successful exercise will account for all such
imagery and experiences in terms of active triggers. It is well to
adopt the attitude that a derivative theme, no matter how
offensive or seemingly inappropriate, validly represents a
sound perception of something that the instructor has done —
usually with respect to the frame of the class. An encoded image
is an adaptive response to a notable stimulus; it is the responsibility of the class and the instructor to *account in logical
fashion* for all such images and themes.

* * *

This, then, is the defined structure of a *self-processing exercise*. It is a set of guidelines for traversing the path from conscious to deep unconscious experience. The presentation of this template should take no more than ten or fifteen minutes or so at the beginning of the first class. For teaching purposes, I have presented a rather extended first look at the process which is more lengthy than it should be when presented to a self-processing class. All the instructor really need do is offer just enough of the essentials to give the class a crude sense of the process. The bulk of the teaching is carried out in subsequent classes, sometimes over years; it involves the elaboration of these basic principles.

Finally, I want to reiterate that self-processing is not analysing. The latter involves intellectual activities of dissecting, connecting, synthesizing, and working over psychodynamic issues divorced from triggers and frames, while the former is a naive process in which themes are allowed to cascade over (frame-related) triggers to reveal unexpected (unconscious) meanings. Only then does one attempt to appreciate and formulate what has transpired.

5. *The first exercise*

To return now to the first class, the instructor has at this point completed his or her overview of the process and has defined its five components. A few brief questions may merit answering, but on the whole, responses to questions are best deferred until after the class has attempted its first exercise and material is available from the presenting student.

The instructor turns the class over to the students and invites them to proceed. The individual chosen to be the initial origination narrator then begins to speak. Whatever follows, the instructor will listen and observe silently until the students' exercise has been completed. If the instructor's comments have been brief enough, the class can be allowed the full forty minutes for an exercise. If a great deal of time has been used up, this first exercise may have to be limited to thirty minutes. In general, it is best to allow the class the full time for their exercise and to keep to the usual frame as much as possible even in this somewhat unconventional first encounter.

6. *The teaching segment*

At the end of the forty minutes, the teacher takes active charge of the class. He or she begins the instruction by asking each member of the class to assess the exercise briefly. The next presenter responds first, and the current presenter goes last. The class is asked to invoke mentally the map of the ideal exercise as a guide for their comments, and they are advised to *stress resistances* to the process, but they virtually never do so. They — their conscious systems — naturally are far more enamoured with and adept at developing pseudo-psychodynamics and isolated meanings than they are in dealing with the inevitable resistances that crop up in doing a self-processing exercise. They seem to be easily blinded to blatant departures from the template and to failed exercises — tendencies that the instructor must, of course, not share with them.

A student's assessment is best done by reviewing in sequence how each of the five components of the self-processing exercise were handled by the origination narrator. Developing the ability to carry out an incisive appraisal of a self-processing exercise is an essential part of the learning process.

Once the class members have evaluated the exercise, the teacher begins his or her work. Essentially this entails reviewing each component of the exercise, step by step, and heeding the advice given to the students to search mainly for resistances to the process. Trading in meaning is natural for the conscious system as long as the themes are disconnected from their triggers and essentially without deep power. The teacher must safeguard against this defensive conscious system tendency.

There is, of course, a lot more to teaching self-processing and it will be covered in the chapters that follow. The first goal is to adhere to the structure of the self-processing exercise and to educate the class. The second goal, that of deep insight, is assured by the successful modification of the inevitable resistances seen during the self-processing effort. The third goal, that of securing and maintaining the frame to the greatest extent possible, follows naturally from the insights generated through the linking process. This, in broad strokes, is the substance of self-processing; we turn now to its further details.

CHAPTER ELEVEN

The focus on resistances

The self-processing teacher needs to have a clear and definitive picture of the ideal ground rules of the self-processing class and the structure of the self-processing exercise, including a knowledge of the essential features of each of the five steps to self-processing insight. With these configurations set mentally, the teacher can use intuition, understanding, inventiveness, and validated principles of technique to modify and correct the typically errant exercises conducted by his or her students.

In this chapter I discuss the general principles related to handling these truly inevitable conscious system resistances and offer some fresh perspectives on this vast topic — viewpoints that have emerged mainly through self-processing therapy itself. The specific issues raised by each aspect of the process will be discussed in the chapters that follow.

THE ROLE OF THE FRAME
IN FACILITATING THE WORK OF THE TEACHER

The ability of the self-processing teacher to step back and incisively observe a self-processing exercise and to identify the main resistances that obstruct its successful completion is more than a simple matter of knowing the template of the process. This basic position of the instructor is sustained by the frame — the ground rules and role definitions of the self-processing class.

Perhaps the greatest support for the teacher comes from the requisite that calls for his or her *relative anonymity*. In substance, this is the role-defining rule that the instructor will *not* be personally revealing, nor render opinions, judgements, or otherwise comment subjectively on the material of a self-processing exercise. Related to this requisite is the *neutrality* of the self-processing teacher — a commitment to work exclusively on the basis of the presenting student's encoded material as it points to both trigger-decoded interpretations and frame-management/rectification responses; ideally, nothing personal is added to these efforts.

Adhering to these ground rules closes off the possibility that the instructor will talk about his or her personal or professional life and effectively prevents the teacher from offering his or her own encoded narratives. A specific constraint is thereby placed on the teacher not to offer to the class his or her associations to the material at hand.

When an individual becomes a narrator, he or she is expressing unconscious, encoded meanings. This behaviour immediately activates conscious system needs to oppose the exposure and revelation of disguised meanings and the directives that they contain to secure the classroom frame. The narrator is always divided — needing to express unconscious meaning and to secure frames on the one hand, and, on the other, needing to conceal and suppress encoded meaning and preferring frame-modified conditions. Because the conscious system has the greater direct power, narrators are always unconsciously invested more in resistance than in revelation.

The instructor's neutral position and control over self-revelations assists him or her in tolerating the build up of encoded meaning in the class without recourse to defensiveness. Of course, no teacher is fully immune from supporting and joining in with his or her students' resistances or from creating resistances of his or her own. After all, the teacher remains the primary object of the telling and often hurtful and disturbing encoded images of the students. The ideal of a resistance-free instructor is an aspiration well worth striving for, but never entirely realized; nonetheless, minimizing a teacher's level of resistance is achievable. The hope is that the instructor will learn his or her thematic and frame-related vulnerabilities and preferred defences, and will be sufficiently well self-processed to be able to catch most of his or her resistances and errors when they inadvertently materialize — and able to correct them and rectify their consequences based on the students' responsive material.

As a result of this situation, one unconscious motive for students' use of disguise, and for the resistances against ultimately achieving insight and securing the frame of the class, stems from wishes to protect the instructor from his or her unconsciously expressed anxieties and to join in with the teacher's consciously or unconsciously disclosed needs for pseudo-insight and deviant frames. The students' resistances are also motivated by needs to preserve the instructor unconsciously as an idealized, god-like figure — a powerful factor in all manner of resistances.

For his or her part, the instructor is always unconsciously motivated to avoid the conscious realization of the often devastating unconscious perceptions of himself or herself conveyed by the origination narrator. This counterresistance in the teacher can be expressed in many ways — e.g., by missing a key interpretation or frame issue, by failing to enforce the process to its fullest, and by a wide range of other mistakes.

These inevitable *target resistances* (i.e., those activated by the instructor because he or she is the *object of* the students' critical encoded perceptions) are difficult enough for an instructor to deal with. The addition of *expressive resistances* (i.e., those that would arise were the instructor to communicate encoded material) would make effective self-processing teaching all but impossible. Such expressions are therefore avoided to the greatest extent possible.

The self-processing teacher must be sufficiently undefended to allow the students' material to become powerful and primitive, and to be incisively attacking and critical of himself or herself when he or she has modified the frame or otherwise erred. The teacher must also be capable of effecting and tolerating secured-frame moments when they become possible. Still another requisite is that the teacher be capable of learning and maturing from the students' exercises and material. This requires an openness to the discovery of one's errors and a capacity to face one's vulnerabilities, limitations, lapses, and psychopathology as they are reflected in non-validated interventions and the responsive direct and encoded material from the students.

Because the self-processing class is created for the illumination and cure of the students, the gains afforded to the teacher must be coincidental and secondary. A direct request for help by a teacher to the class is, of course, a self-revelation and is interdicted. This kind of request would be overloaded with pathological unconscious meanings and would be disruptive to the class — it would arouse conscious system resistances in everyone. On the other hand, in terms of the inherent rewards of doing this work, every successful self-processing teacher grows and changes for the better in the course of this work, mainly because living and working effectively in the world of the second unconscious system and within secured frames inevitably has such effects.

THE TEACHING METHOD

The teaching in self-processing classes is interactive and organized around the four elements of the self-processing exercise and the final linking of triggers and themes. Most of the instruction is carried forward through two means: first, by asking questions of the class that foster the identification of previously missed resistances to the process and then enabling the origination narrator to fill in the missing material in order to complete the exercise; second, by asking selected questions of the students in keeping with the teaching points and healing efforts that are being developed in the context of the material and happenings of the class.

The instructor generally does not simply point out a resistance or ask for material; instead, the Socratic method of asking leading questions is adopted. Except when absolutely necessary, the teacher does not provide the answers to the questions he or she raises or those brought up by the students. Teaching is done in a manner that encourages the students to think actively and to find their own answers.

Towards the end of a class, the teacher must see to it that the class links the main triggers to the most powerful themes in order to generate the interpretations and frame-management responses called for by the material. This too is carried out by leading the students in these directions, though the instructor should, before time elapses, provide any missing components of this part of the work that the class has failed to develop.

TWO BASIC FORMS OF RESISTANCE

There are two essential forms taken by students' resistances. The first are termed *mechanical or gross behavioural resistances* because they are readily identified failures to adhere to the rules and procedures of the process. That is, these resistances can be recognized through a student's self-observing efforts or by a self-processing teacher who is attuned to the essential features of the self-processing exercise. This type of resistance in a presenting student is exemplified by his or her using free rather than guided associations, failing to list triggers, not attempting linking, offering manifest-content formulations, etc.

The second type of resistances are termed *unconscious resistances* because they are obstacles for which the student has no assured means of identification. Repression often is involved in this type of resistance which is exemplified by a student forgetting an important, already identified trigger or his or her failure to recall and use powerful themes from the dream-associational network when linking is developed. These resistances are more subtle than mechanical obstacles, and their identification and resolution requires an extensive development of students' self-observing capabilities.

COMMON RESISTANCES

In principle, the instructor focuses first on the resistances within the origination narrator's exercise. The teacher will query the class so they become aware of the basic components of the exercise (i.e., dream, guided associations, self-indicators, and triggers) that either have not been referred to at all or were insufficiently developed. *A successful self-processing exercise must have two key elements — a strong thematic pool and an identified, usually frame-related, trigger.* It is only after process or mechanical resistances have been recognized and modified that the shift is made to linking, interpreting, and managing the frame.

Common problems include the absence of an adequate origination narrative, weak and thin non-narrative guided associations, and failures to list self-indicators (especially the students' frame-impingements) or to identify the one or two most powerful activating triggers. Students turn to a remarkable amount of intellectualization and isolated formulations of psychodynamics in these classes — this kind of defensive thinking is characteristic of untrained (and many trained) conscious systems.

The instructor is well advised to avoid joining the class in a misalliance by furthering these errant pursuits and sharing blind spots. He or she should keep a sharp eye for the resistance aspect of the process — they never should be far from his or her awareness. Much of the teaching involves removing resistances one-by-one — e.g., by getting a better origination narrative or more powerful guided associations, or by seeing to it that the class list the essential self-indicators and triggers and try their hand at linking. In this way, most self-processing exercises are changed from an obscure set of disconnected images and repressed triggers to the recognition of a key trigger and its responsive encoded themes.

In general, though with many intuitive exceptions, the teaching proceeds systematically from one step of the basic exercise to the next. Each component is examined in its turn for resistances and then elaborated upon so that the missing pieces are filled in. For example, if the origination narrator has not associated to a powerful dream element, the teacher will lead him or her to do so. In following these principles of teaching, the instructor accomplishes two goals — helping the students to become acquainted with their resistances, and moving the self-processing forward by filling out the omitted components of the exercise so that deep insight can be achieved.

COMMUNICATION AND SELF-OBSERVATION

The conscious system has an endless repertoire of resistances. Any departure from the development of the necessary components for linking has a resistance aspect. In general, the conscious system will call on anything that will slow down or obstruct the self-processing effort as it moves an origination narrator and the class (and the instructor) towards trigger-decoded meanings and secured-frame moments. It takes a great deal of conscious system training, conviction, discipline, fortitude, and persistence to master the self-processing techniques and to bring an exercise to fruition.

For the presenting student, self-processing should be a biphasic activity in which the relative freedom of guided associating is balanced against the use of self-observation and an occasional review of the material in light of the self-processing template to ensure the completion of the exercise. Such self-reflective efforts are surprisingly rare among students — again showing the weakness of this capacity. In all, then, self-processing is open, guided, and loose on the one hand, and constrained and regulated on the other — depending on where a student is in a given exercise.

Resisting access to the workings of the second unconscious system is a natural state for the conscious system. Obstacles to self-processing are therefore neither good nor bad, but simply a part of our human and communicative natures. It is as important to leave room for the expression of resistances as it is to help the student master their obstructive use and unearth trigger-decoded meaning.

RESOLVING RESISTANCES

Because modifying resistances is the bulk of self-processing work, it behoves us to look more closely at this aspect of the classroom teaching and intervening. The resolution of resistances comes from two sources — *education (direct removal)* and *trigger-decoded insight.* The first is offered through the delineation and discussion of the components of the self-processing exercise and by identifying the specific resistances that have materialized in a given class. These efforts generally lead the presenting student directly to modify the identified obstacle by filling in the missing element.

For example, when a dream has been mentioned in passing by an origination narrator, but not reported in class (e.g., an omission that often is rationalized by an origination narrator who believes that there is too much dream material to work with), the class or instructor will ask to hear the dream (the rule is that all dreams and narratives that are mentioned in passing must be described in detail). Any failure by a presenter to list all of the self-indicators or triggers and to classify them as to whether they are frame securing or frame modifying (a rule students perpetually have difficulty with — this critical assignment is remarkably alien and threatening to the conscious system) will similarly evoke teaching efforts to have the lapse identified and corrected by the class.

The second source of resolution comes after the resistances in a particular exercise have been removed. One of the positive results of the transposing process is that *linking yields deep insights that illuminate the unconscious basis of an existing or recent resistance.* Indeed, linking alone truly reveals the deeply unconscious sources of obstacles to self-processing. This level of insight enables a student to master the pathological needs and responses to triggers on which resistances are based.

Resistances are not isolated intrapsychic defences, but are *interactional products* in that they are evoked or, at times, unconsciously invited by the interventions of the instructor; they are adaptive, triggered responses in students to the teacher's frame-related and other interventions and silences.

Not infrequently, the development of impediments to a successful self-processing exercise will arise as a response to unconsciously communicated needs in the instructor not to reach a linking insight because it is too anxiety provoking and overwhelming for him or her. This is a common source of failed exercises, and it involves teaching lapses and blind spots in the instructor. Indeed, the existence of unconscious resistances to trigger decoding is so universal that we can offer the maxim that *any self-processing exercise that fails to reach a surprising trigger-decoded insight is likely to have fallen victim to the countertransferences and counterresistances of the self-processing instructor.*

Although all resistances are unconsciously motivated, the nature of the underlying forces sustaining a resistance can be understood only at the end of an exercise when the triggers are linked to the themes. Gross behavioural resistances therefore must be removed consciously during the teaching effort if their deeper sources are to be revealed. Resolving resistances within a self-processing exercise is perhaps the most royal of the royal roads to the second unconscious domain.

The valid identification of resistances is facilitated for the self-processing teacher through his or her non-involvement in the generation of encoded material and by means of adhering to the well-defined structure of the self-processing exercise. The first technical rule of self-processing resembles yet modifies the all-but-forgotten first rule of dynamic psychotherapy: *resistances before frame, and again, frame before content and meaning.*

SOME BASIC PRINCIPLES

We are now in a position to summarize some key principles related to dealing with resistances:

1. Every self-processing exercise will be obstructed to some extent by significant conscious system resistances that render it incomplete.

2. Teaching should therefore begin with identifying and modifying resistances because they preclude effective linking — and both interpretation and frame-management efforts.

3. Resolving resistances occupies most of the self-processing class's teaching time.

4. As a general guide, the search for resistances proceeds in the order of the components of the self-processing exercise — dream, guided associations, self-indicators, triggers, and linking.

5. Once the main resistances are modified and the missing material is filled in by the origination narrator, the linking process is engaged.

6. The unconscious sources of resistances are revealed only through linking the encoded themes to their rightful triggers.

7. All resistances in students and counterresistances in self-processing teachers are interactional products with contributions from both sides of the desk. Students' resistances are responses to specific triggers, often frame-related, as processed in terms of their own inner needs. Similarly, counterresistances are reactions to the frame of the class (an important issue for every instructor) and the specific material and behaviours of the students as they interact with the teacher and his or own inner mental world.

8. Among the unconscious motives for students' resistances, secured-frame anxieties and the need to protect the instructor from painful unconscious perceptions of the implications of his or her errant and frame-deviant interventions play a major role.

PROCESS-ENDANGERING RESISTANCES

There is another helpful classifications of resistances that will enhance our understanding and teaching efforts. The resistances identified earlier — mechanical or process and those that are essentially unconscious — are reflected in failures to follow the template of the exercise. These process resistances are universal and an essential property of the conscious system; they do not, however, entail alterations in the frame of the class.

There are, however, *frame-modification resistances*, which are obstacles that develop because of deliberate or inadvertent departures from the ideal frame; to some extent, all such frame breaks interfere with the success of the process. These resistances arise primarily because of deeply unconscious secured-frame anxieties and are manifest via some type of frame break by a student — e.g., telling a third party about the sessions, missing or being late to a class, failing to pay the fee on time, etc.

Frame-modification resistances may be relatively benign in that they can be worked through and lead to trigger-decoded insights and rectified, or they may be malignant because they jeopardize the success of an exercise or a student's continuation of the self-processing work. The latter are termed *seminar- or process-endangering resistances*, and they include all efforts by a student to disrupt or inadvertently or deliberately to defeat or abandon the process.

This last type of resistance has many forms. At one extreme is the simple decision not to enter a self-processing seminar or to quit prematurely, usually without insight into the unconscious reasons for the decision. It is seen, too, when an origination narrator deliberately conceals material that has come to mind or decides in some other conscious way not to comply with the requisites of the exercise and process.

These are all examples of *malignant forms of gross behavioural resistance* that reflect a conscious decision to either interfere with or bring to a halt the effort to engage in self-processing. This group of resistances is quite difficult to deal with because typically the student's actions deprive the instructor (and student) from access to the material from a self-processing exercise that is needed for the deep insight through which the resistance knowingly could be resolved. Often, there are no available or only heavily disguised representations of the key triggers that are evoking these behaviours and/or little material to convey the encoded themes that would illuminate the *unconscious sources* of the disruptive behaviour. Indeed, although the manifestations of these seminar-jeopardizing resistances are on the surface, their deeper causes can be known only through linking; yet it is this very pursuit that is being defeated when these resistances are activated. Left to manifest contents and to conscious system speculations and discussions, the teacher is almost always unsuccessful in his or her efforts to help the rebellious student remain in class.

There are several common sources of these disruptive actions by students. The most frequent is the presence of a blatant and unrectifiable frame deviation which the student unconsciously finds intolerable (he or she seldom is aware of the key provocative triggers, or, if the triggers are known, their critical implications elude awareness). Unconsciously, these students often enter a self-processing class because the deviation protects him or her from a fully secured frame and its attendant unconscious meanings and death anxieties. They tend to be severely secured-frame sensitive — and severely deviant-frame sensitive as well. While they appear to be quite paranoid, there is a realistic core and trigger for their feelings of persecution — and these feelings seldom can be modified. Although the teacher can try to maintain the remainder of the frame in a secured state, this effort also is a threat for these very easily traumatized students. The prospect of a secured-frame moment and the decoding of unconscious meaning terrifies these students, and they obstruct the process. All of this transpires with little awareness of the key issues.

Examples of deviant triggers that can create this problem are the presence of two friends or relatives in the same self-processing class, or of a student who had met the self-processing teacher socially. There is, then, considerable truth to the negative encoded perceptions of the teacher under these conditions, in that he or she realistically is dangerous and betraying, harmful and seductive. However, most students will stay with the process long enough to encode material in response to these frame-deviant triggers so that, through linking, they are able to work over and deal with the deeper meanings of the issues they raise — and offer models of rectification where possible. On the other hand, the disruptive student, who is usually someone who has been over-traumatized by early assaults or seductions and/or death-related experiences, cannot tolerate working with much in the way of derivative meaning — it is too terrifying, even in encoded form. They will invent or find a wide variety of provocative excuses to abandon the process — and usually the class.

Another frequent cause of this relatively rare syndrome arises when there is a basically deviant frame in which a secured-frame moment is experienced by the student. Having contracted for a deviant frame, and expecting only more of the same, these fragile students cooperate with the teacher as long as the altered frame remains altered. But when the instructor secures an aspect of the frame, this type of student becomes exceedingly (and usually unconsciously) anxious and unknowingly acts accordingly. For example, when a request to change the time of the class is denied based on the encoded material from an exercise, this kind of frame-sensitive student will become grossly disruptive without any awareness of the deeper causes.

Because they dread secured-frame experiences and meanings and also fear that their own derivatives will support the secured frame and reveal abhorrent deeper meanings, these students will refuse to go forward with the process. Often, they are convinced unconsciously that they will not survive the secured frame; unconsciously, too, they appear to believe in the reality of the brutal and awful images connected with their view of a secured frame as entrapping, smothering, and mutilating. These extreme convictions have the attributes of *unconscious delusions*. For such students, staying in the secured frame and participating in the self-processing exercise is to risk overwhelming levels of anxiety and morbid encoded images whose decoded meanings are terrifying — unconscious perceptions of the teacher as a murderer, cannibal, and such, much of it linked to early life traumas and persecutory or deserting (dying) genetic figures. The problem is compounded by the fact that, as noted, these secured-frame anxieties are almost never experienced consciously. The result is blind action — and often the decimation of the self-processing work.

Students for whom secured frames are overwhelmingly persecutory behave in frame-deviant ways that often seem entirely irrational and provocative to the self-processing teacher. Nevertheless, the student consciously rationalizes these actions and justifies them by alluding to some behaviour of the teacher that they see as causing the resistance. The situation usually is of crisis proportions because the loss of the student is imminent, the abuse of the teacher considerable, the student's communication of derivatives minimal or non-existent, and effective self-processing all but impossible. Given this emphasis on the dysfunctions of the student, we must be mindful that *this ominous situation is, as always, an inter-actional product and that the teacher has in some important way contributed to the impasse — usually via an unrectifiable frame deviation.*

DEALING WITH
PROCESS-ENDANGERING RESISTANCES

How then does a self-processing teacher deal with this kind of crisis situation? The following guidelines may help to answer this question:

1. *Understand that malignant gross behavioural resistances threaten the continuation of the student's participation in the self-processing class; they are always ominous.*

These resistances take precedence over all other concerns of the class, but this does not imply that they should be dealt with manifestly and head-on — such efforts are virtually never successful in righting the situation. Making use of insights derived from a self-processing exercise is by far the best remedy.

Recognize that the chances of reversing this kind of decision to abandon self-processing are very small — no matter how much is communicated by the student and worked over in class. Accepting the idea that there are realistic limitations to your efforts as a self-processing teacher is humbling but necessary even as you try to resolve the crisis.

2. *Try to do everything possible within a non-deviant frame to keep the student in class and to allow sufficient time for the student in question to be the origination narrator for a self-processing exercise.*

The linking that then occurs as part of a completed exercise should powerfully illuminate the unconscious perceptions and frame alterations that are prompting the attempt to disrupt or leave the class. A strong secured-frame moment in the context of an unrectifiable frame deviation is the most common configuration in these crises.

In principle, look to the frame at such moments; it usually holds the key to the problem. Try to develop as much narrative material as possible — powerful images unconsciously are at issue and are needed for the linking effort. Finally, whatever the background trigger, be sure to take a *currently activated trigger* as your initial point of departure for your interpretations and frame-management efforts — tracing the situation from there back to earlier frame modifications and the like.

3. *Be prepared to invoke heroic measures, but also try to avoid the temptation and the student's pressures to re-structure the work towards a manifest-content, conscious system approach.*

Although true healing comes only from trigger-decoded insights, it may be necessary to resort to extreme forms of confrontation. They are, however, only rarely helpful, so the teacher must safeguard against intervening primarily to vent his or her anger at the provocative student. The guidelines of self-processing teaching specifically protect the instructor from undue expressions of countertransference. Departing from these principles is always risky, yet it is justifiable when all else fails — and only after all else has been tried.

4. *In assessing the sources of the disruptive behavioural resistance, look to both the student and yourself.*

Look first for your own inevitable frame-related contribution to the student's flight, and only then at the student's motives. These moments always have legacies from both sides of the situation.

5. *Using the material available from the presenting student, secure all of the deviations that can be corrected.*

Keep in mind the importance of using the material from the exercise, however thin it might be, as the basis for your response. The more the teacher uses insights from linking, the more effective his or her handling of the crisis is likely to be — and the greater the chances of keeping the student in class.

6. *If the secured frame is at issue, the material from the exercise should make the interpretation of the student's deeply disturbing unconscious perceptions of the secured frame feasible.*

The disruptive behaviour is taken as the main self-indicator, and the linked material (trigger and themes) is used to explain the unconscious basis of the resistance. *Under secured-frame conditions, the student expresses as much unconscious fantasy and fear as perception,* and both should be taken into account in interpreting the material.

7. *The closer the teacher adheres to the principles of self-processing during these crises, the greater the likelihood that the student, even if he or she leaves prematurely, will accrue some benefit from the class and the handling of the crisis — an assessment that is, of course, difficult to confirm given the flight of the student.*

Nonetheless, in principle at least, students acquire ego-strengthening introjects when teachers maintain their integrity and stick to their validated principles; the introjects are far more disruptive when a teacher departs from this position — no matter how necessary.

A CASE IN POINT

Mr. Everett was in a self-processing class with Dr. Parker, a male psychologist. Ms. Barnes, a co-worker and friend of Mr. Everett, was also in the class; they had both responded to an advertisement.

From the beginning of the seminars, Mr. Everett was sceptical of the work that Dr. Parker was doing. He raised many objections to the latter's formulations and interpretations, and took to openly challenging his qualifications as an instructor, finding much fault with his self-processing methods. The material from the exercises led by other students did not allow Dr. Parker to define effectively the underlying sources of Mr. Everett's resistances in terms of deep unconscious meaning.

When Mr. Everett's turn came to be the origination narrator, he could not remember a dream. Although he knew that it was his responsibility to make up a story in order to create an origination narrative, he said he didn't know how to do it and refused to try. Instead, he free-associated loosely with little sense of meaning — manifest or encoded.

Half-way through the exercise, two of his classmates insisted that he make up a story, and he reluctantly said, okay. A man is at a country fair. He meets a woman at a hot dog stand. They talk and go on rides together, and then she disappears. The end.

Associations to the story were sparse. Mr. Everett recalled that he likes fairs, but he hadn't been to one in years. He told the class that he couldn't associate to the woman. When asked by a classmate, he was unable to think of any triggers for these images from either his everyday life or the self-processing class.

When the time came for Dr. Parker to attempt to develop the material further, Mr. Everett became uncooperative and challenging. Dr. Parker did not respond to the negativism (it would have been a manifest-content, non-derivative dead end), but simply pressed forward and encouraged more associations to the origination narrative. Reluctantly, Mr. Everett recalled being at a country fair with his mother when he was seven years old. He refused to elaborate.

When pressed for a specific story (following the principle of using a general recollection as a marker for an unmentioned and probably meaningful specific recollection), Mr. Everett begrudgingly remembered that his mother cried a lot that day at the fair. He had gone with her on the ferris wheel and had felt trapped in the seat, afraid he might fall out. They also had gone into a hall of mirrors and his mother had disappeared; he remembered being very frightened and crying. When she suddenly materialized again, she told her son not to miss her if she disappeared again later on, that things like that had good reasons for happening and they had nothing to do with him. At the end of the day, she had made him promise to keep their conversation a secret. Mr. Everett recalled being scared and completely bewildered.

At this point, Mr. Everett expressed a sudden urge to leave the class. He fell silent for a long while and would talk only when his classmates pressed him to do so. He then revealed that soon after the incident he had just described, his mother had committed suicide. It emerged later, he added, that his mother had been having an affair with a man she had known from work, and that she had been unable to deal with the turmoil created when Mr. Everett's father had discovered the infidelity.

Angry that he had revealed this secret, Mr. Everett fell silent again. He refused to participate further in the work of the class. He announced that he was going to make this his last session.

Unable to engage his further cooperation, Dr. Parker worked with the other members of the class. The main self-indicators for the moment, they realized, were Mr. Everett's refusal to communicate in class and his decision to quit the seminars — both were, of course, frame-modifying resistances.

There were several active triggers. First, there had been a request in the last class that the time of the class be moved thirty minutes later. Based on the material from the exercise, Dr. Parker had held the frame as set and had obtained encoded validation of his decision. This was a frame-securing trigger and a secured-frame moment.

The second trigger was a background trigger, namely, Dr. Parker's decision to include in the same class both Mr. Everett and someone with whom he had a personal relationship, Ms. Barnes. Clearly, this was a frame-deviant trigger that had been worked over, but not rectified, when Ms. Barnes had presented. She had been cooperative in doing the work of the class, and the exercise had indicated that the frame alteration was a disturbing modification in anonymity, confidentiality, and privacy for the two friends and, by extension, for the entire class. Nevertheless, no frame-securing solution had been reached; Dr. Parker might have missed the derivatives that were pointing in that direction.

Dr. Parker interpreted Mr. Everett's non-cooperation as a response to both triggers. The frame-securing moment had stirred up unbearable anxieties related to entrapment and death, as reflected in the memory of being trapped on the ferris wheel and his mother's suicide. On the other hand, the frame deviation portrayed by the adulterous couple was being experienced unconsciously as an illicit affair with a potential to cause harm — suicide — and as a deadly violation of the ground rules. Upset by the mixed frame-related messages from the instructor, in terror of the frame-deviant destruction directed towards himself and Ms. Barnes, and fearful of the securing of a different aspect of the frame, Mr. Everett was trying to remove himself from the process as if he were trying to save his life.

In response to these formulations, Mr. Everett chose to speak again. He at first argued with some of what Dr. Parker had said, but the teacher responded by simply asking for a fresh association to the origination narrative. (He again was following the principles of avoiding conscious system discussions and arguments, and of asking the student to allow the voice of the second unconscious system to speak, which it does only through specific, fresh encoded stories.)

Begrudgingly, Mr. Everett returned to his sparse origination narrative and associated to the image of meeting the woman while eating a hot dog. He and his father had liked going to a local delicatessen and eating hot dogs together, often keeping it a secret from his mother who objected to eating between meals.

Mr. Everett suspected that his father had actually known of his mother's affair for a long while before confronting her. Had he wanted to, he could have nipped the relationship in the bud, instead of letting it go on until the situation became hopelessly entangled and his mother began to think of marrying the other man, who also was married. Mr. Everett had a strange feeling that his father had acted in a crazy way in the situation. Besides, his mother should have been strong enough to make a decision to stay with his father or leave him for the other man; keeping both relationships going was a disaster.

With the help of Dr. Parker, the class trigger-decoded this fresh material. It validated interpersonally the teacher's trigger-linked interpretation through the positive memory of sharing food with the father. But in encoded fashion it also brought up Dr. Parker's failure now and earlier to rectify the critical frame deviation of having two friends in the same class. Dr. Parker could have done something to nip the deviation in the bud, and his failure to do so only heightened the tension and destructiveness of the situation. He should have chosen one or the other student, and not kept both in the class. His failure to rectify the frame was in some way crazy on his part.

At this juncture, Dr. Parker finally explored the frame-securing alternatives with the class, and the adaptive decision they reached was based on the unconscious directive from Mr. Everett that one party should be removed from the situation — it was encoded in the choice he felt that his mother should have made. Because Ms. Barnes had committed to the class before Mr. Everett, he and the class decided that Mr. Everett should leave the class after the present exercise, and that Dr. Parker should return the remaining tuition fees to him (an unusual, but necessary, frame-modifying/frame-rectifying trigger that acknowledges the instructor's accountability for the errant initial frame deviation).

In response, the class engaged in a further conscious system, intellectual discussion in which they expressed their upset over Mr. Everett's leaving; they understood the need but were disturbed nevertheless. Dr. Parker intervened again and by-passed this communicative resistance (ideally, the class should have expressed their conscious feelings and then asked Mr. Everett for a fresh guided association to his origination narrative). Because time was short, the teacher simply asked for a final association to the original story.

In answer, Mr. Everett recalled another fair that he had gone to with both of his parents. He remembered their fighting terribly, to the point where he was embarrassed and wanted to disappear. His father had allowed him to ride the ferris wheel alone, and he liked doing it.

Although not a very strong image, the class took this association as an encoded cognitive validation of the frame-rectifying decision that their teacher had made. Mr. Everett was legitimately embarrassed by the turmoil that the deviation had been creating, and he had every right to leave the class. The validity of Dr. Parker's decision to dismiss Mr. Everett was encoded in the image of the father allowing his son to enjoy a ride on his own. Hopefully this act of rectification by Dr. Parker would set Mr. Everett and the class free in other ways as well.

The solution in this case was rectification of the frame through the least harmful frame alteration, which entailed asking the most deviant member to leave. Often, the teacher has no choice but to accept a termination solution in the face of intractable resistances or an otherwise unrectifiable frame deviation. As was the case here, these two issues often go together — the uncorrected frame break creates the unmanageable resistances. In this situation the most disruptive trigger was Dr. Parker's allowing two friends to be in the same self-processing class — a frame break that betrayed and harmed both of them.

The hope is that the rectification of this frame deviation was experienced in the students' deep unconscious systems as sound, sane, and constructive, and that it afforded them a fresh positive introject of their instructor and a segment of deep insight. If Mr. Everett left with this kind of experience in hand, he probably gained a great deal despite the background of hurt and turmoil.

* * *

Work with the more usual process resistances is a lot more peaceful than the kind of turmoil that surrounds class-endangering resistances. The techniques necessary for the resolution of all types of resistances depend on the instructor having a clear picture of each of the five steps to a successful self-processing exercise. With this in mind, let us turn now to the details of each step.

CHAPTER TWELVE

The origination narrative

The fountainhead — the power source — of every self-processing exercise is the *origination narrative*. The choice of which narrative to use is left entirely to the presenting student — the *origination narrator*. In most cases, this takes the form of a recent dream, and, as noted, the next best choice is a brief fictional story composed at the beginning of the exercise. Whatever form it takes, this first narrative *is to be the primary source of the presenter's guided associations*.

While the choice and contents of the initial narrative are entirely the responsibility of the student, the instructor can, during the teaching period, identify resistance aspects to the story and raise other teaching issues. He or she is guided by the template of an *ideal origination narrative*. Indeed, as we will see, each of the five steps in the self-processing exercise has its own essential optimal characteristics.

THE MAIN SOURCES OF ANXIETY

In keeping with the need to keep an ear towards resistances first, I will begin this discussion by reminding us of the main anxieties connected with effective self-processing. The first sources lies with the material itself. Even though derivatives are disguised, they are a source of great terror for the conscious system. Derivatives encode terrible unconscious perceptions of the powerful, idealized, and fearsome instructor and of the students themselves. They therefore are treated as dangerous communications despite their disguise and constructive potential. In all, then, there is a universal dread of encoded expressions in all of the participants in a self-processing class — a fear that the self-processing teacher must overcome to the greatest extent possible.

The second major source of anxiety is, of course, the secured frame. This silent fear is linked to the dread of unconscious meaning in that derivative material consistently points to the necessity for secured frames. As noted, this type of frame provides a marvellous hold and support for both the instructor and the class, but at the same time it stimulates morbid anxieties — related mostly to personal death and entrapment (see chapter eight).

Lastly, the deviant frame, though welcomed by the conscious system, is also a source of anxiety in that it impairs the holding qualities of the ground rules and teacher who manages them. Altered frames universally possess destructive and persecutory qualities — frame modifications are harmful even as they satisfy denial and other defensive needs. In general, frame alterations are a source of unconscious mistrust of the teacher and are the stimulus for many types of dysfunctions that are seen in both students and teachers.

These frame-related anxieties ultimately pertain to death anxiety, which is the great disturber of the self-processing class and its participants. Death anxiety has two fundamental forms: first, *secured-frame death anxieties*, which reflect the inevitability of death in the face of sound holding; second, *deviant-frame death anxieties*, which arise from the actual harmful aspects of every break in the frame. In each instance, these anxieties are universal and are shared by student and teacher. Ideally, the main differences between the two should be that the instructor has, through self-processing, significantly reduced and neutralized his or her level of secured-frame death anxiety and the need to exploit others through frame modifications. This frees him or her to work effectively with students in this critical area.

In light of these issues, it is well to be reminded that we pay an enormous price for our defences against the realization of secured frames and deep insight. Were it not for their invaluable healing properties, few conscious systems would dare take on this much-needed pursuit.

THE ORIGINATION NARRATIVE: COMMON RESISTANCES

As for the origination narrative, in principle, the *ideal* power source is a medium-length dream that is less than a week old (i.e., one that has been dreamt since the last self-processing class). The dream should have at least one or two strong manifest elements and should be sufficiently varied in its themes and long enough to allow for a diverse network of guided associations.

In general, a presenting student's failure to remember a recent dream can be taken as a resistance largely because experience shows that this void usually signals a trigger-activated dread of encoded meaning and of some aspect of the frame. Of course, the student can readily modify this obstacle by composing a narrative in class, but the teaching is done with an ear for the deep sources of the original resistance. The most common cause is a secured-frame moment and its attendant anxieties.

If a dream is very brief, it seldom will provide a sufficient number of discrete elements to generate a rich and varied thematic pool. This deficit is a resistance that can be dealt with, first, by having the student press each minute detail in the abbreviated dream for associated narratives — often enough, a short dream proves to be a richer source of material than might be expected on first hearing. The second alternative lies with having the student produce *a supplementary origination narra-tive* in the form of a brief story or another recent dream — to which he or she then associates.

Another not uncommon resistance is expressed in an over-abundance of origination material. If a dream is overly long or if there are several dreams, it is impossible for the presenting student to associate to all of the available elements. Neverthe-less, in principle, *any dream that a presenting student recalls must be told in class*; as narratives and potential sources of guided associations, they are not to be suppressed. If a dream has been alluded to but not told, the instructor is obligated to ask for that dream and for associations to it during the teaching time. Indeed, the conscious system cannot effectively second-guess the process and elect to modify it — this type of decision almost always is a product of resistance.

In general, multiple dreams tend to evoke scattered guided associations and make it difficult to discover common, organiz-ing threads and to find a single compelling trigger that will organize the thematic pool. The best strategy when faced with several dreams or a single but very long dream is for the origination narrator to concentrate his or her associations on one dream or on one segment of a long dream at a time. In addition, the guided associations should be derived mainly from the *strongest elements* in the dream (see chapter thirteen). This approach allows for diversity yet helps to increase the chances of developing a powerful set of themes that are likely to be related to one or two important triggers.

A CLINICAL EXCERPT

Mrs. Evans was the origination narrator for her long-standing self-processing class with Mr. Daniels. She began the class by saying that she could not recall a dream that week. She had no idea how to make up a story and felt stuck. Although she looked beggingly to the instructor, Mr. Daniels remained silent. Mrs. Evans then struggled for a while and remembered a small dream fragment from the

previous night in which she is with a childhood friend,
Ernie, in front of a movie house.

For some time, Mrs. Evans talked freely—i.e., she was
using free rather than guided associations—about a
variety of subjects, ignoring the dream fragment. When
one of the other students in the class finally pointed out
that she was intellectualizing and not using guided
associations, and that she was ignoring her dream, Mrs.
Evans took up the dream fragment and began to associate
to its sparse elements.

The movie house recalled a film she had seen recently in
which a professor had had an affair with one of his
students. Ernie was a sociologist who had written several
books and had taught and lectured all over the world. Mrs.
Evans would hear about him from time to time and felt
envious of his successes.

During the balance of the exercise, further guided
associations were sparse. The class failed to list their self-
indicators and made only a perfunctory attempt to search
for triggers, and these efforts proved to be uninformative.
Linking was not attempted, and, of course, no deep,
trigger-decoded insight came forth.

During the teaching segment, Mr. Daniels first established
through a series of questions that Mrs. Evans—and the
class—was in a strong state of resistance. They were then
able to recognize the deficits of their exercise and to grasp
the idea that some as yet *hidden (repressed) trigger* must
be at the root of these difficulties. They recognized that the
sources of these resistances could be understood only if
they pressed past each specific resistance and completed
the exercise. The forms that the resistances had taken
could be identified, but their unconscious sources could
be ascertained only when the evocative trigger was
unearthed and linked to a more complete pool of strong
themes.

The realization that the class had uncharacteristically
departed from the structure of the exercise at almost every

turn suggested that one or more very powerful triggers must have been provoking this maladaptive lapse into conscious system ignorance and blocking — and dramatic failures in the student's self-observing functions. Nevertheless, as I have indicated, these resistances are interactional products with contributions from both the students themselves and their teacher — the key adaptation-evoking trigger needed to be identified.

The class elected to have Mrs. Evans create a supplementary origination narrative by composing a fresh story. Reluctantly, she made up a tale in which a group of mountain climbers try to scale Mt. Everest. Ignoring the risks, they decide to use a path to the top that had been closed to climbers. They camp one night high on the mountain, and a storm comes up that blocks further ascent and cuts off their escape route. One by one, the members of the party go for help but fail in the effort. In the end, only one member of the group is found alive.

Mrs. Evans associated to the story by recalling a slide lecture she had recently attended on a successful climb of the Matterhorn some years earlier. One member of the party had fallen and his leg had been caught in a crevice, but he had been freed. The lecturer described some of the pleasures of the isolated camps where the climbers entertained each other with stories, tales, and the like. In fact, one of the stories had later formed the basis for a successful novel. But there were problems, too. One night, two members of the group had quarrelled and one had nearly killed the other.

The storm brought up a book Mrs. Evans had read about the Brazilian jungle. There were many animals flourishing in the jungle, some of them rare species. But a severe storm had come up and caused flooding that prompted the animals to flee into unfamiliar territories. Many of these animals were trapped by poachers or killed by predators.

The class could see that Mrs. Evans's associations to the story she had made up were far more *powerful* than those she had made to her dream fragment, and that both of these dream-associational networks were stronger than all of the material she had generated in free associating. They realized, too, that it now was time for them to come up with a list of their self-indicators — especially their own impingements on the frame of the class. These frame-related encroachments would be targeted for explanation when linking was attempted. They might also provide clues to the missing trigger(s) in that *students' frame-related behaviours usually are stimulated by and often mirror the frame-management efforts of the instructor.*

It happened that Mr. Daniels was quite aware of the two triggers that were at the root of the day's exercise. With much patience and careful questioning he teased out from the class both sides of the key equation — the frame-related self-indicators and the frame-management triggers. For those who have not observed their conscious minds in action in the emotional domain, especially in a self-processing class, the missing indicators and triggers will seem so obvious as to make the class's difficulties seem ludicrous. But instead of wonderment at the class's imperviousness, it would be far wiser to realize that we are observing the conscious system in action — again, it is a system that is exceedingly defended and blind.

There were two intertwined self-indicators and triggers, each the mirror image of the other. First, the class had completely overlooked the fact that this particular seminar was the first of a new series. This moment of renewal, if it is transacted without complicating factors, is always a secured-frame moment. It is an exquisite time for processing secured-frame issues and anxieties. In addition, students' reactions to the offer of a fresh set of classes often will include a reworking of the essential history of the class, including all significant prior deviations — e.g., a deviant recruitment procedure, if that was how the class came together. In this instance, the class had been formed out of a course on Freud's case histories that the instructor had taught at a local college.

Mrs. Evans's dream fragment and eventual associations to it certainly encoded a response to this particular background trigger in referring to a teacher and lecturer — *bridging themes*. It also touched on one implication of the transfer of the students from a class on Freud into a self-processing seminar — it is a seductive, sexually tinged act (for the second unconscious system — and validly so). However, this formulation is organized around a *background trigger*. Because the deep unconscious system reacts primarily to *contemporaneous stimuli*, every background trigger must be traced to a currently active evocative stimulus. In principle, every self-processing exercise must be centred on a *current trigger* which will then account for the activation of earlier related triggers, as well as the dream-associational network and its ties to both psychodynamics and genetics. The human mind works always from the present to the past.

> The class at first reasoned that the old but unrectifiable and therefore ever-active deviation must have been aroused by the renewal of the class' contract with their teacher. At this juncture, Mr. Daniels raised two issues: first, what was the class's and the presenting student's unconscious response to this renewal process? And second, was there another currently active trigger in operation — frame securing or deviant — that also had aroused the recollection of the initial frame alteration through which the class had been established?

> The class quickly saw that the images and themes were both frame securing (the entrapment of having one's leg caught in a crevice) and frame modifying (the affair and being forced to leave one's accustomed space); this suggested that both kinds of triggers were active. Suddenly Mrs. Evans recalled that the other night she had been at the school where she had taken the Freud course with Mr. Daniels. She had seen the course listed on the bulletin board for the new semester and, well to tell the truth, she added, she had peeked into the classroom to see what Mr. Daniels was doing.

In one stroke, Mrs. Evans had provided a key self-indicator (a frame-deviant impingement on her part) and a key trigger

(Mr. Daniel's public exposure). On the trigger side, Mr. Daniels ideally should not make himself available for possible contact by class members in any public setting; he must therefore take responsibility for teaching the new class and for affording his student the opportunity to see him in class. On her side, Mrs. Evans must take responsibility for looking in on Mr. Daniels, and she needed, through the exercise, to discover her unconscious motives for doing so. However, the *prior trigger* that had evoked her behaviour also would have to be identified to complete the picture and do justice to the circular interaction between students and their self-processing teachers.

At this juncture, Mr. Daniels helped the class interpret Mrs. Evans's unconscious view of the incident at school and her unconscious perceptions of him on the basis of his self-exposure. The experience unconsciously was seen as one in which they both were deviant-frame endangered by taking the wrong path and having contact outside of their proper territory. Unconsciously, the frame break also was experienced as a form of inappropriate sexual contact between student and teacher. Unexpectedly, Mrs. Evans now remembered that Ernie was known to be a seducer of women when he travelled. He was also the butt of many jokes because he was an avowed nudist.

Without having to be asked, Mrs. Daniels had provided encoded cognitive validation of the teacher's and the class's formulations of the links between the current and earlier triggers and the themes in this dream-associational network. A current trigger had indeed recalled an earlier, similar evocative stimulus — the present frame break had aroused the memory of the earlier deviation.

The class seemed quite content with their efforts and was ready to relax when Mr. Daniels reminded them that they were avoiding the other active trigger for the class. He asked what it was, and one member tentatively brought up the fact that Mr. Daniels had renewed the contract with the class and had accepted their cheques and defined the dates of the next ten classes (this was the correct way to identify this secured-frame trigger, simply by describing the intervention of the teacher). The search was on for themes to link with this much-evaded trigger.

Slowly, and with considerable teaching help, the class realized that the anxieties related to the secured-frame moment were embodied in the story Mrs. Daniels had composed, and her associations to it.

Without exception, the secured frame is unconsciously experienced in two ways — as a growth-promoting and caring hold and as a dangerous entrapment where violence and murder will occur.

This mixture of themes is strikingly present in Mrs. Evans's material. Notice again that they are not evident in the network associated with her dream fragment, but became abundant when Mr. Daniels and the class pressed Mrs. Evans to resolve her resistance against telling a second origination narrative. This is a classic example of how modifying a resistance fills out a component of the self-processing exercise.

The class did most of the linking between the teacher's securing a fresh series of seminars and these last encoded images and themes. The secured frame had been experienced unconsciously by Mrs. Evans, as spokesperson for the class, as a nurturing moment in which the students could be creative (the telling of tales and writing a novel) and flourish (the animals thriving in the Brazilian jungle). But it also was entrapping and would lead to death (the trapped climbers stuck in their camp and the death of all but one of the climbers; the trapped animals that were killed by poachers and predators; and the fight and near death of the two isolated climbers). That which holds and enriches us the most in emotional life is also that which unconsciously we believe endangers us the most — and at the very least reminds us personally that death inevitably follows life.

Time ran out before Mr. Daniels could get one last validating association from Mrs. Evans. There was both reality to this lapse in procedure (the classwork had been very arduous) and a counterresistance (undoubtedly a result of his own unresolved secured-frame anxieties).

This had been a difficult class that had, nonetheless, under his guidance, reached some compelling insights through the linking process. The strong resistances experienced by Mrs. Evans and the class had been evoked by both a frame-securing trigger (the creation of a new series of classes) and one that was frame-deviant (the exposure of Mr. Daniels to Mrs. Evans in the school). Experience shows that mixed triggers of this kind often are the source of almost intransigent resistances — especially when a strong frame-securing moment is part of the picture.

The use of the formal techniques of teaching self-processing enabled Mr. Daniels to help Mrs. Evans and the class to modify these obstacles and to allow the underlying unconscious perceptions and experience to emerge in decodable form. It is virtually certain that none of this repressed material would have emerged in most psychotherapy sessions. Left to their own resources, students favour communicative resistances over communicative expression — especially when secured-frame anxieties have been aroused. These students had succumbed to their resistances in part because unconsciously they had been signalled to do so by their teacher. Only active self-processing teaching could bring forth the fullness of the derivative material and triggers needed for deep insight under these circumstances.

CHAPTER THIRTEEN

Guided associations

The teaching issues in the area of guided associations are among the most complex in the self-processing exercise. In the vignette just studied, we saw a student abandon the process of guided associating entirely, but it also is common to come upon resistance-dominated associational networks that are repetitive, sparse with regard to powerful images, scattered and difficult to organize around central themes, seemingly unconnected to known triggers, and overfilled with intellectualizations.

Building a *dream-associational network with strong imagery and themes* is an essential part of the self-processing exercise. The narrative network is needed for linking to triggers; a powerful thematic pool will carry a strong and emotionally important message, while weak networks tend to be inconsequential.

THE CONCEPT OF POWER

Studies done in self-processing classes and in our formal scientific research have revealed the importance of *power* in one's

mental economy, emotionally charged choices, symptom formation, and healing. Research-wise, it proved possible to develop
several mathematical measures of direct and cyclical power, as
well as the power of deep influence and of communicated
themes. The resultant findings lent credence to the idea that the
exercises in the self-processing class are quantifiable with respect to overall power. This encouraged the thesis that power
could also be measured crudely on the clinical level, and this
position has held up well in the course of this work.

In principle, powerful triggers evoke strong unconscious
(and, on occasion, conscious) needs, conflicts, and experiences
that are the primary determinants of emotional conflict and
functioning. Communicatively, powerful unconscious emotional issues are reflected in vivid and compelling stories,
images, and themes that reflect psychodynamics with major
consequences for emotional life. Frame issues in particular
evoke strong images that reflect powerful facets of unconscious
experience — and the pressures they exert on emotional adaptation.

In simple terms, certain experiences and adaptive responses empower emotional life far more than others. They are
termed *powerful issues and forces* — nontrivial factors in self-
processing, emotional functioning, and daily living. And strong
issues — triggers — evoke strong narratives which need to be
unearthed during a self-processing exercise so they can be
linked to triggers in order to reveal the most compelling forces
in emotional adaptation and existence. *No self-processing exercise can be completed and no significant deep insight achieved
without a pool of grim and powerful themes.*

Every meaningful narrative pool is characterized by the
presence of one or more strong images and set of themes, and
every successful self-processing exercise involves emotionally
serious issues. The deep wisdom system deals with potent and
painful emotional concerns, images, conflicts, etc.; it is a system designed for handling compelling problems, and it does not
deal with casual or minor stimuli or triggers — the latter are
subjected to conscious system processing. There is a serious
and often awful side to emotional life, and self-processing is
designed to access and favourably modify how we deal with it.

We turn now to a list of powerful themes or images. In
developing this lexicon, we should bear in mind that themes

organize first and foremost as encoded perceptions of the teacher and that strong themes are responses to strong triggers. As we review these signs of power in the communications from a presenting student, we should remember that the material from an origination narrator reflects both conscious and unconscious adaptation, and that in the self-processing class, students are adapting primarily to the (frame-related) interventions of the teacher. We are by no means dealing with fantasied themes or isolated, mental images; strong themes are a sign of strong and real adaptive issues within the self-processing class itself — and often secondarily in the everyday life of the students as well.

The list of powerful themes includes the following:

1. *Sexual themes*

Explicitly sexual imagery reflects a basic instinctual drive and an aspect of human life that is, on some level, a universal problem for every human being. Overt sexual imagery signals unconscious perceptions of the teacher that, as a rule, have been evoked by interventions that usually are not overtly seductive, though they are latently and unconsciously so; they are unconsciously and validly experienced by the student's deep unconscious system as such. For example, every break in the frame is experienced unconsciously as a perverse sexual act and incestuous seduction. As a result, *frame modifications by the instructor are a major class of triggers for strong sexual imagery in a student's dream-associational network.*

In principle, then, manifest sexual dreams of any kind and/ or erotic guided associations to dream elements generally signal an active frame alteration by the teacher. Similarly, conscious sexual fantasies about a self-processing teacher call for scrutiny of the classroom frame in search of the frame-deviant trigger that has evoked this kind of undisguised and blatant imagery. Indeed, the communicative position does not embrace the idea that sexual feelings towards a therapist or self-processing teacher are inevitable forms of so-called erotic transference. On the contrary, in a relatively secured frame, manifest sexual images of, and conscious sexual fantasies about, a therapist or self-processing teacher are quite rare, although under deviant-frame conditions they are exceedingly common.

Sexual images that arise in associating to a dream should be accounted for through one or more frame-related triggers. Segments of manifest dreams with blatant sexual content are important images, and they should evoke guided associations from the presenting student.

2. *Themes of violence, aggression, harm, injury, and illness*

Another group of generally strong encoded themes is that of violence, destruction, harm, assault, illness, and injury. The importance of this group of themes stems from several factors. First, as is true of openly sexual material, these themes tend to appear when frames are modified; they also emerge in the form of enclosing images when frames are secured. In the first instance the themes arise because deviant-frame interventions by self-processing teachers are validly experienced unconsciously as assaultive and traumatic. In the second case, the violence relates to fears of entrapment and death anxiety — the issues raised at secured-frame moments.

A second general reason that these themes are important is that they tend to reflect early childhood traumas that have played a critical role in the development of an individual's emotional dysfunctions — a point that holds true for sexual themes as well. The emergence of themes of violence and illness suggests that in some way the self-processing teacher has traumatized the presenting student (and the class) in a manner that repeats an early trauma or traumatic relationship. Not infrequently the genetic material will be recalled during the self-processing exercise, serving the dual purpose of encoding valid perceptions of the implications of the teacher's assaultive, adaptation-evoking interventions and providing the early childhood link to the current situation in the class.

3. *Themes of death*

Manifest allusions to death, whether due to natural causes, accidents, suicide, or homicide, are always a sign of great derivative power. As noted, they arise in deviant frames because of the harmful qualities of these frames, and they are a consistent aspect of responses to secured frames which evoke encoded affirmation that typically is followed by images that reflect fears of entrapment and personal death.

4. Allusions to rules, frames, and boundaries

Frames and boundaries inherently are powerful entities emotionally, and their appearance in an origination narrative signals another strong area of meaning — one of prime importance to the second unconscious system. Because the conscious system tends to overlook and avoid frame allusions, the self-processing instructor should be especially alert to their appearance in a manifest dream — and in the guided associations to the dream. They are remarkably common in such material.

It is good practice for a class to develop the habit of monitoring and listing all of the frame allusions in a dream-associational network, always noting whether the image is or implies frame securing or frame deviating. This is an essential way of clarifying the status of the frame during a given session and to develop an appreciation for the importance of this dimension of self-processing therapy — and of life. Often, the search for triggers is guided by this assessment in that frame-deviant images suggest an active frame-altering trigger, while frame-securing images suggest the opposite.

A special class of frame-related images pertain to *themes of dishonestly, criminality, lies, deceptions, and the like.* They are important themes in that they often encode a corrupt or illicit, usually self-serving, frame-deviant trigger from the instructor that very much needs to be discovered, and both interpreted and rectified if possible.

5. Events that did not or cannot occur, or are extremely unlikely, in reality

There is, in all humans, a deeply irrational psychotic core and set of primitive anxieties that stem from such factors as early and later primitive modes of experience, unresolvable intrapsychic and interpersonal conflicts, efforts by others (usually, but not always, unconsciously) to drive a person crazy, and the maddening aspects of being given the gift of life with the conditional inevitability of personal death. As a result of these factors, many manifest dreams and guided associations contain elements that are entirely imaginary and impossible or very unlikely in real life. These images are called *mini-psychotic images* to reflect their lack of contact with reality and the ease with which the presenter recovers that contact. Examples include allusions to dead people coming back to life, humans flying or being in two distant places at once or one moment after the next — even guided associations that come from works of fiction or fairy-tales.

This phenomenon is also expressed in everyday life in momentary lapses, as when a person forgets his or her telephone number or home address, cannot remember where his or her car was parked, or otherwise suffers a brief break in contact with reality. These latter interludes are called *mini-psychotic moments*, and they too are far more common than is generally realized.

Mini-psychotic images appear in everyone's dreams and guided associations at one time or another. Their importance lies in the clinical finding that they reflect underlying psychotic or extremes of anxiety. As a consequence, their presence in a manifest dream calls for guided associations (strong dream elements generally evoke strong guided associations). However, not surprisingly given the intensity of the underlying anxieties, these dream elements prove to be difficult for students to respond to with specific narrative tales. Nevertheless, the instructor should not avoid obtaining associations to these images lest the student consciously or unconsciously perceive that the teacher's own psychotic anxieties are interfering with the pursuit of the self-processing effort.

6. *Genetic allusions*

References to early childhood experiences, especially those that are meaningful and/or traumatic, are key elements in any derivative–thematic pool. Every complete self-processing exercise should touch upon the earlier roots of the presenting student's current encoded perceptions of the interventions of the instructor. The proper formulation identifies the genetic material as reflecting ways in which the instructor on some level has repeated the hurtful (or helpful) behaviours of the earlier figure.

The human mind operates primarily through adaptive perceptions, conscious and unconscious, and not primarily through the projection of genetically derived fantasies. The existence of *genetic roots* that affect the nature of current experiences and behaviours is a valid concept — we do react in the present in light of the past. The effects of the past create a strong *selective factor* in human experience — one that interacts with the actuality of external impingements (triggers).

Past events and relationships imprint sensitivities to particular meanings and issues in human interactions; they do not, as a rule, cause misperceptions and distortions. Even when they do cause misconceptions, the error usually is difficult to recognize with certainty — the conscious system inherently has difficulty with such assessments — and they are in general of minor import. No organism could survive without a strong core of valid and reliable perceptual capabilities.

* * *

Sexuality, violence and illness, death, frames, unreality, genetics — these are the adaptationally evoked themes or areas of experience and issues that deeply empower emotional lives. Powerful themes are different from themes with emotional impact or strong affective qualities — moments of sadness, loss, anger, and the like. Many experiences have emotional import but lack inherent power; their deep influence arises from the conflicts and issues they arouse, and these then emerge in the forms outlined above. Themes of separation are not on the list because they show little power *per se* as encoded themes, even though they have considerable strength as adaptation-evoking triggers to evoke powerful imagery.

Every powerful manifest element of an origination narrative should be the source of one or more guided associations — as noted, *powerful manifest images generally lead to powerful associations*. Every meaningful thematic pool should have several of these themes as part of their contents, available for linking to activated triggers. The absence of a weighty amount of thematic content is a process resistance that must be modified during the teaching segment of a class. And, finally, let us recognize again that powerful themes speak first and foremost for powerful triggers.

PRINCIPLES RELATED TO THE HANDLING OF GUIDED ASSOCIATIONS

The efforts of the students and their instructor with respect to guided associations are directed by both intuition and informed educational guidelines. The following are the main principles that apply to this component of the self-processing exercise:

1. *Maintain the distinction between free and guided associations.*

Students tend to prefer free to guided associating because of the weaker qualities of the former — a characteristic preference of the conscious system. Based on the material of an exercise, the instructor should be prepared to demonstrate the differences between these two efforts. The teacher must, of course, first allow the presenting student full play of his or her meanderings and resistance. But then, during the teaching time, the instructor should intervene by asking questions that are likely to lead the origination narrator to generate a strong set of guided associations. When a student has used both free and guided associations, the class is asked to compare the two sets of images and their themes; virtually without exception the guided material will be far more powerful than the unencumbered associations.

The teaching should also include a discussion of why guided associations are preferred to free associations. The main point is that, clinically, it has been found that the origination narrative is a very special condensed set of images, and that associations based on dream elements lead to the strongest thematic material possible. In theory, free associations tend to move towards weak narratives and intellectualizations that reflect the basic defensive position of the conscious system — a point that deserves elaboration at the proper moment in a class.

2.   *The ideal guided association begins with a dream element and spins off a fresh, detailed narrative from there.*

The search is for narrative associations that change the time, place, and personages of the original manifest dream image so that the associated story is radically different from the original image — the more diverse the imagery, the richer the dream-associational network. Often, the origination narrator will begin with guided associations that involve the people, places, or time period alluded to in the manifest dream element and move on to associate with specific stories that shift further and further away from that starting point. This kind of guided associating almost always produces a rich and varied yet unconsciously connected *thematic or narrative pool* with compelling expressions from the deep unconscious wisdom system.

3.   *The completed dream-associational network should have several powerful stories and themes.*

Guided associations are generated for linking with triggers. The deep unconscious system deals with serious emotional issues in a brutally frank manner; this implies that it will create dream elements that potentially connect to and will arouse associations with considerable power — including one or two genetic images. Strong themes are needed for insights of consequence; the self-processing teacher must press for associations from the origination narrator until they materialize. *Narrative power and variety* are essential features of a workable dream-associational network.

4.   *An ideal set of guided associations has two types of themes.*

The first are termed *bridging themes* because they provide images that clearly link the dream-associational network to the active triggers. For example, if the teacher has secured the frame by moving a student from a self-processing class to a self-processing tutorial, there might be a story of someone living in a group house who had recently rented his or her own apartment. Or if a teacher erroneously increased the fee for a self-processing class, there could be a story of someone who overcharged a customer for a purchase. Whatever their dynamic qualities and meanings, bridging themes serve primarily to make unmistakable the connection between the themes and the trigger.

The second set of themes are called *power themes* because they reflect the most compelling unconscious meanings of an adaptation-evoking trigger (bridging themes typically are not especially powerful). Thus, a secured-frame moment might also lead to stories of being trapped and attacked in the new apartment (a reflection of mobilized secured-frame anxieties), while the trigger of the fee increase might lead a student to a story of cannibalism. Both types of themes — bridging and power — are needed for an effective linking effort and for deep insight.

5. *Be sensitive to allusions to general stories and broad recollections of particular time periods in order to ask for specific events and narratives.*

The general recollection is an incomplete or unfinished story; it is to be taken as a significant *marker of a specific and important unmentioned narrative*. Almost always there is a definitive event connected to the general incident or period alluded to; it is that story that needs to be told by the origination narrator. The deep unconscious wisdom system speaks primarily and most forcefully through *specific and detailed narratives*; the conscious system is the great generalizer. Moving from the general to the specific is a frequent pathway to important encoded material; the instructor should make certain it is traversed.

6. *Allow the presenting student as much freedom, spontaneity, and opportunity to determine his or her guided associations as possible.*

The teacher should not, in principle, try to avoid or interrupt expressions of resistance. They must be allowed free play and then recognized, discussed, modified, and interpreted. In a similar vein, the instructor should not, until absolutely necessary, set the course for a presenter's supplementary guided associations during the teaching period. The choice of what element to associate to is left to the student until quite late in the session when time pressures create a need for more pointed efforts by the instructor.

In principle, the instructor's main responsibility is to see to it that eventually, *all of the strong manifest images in an origination narrative have been associated to* — students often fail to do so — and to make sure that a powerful and varied thematic pool has been developed before linking is attempted.

When other class members try to direct the source of a presenter's associations, they must be allowed to see where their efforts take the origination narrator — whether to a seemingly meaningful associated narrative or to a weak story or non-narrative response. Most directives of this kind, as is true of almost all gratuitous interpretations from students, prove to be ingenious efforts by a conscious system to render the presenter even more defensive than he or she is at the moment — they are as a rule relatively unfruitful. Rather than evoking strong disguised images, these efforts tend to lead to themes of people who are interfering with a proper pursuit of meaning — an encoded response to these resistance-promoting suggestions. The wisdom of what to associate to in a dream lies with the presenter; only rarely can someone else help — and then mainly because a non-presenting student has asked for guided associations to an overlooked strong element in an origination narrative.

7. *The associating process should be as loose and naive as possible, striving always, without thought of triggers, to generate as many narrative images and themes as possible.*

Guided associations are developed as the first step in a self-processing exercise because they should be naive and expressed without thought of triggers or frames. They should be spontaneous and unforeseen, a product of the wondrous imagination and thinking of the adapting human mind. Associating with triggers in mind — and doing so is rare — tends to be intellectual or to produce obvious, barely disguised images. Loose and innocent associating is far more inventive and is the best source of meaningful carriers of encoded meaning.

There is always a potential for more associations, so the main teaching issue is whether there seems to be enough strong, varied, yet coalescing images and themes in a narrative pool for meaningful linking. The decision usually depends on the instructor's knowledge of the key trigger and his or her assessment as to whether a given derivative or thematic pool sufficiently reveals the students' unconscious perceptions and reactions to the implications of that trigger in unexpected and telling ways.

8. *Strong themes imply both strong triggers and powerful inner issues.*

In principle, every powerful image in a dream-associational network should be linked to and accounted for in terms of an active adaptation-evoking trigger.

* * *

The basic goal of the work with guided associations is to generate a powerful, varied, yet coalescing set of themes that can be used for linking with triggers. Once such a network of themes has materialized, the students are advised to tuck the themes away in the back of their minds in order to save the thematic material for later linking to the identified triggers. In class, once the teacher believes that the student's dream-associational network is relatively complete, the instructor advises the presenting student that he or she can add a new associated narrative at any time as the process continues to move forward. The instructor then turns next to dealing with the *self-indicators and triggers* — efforts to which we now turn.

CHAPTER FOURTEEN

Self-indicators and triggers

The instructor has now ensured the best possible thematic pool for the exercise. With this accomplished, he or she should next deal with the students' side of the background equation: the *self-indicators or markers*. As we know, this refers to their current emotional issues (mainly those of the origination narrator) and especially to any impingement that a class member has made on the frame of the class.

The principles related to identifying self-indicators are fairly straightforward. They begin with the need to list the main active self-indicators, especially those related to the frame of the class. As noted, frame-related self-indicators must be classified in terms of their frame-securing or frame-modifying attributes, as the case may be. Summing up indicators gives everyone a sense of the emotional state of the origination narrator and the other class members, and their current position *vis à vis* the frame of the class. The summary statement should be made by the class and later confirmed or reworked by the instructor. Beyond that, the following points may be of help:

1. *Cull out all allusions to the origination narrator's current emotional issues and seek out any additional problems.*

Recall that self-indicators include a wide spectrum of physical and emotional symptoms, interpersonal or characterological difficulties, acute crises, and emotionally charged decisions and issues. It is therefore important to list the active indicators in order to provide a sense of the emotional state of the presenter — and, secondarily, the others in the class. Any student who is in a state of intense emotional need should be free to express his or her personal self-indicator.

In terms of non-frame dysfunctional indicators, two classes should be noted: first, the *symptomatic indicators* noted above, and, second, the *resistance indicators* discussed in chapter eleven. Each form requires a separate listing and should be marked for deep insights that will illuminate their unconscious structures. In principle, *the unconscious basis of a self-indicator should be clarified by the communicative insights gained through the linking process.* Very often an emotional problem can be traced to an active frame deviation by a self-processing instructor; frame-related interventions also are likely to be a significant factor in any emotional decision a student is making. On the other hand, improvements in emotional functioning are typically related to frame-securing efforts and validated interpretations of the self-processing teacher. As is true for therapy, then, both positive and negative self-indicators are targets for deep insight and should be illuminated when the themes are linked to their triggers.

2. *List all frame-related indicators separately.*

The students and instructor should have a clear sense of where the students stand in respect to the frame of the class. Often, there is a mixed picture and this is discovered only when the list of frame impingements has been completed. This tabulation should include frame-related behaviours by any member of the class; not infrequently, one student will have secured an aspect of the frame while another has modified it. The listing also is necessary because of the tendency of the conscious system to repress major frame-securing and frame-deviant triggers which often are discovered only through the identification of a related, often mirror-image, self-indicator — typically, a student's frame alteration parallels a frame alteration by the teacher.

The ground rules and frame of the self-processing class, and the behaviours of both the students and their teacher, are, as noted, the most cogent organizers of their material and their encoded communications and emotional states. Indeed, the situation is quite different when the class is in a frame-modifying mode as compared with frame-securing. The anxieties, issues, resistances, and degree of emotional health are distinctive for each basic configuration. Students' frame alterations suggest pathological modes of adaptation and usually are a response to their teacher's frame modifications; only rarely are they a reaction to a secured-frame moment. On the other hand, secured-frame anxieties are pathological only in the extreme, at which point they are quite disruptive for the students and require sound interpretive efforts by the teacher.

3.　*In listing the self-indicators, maintain the attitude that they are related to triggers, thereby ensuring a balanced, interactional approach.*

It is important to convey the sense that self-indicators are related to triggers — i.e., that the students' dysfunctions, improvements, and frame-related behaviours are connected to and are a factor of the interventions of the instructor. Most frame deviations by a student have their counterparts in a frame deviation by an instructor. On the other hand, frame-securing interventions and sound interpretations tend to evoke frame-securing and healthy responses in students — much to their benefit. As a rule, self-indicators and triggers are systemically intertwined.

A self-processing class is a fair, bipersonal domain in the sense that everything experienced by a student or teacher is understood as an interactional event with strong inputs from both sides. The teacher has the greater responsibility for the frame of the class and for assuring non-destructive behaviours, but the student must be responsible for his or her actions even though they are deeply motivated as reactions to the teacher's interventions (triggers). There is a fine balance here: the instructor must, based on the material of an exercise, acknowledge his or her full contribution to a self-indicator and to the experiences of the class, while the students must recognize that they have many options in dealing with an instructor's inputs — even when they are frame deviant or erroneous. Accountability exists for everyone.

One of the more self-defeating attributes of the conscious system is its tendency to seize the frame breaks and destructiveness of others to justify frame breaks and damaging actions of its own. Rare indeed is the person who will react to a frame-deviant intervention by a teacher with a frame-securing response.

In respect to teaching attitudes, it is well from time to time to remind students who are listing their frame impingements that whatever they may be — and no matter how disruptive — *they are in some real and justified way a response to a stimulus or trigger from the instructor*. This perspective legitimately diminishes the inappropriately self-accusatory and guilty attitudes of students who have had lapses and otherwise modified the frame of a self-processing class, qualities that are likely to disrupt the working-through process.

4. *Frame-altering self-indicators in particular should be marked for deep understanding through the linking process.*

The students' frame-related behaviours, especially those that are frame-deviant, should be marked as targets for deep insight in light of the prevailing triggers and encoded material. The self-processing exercise should yield this kind of understanding, which the student can then use as a model with which to deal with comparable everyday emotional issues.

* * *

These, then, are the key precepts related to the dealing with students' self-indicators. With these issues well defined and summarized, the instructor turns to the final piece needed for the linking process — his or her own side of the equation, the triggers.

TRIGGERS

No self-processing exercise can be successful without identifying all of the active and important interventions (triggers) of the teacher. The list begins with those that are most recent and powerful, and extends back to past triggers that have been activated by current stimuli. Here, too, some precepts will guide us.

1. *There are two classes of triggers.*

The teacher's interventions fall into two basic categories, a distinction of considerable importance for teaching techniques. The first are termed *impression triggers* and the second are called *frame-related triggers.*

The first category involves all interventions that are unrelated to the frame. It includes an endless number of possible ways that the teacher has commented and behaved, and all of their properties — facial expression, tone of voice, timing, body movement, and the like. Also included are such facets as what the teacher has chosen to comment on or avoid, the nature of a comment (whether it was a question, clarification, confrontation, off-hand remark, interpretation, personal opinion, directive, reconstruction, etc.), how he or she expressed what was said, the attitudes the remark reflected, and a host of other properties that accrue to the manifest teaching efforts of the instructor.

A student's direct impressions of the implications of a teacher's non-frame comments are always a mixture of his or her own conscious experience (which is very much under unconscious influence) and the actual message and intentions, conscious and unconscious, of the instructor. Unless the remark was extreme and certain to have had a deep impact, these impressions tend to be conscious system issues and seldom are matters of significance unconsciously.

Often the intervention selected by a student for an impressionistic response serves in an important way to avoid a frame-related trigger. In addition, the possibilities of conscious system distortion and bias are enormous — on both sides of the issue. Nonetheless, the teacher should be attentive to a student's complaints regarding an impression intervention and strive to recognize all valid criticisms. These triggers should not be dismissed, nor should the instructor fail to explore their truth value on his or her own. But, in any case, they should not be dealt with in class on a manifest-content, conscious system level.

Eventually, as noted, the validity of a student's (and teacher's) surface impressions must be checked out through an assessment of the presenting student's derivative material. As is true of all aspects of self-processing therapy, the second unconscious system is the ultimate arbitrator of the truth value of all conscious impressions. It is likely that it is no coincidence that frame-related triggers tend almost always to be sharply definable, while other kinds of triggers are far more indefinite — this is another special attribute of ground rules and frames. A feeling that a teacher's remark was hostile or seductive is far less likely to be a valid belief (though, of course, it may well be) than claiming that he or she was late to class or made a personally revealing comment.

Students should be allowed and encouraged to express themselves when something disturbs them consciously about a comment or behaviour of the teacher. However, the teacher must proceed with due caution in dealing with these communications in that he or she should not respond with direct comments of his or her own. In particular, the teacher should not directly refute an impression even when he or she believes that it is baseless and grossly distorted. Instead, it should be left to the wisdom of the students' second unconscious systems to have the final say on the matter.

In essence, then, a student's conscious impressions of the teacher are to be taken seriously but not discussed, disputed, or confirmed directly unless the linking process reveals unconscious perceptions that are comparable to the conscious system appraisal. Self-processing must be transacted in terms of encoded rather than direct communications; shifts to manifest exchanges are always detrimental to the process. A valid conscious impression will find support in encoded material, while one that is invalid will be unsupported or contradicted by the derivative images.

The second group of triggers pertains to the teacher's management of the ground rules and frame of the class — they are termed *frame-related triggers*. It cannot be stressed enough that these triggers must always be listed in full in each self-processing class and *classified as frame securing or frame modifying*. The most powerful one or two of these triggers should be used first for linking to the available themes. Secured-frame issues take precedence over most deviant-frame issues, although all active frame-related interventions must be accounted for and linked to the strongest themes in the narrative pool. Background triggers connected to those that are currently active are listed as well, but the compendium must always centre on contemporaneous triggers. *Interpretations always should begin with linking themes to currently active triggers* — and from there, they may touch on relevant past triggers.

A full listing of triggers and their main implications should be made by the class — and the instructor — towards the end of each exercise in preparation for the linking process. In addition, the class must be open to searching for triggers that have been missed and for implications of known triggers that have been overlooked. In principle, once a frame-related trigger has been identified, its implications should be thought through as a way of anticipating the kind of likely unconscious responses the students will express. Beyond that, the themes will speak for themselves, and often they will reflect meanings that have not been anticipated. *The more that is known of the ramifications of an identified trigger, the easier the linking process will be.*

2. *There are two approaches to listing triggers and both should be used.*

The first effort simply involves listing all of the prevailing triggers by trying to recall directly and consciously what the teacher has said and done of late, especially with respect to the frame — this is called *the method of direct recall.* The second approach uses the themes as a guide for the recognition of the active triggers — this is called *the themes-to-triggers method.* In principle, the most immediate and powerful triggers should head the resultant list, then less strong, active triggers, and finally all pertinent, reactivated background triggers should complete the agenda.

This part of the teaching effort usually begins with the instructor asking the class to identify all of the current triggers — moving from strongest to weakest. The class members then choose their method of trigger identification or may opt for a mixture of both approaches. When they have completed their list, through interactive teaching, the instructor should see to it that any missing trigger of note is recovered by the class members.

It is quite common for a major trigger to be omitted from the students' list, or for a critical trigger to be mentioned but inexplicably dropped, or its most telling implications minimized or missed. The usual rule has the instructor beginning his or her teaching efforts in this area by encouraging further attempts at the direct recall of triggers. If an important trigger still has not been identified, the teacher next invokes the themes-to-triggers method to help the class discover the repressed stimulus.

Every effort must be made to have the class do this work without direct answers from the teacher. The discovery of an important but repressed trigger is a telling experience for the class members, and it enables them to experience and realize their personal areas of anxiety, defensiveness, and vulnerability — as well as the rather universal defensiveness of the conscious system.

3. *The most powerful triggers must be identified first and readied for linking.*

The usual trigger list contains three or more active triggers. On some occasions, a single trigger — a strong and recent frame-related intervention by the self-processing teacher — dominates the situation and lends itself to linking in a most propitious manner. In most cases, however, the class must choose among several triggers and select one at a time for linking, beginning always with the one that seems most compelling for the second unconscious system.

To reiterate, in principle, frame-securing triggers are first in importance, and blatant frame alterations next. In the latter category, repetitive frame breaks are especially strong, as are those that flagrantly modify the frame of the class or alter an aspect of the frame that had been secured. Examples of important deviant-frame issues include accidental or deliberate physical contact between a student and teacher; a change in the fee for, or the time of, the seminar; the introduction of a new member to the class; and much more. In most cases, the strongest trigger is easily identified, though on occasion there may be two equally strong candidates and, of course, both must be used for — and are likely to work well in carrying out — the linking process.

Finally, *all of the powerful themes in a dream-associational network must be accounted for through a meaningful and sensible link to an identified trigger.* Not infrequently, a strong theme will defy linking; *this usually means that a critical trigger is being repressed or denied.* There are times when, despite all effort, this missing trigger does not surface. The class should then make note of the unexplained themes in the hope or expectation that future exercises will reveal the trigger(s) to which they are related.

CHAPTER FIFTEEN

Linking triggers to themes

The entire self-processing exercise culminates in the *transposing or linking process*, in which a trigger is selected, its implications identified, and the themes of the narrative pool are extracted from their manifest context and allowed to connect to or cascade over the trigger and its ramifications. The basic assumption is that these themes are constituted as *valid encoded perceptions* of the teacher in light of the meanings of the adaptation-evoking triggers that he or she has created. Those images that do not formulate sensibly as unconscious perceptions of the teacher are almost always *encoded models of rectification or correctives* and, secondarily, self-perceptions of the self-processing student himself or herself and, more rarely, of other members of the class.

The linked statement is made by transposing pertinent themes from their manifest context into their latent, trigger-related context. The statement that links triggers to themes is always narrative in nature and structured in terms of cause-and-effect; it is descriptive rather than technical. It begins with the teacher's intervention, *simply and descriptively stated*, and moves across the relevant themes, formulating them as logical adaptive responses to the meanings of the activating trigger. The model interpretive statement from a teacher goes something like this: "I did this or that, and you experienced it in that and this way, and you then reacted to that experience in this and that manner and recommended that and this corrective to resolve the situation." Indeed, we can propose a model of this kind because it captures the adaptive functioning of the second unconscious system which is consistent in ways uncommon for conscious coping.

These general principles apply most clearly when a frame-deviant trigger is at issue and the response is almost exclusively developed in terms of encoded perceptions of the teacher. But when the trigger is frame securing in nature, there is a more complex response: first, there are indications of encoded confirmation (which are essential for the validation of the teacher's secure-frame management efforts and the related interpretations); second, there are encoded images that pertain to both the teacher and the student himself or herself. *Under frame-securing conditions, both unconscious fantasies and unconscious perceptions are expressed* — perceptions of the sound hold and the restricting aspects of a secured frame and fantasies of the consequent seemingly overwhelming dangers of entrapment and annihilation. These latter images may seem distorted or unconsciously overstated, but they make considerable sense when secured-frame experiences are understood always to mobilize natural death anxieties and related concerns.

The human mind is primarily an adaptive, perceptive, and processing apparatus, and only secondarily activates fantasy formations and general expectations and fears. The encoded messages from an origination narrator involve first and foremost unconscious perceptions of the teacher. The key formulations therefore are *not* couched in terms of a student's projections and fantasies, but are stated as introjections and reflections of unconscious experience. As noted, those images that do not meet these criteria are usually correctives or models of rectification — directives as to how the teacher should secure an altered frame. It is quite surprising to observe the extent to which both students and teachers naturally veer away from valid unconscious perceptions of the instructor — considerable alertness is needed to see to it that linking in these terms does materialize.

The following teaching principles pertain to the linking process:

1.   *Be prepared to both manage the frame and interpret.*

Because a frame issue almost always is the key trigger for the linking effort, the interventional/linking process should include two elements: first, a frame-management response developed from the themes and derivatives of the exercise; second, an interpretation of the student's encoded perceptions of the teacher's existing frame-related efforts.

2.   *The students should be guided to do their own linking before any interpretation or frame-management response from the instructor.*

The teaching of self-processing is, to the very last, basically a method in which the student is queried, challenged, and subtly directed so as to evoke active responses on his or her part. Therefore, when the time has come for linking triggers to themes to yield encoded perceptions and frame-management correctives, the students should be helped to develop these formulations on their own before the teacher offers his or her own ideas and interventions.

Students find linking the most difficult part of a self-processing exercise; at best, they usually develop only fragments of the full picture. In time, they do learn how to connect a fair portion of the thematic material to their triggers, but the conscious system tendency towards non-adaptive, non-interactive isolated formulations is quite strong. Thus, almost always the instructor will have to supplement the rudimentary linked insights of the class members, if any, with his or her own formulations of the material. Not infrequently, the class leaves the most powerful themes out of their transposing efforts, and the teacher must tie these strong images to the most active triggers — always doing so in cause-and-effect, adaptive terms.

3. *No interpretation can be accepted as valid without encoded confirmation.*

Once the class or a teacher has stated a particular intervention, the presenting student should be asked to generate one or two fresh associations to a manifest element of his or her choice taken from the prevailing origination narrative. These spontaneous associations serve unconsciously as the means of confirming or disconfirming the interpretations or frame-related interventions that have been developed — and they do so remarkably well. Conscious acceptance, support, or extensions of an intervention do *not* constitute affirmation from the second unconscious system and have little meaning or relevance in self-processing classes.

The two forms of confirmation are *interpersonal validation*, which is transmitted via narratives about well-functioning or helpful figures, and *cognitive validation*, which emerges via the generation of fresh *disguised* images and themes that extend in unexpected but telling ways the interpretation at hand. Similar principles apply to the need to validate unconsciously the teacher's — or student's — frame-management efforts.

If validation does not materialize, this must be acknowledged by the instructor and a search begun for the source of the erroneous formulation. This is carried out through a re-examination of the five components of the exercise, although almost always *the problem lies with having missed a critical trigger and/or having selected the wrong trigger for linking.* The main effort, then, should involve the quest for a missing trigger so it can be put to use in the linking process by tying it to the available themes.

4. *The teacher must be certain to carry out the linking process for any secured-frame trigger that is active in a given class.*

This precept is stated specifically because of the universal resistance against dealing with secured-frame triggers and the anxieties they create. Securing frames and interpreting secured-frame anxieties through the linking process arguably are the most difficult yet healing interventions a self-processing teacher can make.

5. *If there is a frame-related trigger that has occurred just prior to or during a class, it must be included in the linking process.*

If someone enters a classroom unannounced (regardless of the circumstances, the teacher is held accountable for the frame break) or if a teacher brushes against a student as they enter the classroom, the class is dealing with an *immediately activated trigger* to which the second unconscious system is certain to react. On the other hand, the conscious system tends to overlook these traumatic, close-at-hand triggers — their immediacy poses a great threat to all concerned.

While we might expect students consciously to avoid these stimuli, clinical experience has shown that this class of triggers is very often by-passed by self-processing instructors as well. This occurs because the conscious system is an emergency-reaction system, and the deep unconscious system — and the pursuit of its derivatives — tends to shut down in the presence of an acute trauma or crisis, affording almost all available mental energy to the conscious mind. Clearly, then, the self-processing teacher should be on special alert for such incidents. When they occur, he or she must make an indelible mental note to be certain to include the trigger in the classroom work and, especially, the linking process.

Under these conditions, a presenting student's associations to his or her origination narrative will *condense* responses to the triggers still active from recent classes (they would be the triggers that evoked the origination narrative in the first place) and the unexpected, immediate trigger (this would be an added stimulus for the student's *guided associations to the dream*). Linking must be done with both of these sets of triggers, especially the one that is most recent.

6. *When there are two or more compelling triggers, be certain that the class carries out the linking process for each of them.*

The conscious system tends to overstate responses to one trigger as a trade off against linking to another, often more powerful and disturbing, trigger. The self-processing instructor must be alert to this kind of disarming communicative defence and set it aside so that the class can engage in linking to all known strong triggers and to all of the triggers that most clearly interdigitate with the thematic pool.

7. *The linking process should evoke surprise in the simplicity and self-evident qualities of its newly generated trigger-decoded message.*

There is a special quality to a successful linking effort that is difficult to describe, yet remarkable when experienced. Images should link to triggers in ways that are disarmingly simple and obvious once articulated; there are very few fancy or esoteric linked deep insights.

The key to this feeling lies with the fact that most linking is done with triggers whose presence or meanings have been overlooked or minimized by the defensiveness of the conscious system. The themes are there, and so is the trigger; it is *the connection between the two* that has evaded the conscious system and has the power to produce unexpected insight. The sudden realization that a previously overlooked and now obvious trigger connects dramatically with a thematic pool whose coalescing meanings were undetectable in the absence of their adaptation-evoking stimulus produces the unique kind of "Oh my, how did I ever miss that?" which is so characteristic of the punch lines of self-processing exercises.

8. *The self-processing teacher should remember that interpreting deviant-frame triggers must be supplemented by frame-securing interventions if an exercise is to be completed successfully.*

Interpretations of the encoded perceptions of a teacher in light of deviant-frame interventions (triggers) is insufficient. These efforts must be supplemented with frame-securing measures that are orchestrated by the encoded directives of the origination narrator. In principle, altered frames must be both interpreted and rectified at the behest of the origination narrator's derivative material.

9.   *When a theme is linked to a trigger, the result should be stated as a rather straightforward and logical explanatory, adaptation-oriented narrative that speaks plainly of cause (the implications of the teacher's trigger) and effect (the encoded perceptions and directives of the student).*

An interpretive statement (and a rectification of the frame) should make good sense and be easy to follow. It should begin with a trigger and describe the series of sensible adaptive responses that are encoded in the thematic pool. The intervention should provide a sense of unity to seemingly disparate themes and should include most, if not all, of the strongest available derivatives in its explanation.

10. *Once linked insights have been confirmed, it is helpful if the students' material allows the class to anticipate reactions to the frame-related experience and encoded perceptions that have been evoked by the teacher's triggers.*

The classroom experience and the self-processing teacher have a deep impact on the lives of students. The instructor should at all times be mindful of these real effects and their possible consequences. The students' material should, if possible, be used to show them the need to be on the alert for expressions of their own secured- or deviant-frame anxieties in their daily lives. The instructor must, however, avoid extraneous remarks and directives or warnings that stem from his or her own anxieties — the work is always done at the behest of the students' derivative material.

* * *

These, then, are the main principles that guide a teacher's work with the linking or transposing process. Linking is the ultimate expression of emotional meaning and of a teacher's healing and teaching skills. It must be a well-honed capacity because students have great difficulty carrying out this part of the self-processing exercise on their own. Still, trigger-decoded interpretations and frame-securing interventions are the essential sources of healing in a self-processing class — and in life. Linking brings them to their utmost fulfilment.

A FINAL VIGNETTE

We turn now to a final vignette from a self-processing class, one in which I will stress the linking process in particular.

> Ms. Walker was the origination narrator in a three-person class run by Dr. Green, a male psychologist. Ms. Walker's origination dream was about a man who was something like a pied piper. He was playing the flute, and children were following him. There was the look of a maniac on his face. The children were about to be murdered when she woke up with a start.
>
> After presenting the dream, Ms. Walker recalled a newspaper story of a physician who was something of a Jekyll and Hyde — a respected doctor by day, but a frequenter of brothels by night. He preferred group orgies, often engaging in sex with three or four women at a time. The flute brought to mind a man who conducted a symphony orchestra and insisted on having a sexual liaison before accepting someone into the orchestra — man or woman. Eventually, the man had had a nervous breakdown and was hospitalized for a paranoid break in which he believed that a mob was out to murder him.
>
> There were more guided associations to this dramatic origination narrative, but these images will suffice for our purposes; their considerable *power* is self-evident. Ms. Walker was unaware of any active self-indicators, although

another student pointed out that this was the next-to-last class in this first series of twelve seminars. Ms. Walker then realized that there was a related frame-securing trigger in that Dr. Green had offered the class a fresh contract of twelve meetings. This meant that there was an additional frame-related self-indicator in the students' indecision about continuing the class — one that bordered on resistance and on a potential frame modification (the seemingly premature termination of the self-processing class). A go around the class revealed that there was much uncertainty about each class member's decision in this regard.

Before the class's exercise time was up, Ms. Walker suggested that they try to find a trigger to link to the themes in her dream-associational network. However, when they attempted to invoke the frame-securing intervention of Dr. Green's offer to continue the seminar, they were unable to develop any sensible connection between the images and the trigger. Even recognizing that the themes were far more frame-deviant than frame-securing did not bring them closer to finding a missing trigger. Ms. Walker did, however, add another association to her dream: she recalled a story about a music teacher who was so gifted that three of his students became world famous pianists in the same year. The class again tried to link this and the other themes to a trigger, but came up empty.

With the class's forty minutes elapsed, Dr. Green took over. First, he reviewed the attributes of the dream and agreed with the class that it seemed to be of workable length and that it had some strong manifest elements. When asked what they were, the class identified as the strongest images in the manifest dream the unlikelihood that the dream could have occurred in reality, the crazy look on the flautist's face, the decompensation of the orchestra conductor, and the theme of murder.

Next, Dr. Green asked for an assessment of Ms. Walker's guided associations. The class saw the material as suitably guided by manifest dream elements, and as narrative, diverse, and powerful. The strength of the material was located mainly in the stories about the doctor who went to brothels and preferred group sex, the sexual payment that the conductor extracted from those who wanted to join his orchestra, and the nervous breakdown that the man had suffered. The class realized that the violence that dominated the manifest dream surprisingly had evoked associations concentrated on themes of illicit and inappropriate sex and seduction.

In this instance, Dr. Green knew the key trigger and he felt that he had a rich derivative network to work with. He decided to concentrate his efforts on the identification of the main triggers (the class had missed at least one vital trigger) and the linking process (this needed extensive work). But before leaving the subject of Ms. Walker's associations to her dream, he turned to a strong manifest dream element to which there had been no associations — there was a piece missing that needed to be filled in. He therefore asked the class what strong dream image had been neglected, and one of the students remarked that Ms. Walker had not associated to the image that had woken her up — that of the children about to be murdered.

Dr. Green complimented the student for his perceptiveness and suggested to Ms. Walker that she associate to this consciously avoided but very powerful dream element. After some rumination, she remembered a news story in which an artist of some talent had murdered a family that included two children. The man had proven to be a psychotic killer. The class noticed the repetition of the themes of murder and madness, but the students admitted that they still had no idea what trigger could have prompted these images. They knew that powerful themes needed to be accounted for through a compelling and probably frame-deviant trigger, but they were stymied.

Dr. Green did not pursue that question for the moment. Instead, he took up the issue of the class's self-indicators. (It is well to build the classwork in sequence, going from dream to guided associations to self-indicators and then to triggers and linking.) With the help of his queries, the class brought together their position on the frame, which was quite indefinite. They had not decided whether they would continue the seminar or terminate it. Dr. Green suggested that this uncertainty spoke for a comparable uncertainty in his own management of the frame (again — in general, self-indicators tend to mirror triggers). The key problem in the exercise was to discover the mixed triggers that would account for this unconscious image of himself — and the prevailing themes.

When nothing more materialized, Dr. Green finally took up the question of the strongest activated triggers. Again with his help, the class identified the two methods of getting to triggers — direct recall and the use of clues from the themes. The class opted first for direct recall. They mentioned again Dr. Green's offer to continue the seminars — a secured-frame intervention — but they could find nothing noticeable beyond that. Ms. Walker suddenly thought of the means by which the students had come together: they were all therapists who had been recruited by Dr. Green for a seminar on self-processing. Had they felt seduced in some way? It was difficult for her to say.

Dr. Green noted the mechanical quality of his student's comment and suggested that in part the coldness came about because she was alluding to a background trigger. A sound communicative principle states that all presently meaningful background triggers are aroused by a currently active, adaptation-evoking trigger. What then was that stimulus?

The class was still at a loss, so Dr. Green suggested that they turn to the thematic network for clues to the missing trigger. With some assistance and effort, the class identified the themes of murder, illicit sex, recruitment, madness, as well as those of creative teaching and creative talent. Their unconscious picture of Dr. Green appeared to be mixed, but how were they to account for the imagery? What was Ms. Walker's deep unconscious wisdom system trying to tell them?

In time, the class came to realize that the renewal offer by Dr. Green was a secured-frame trigger that they had identified earlier, but had failed to use for the linking process. They then tied the themes of entrapment and murder by a creative, growth-promoting person to that trigger; the interpretation spoke for itself. To state it briefly, in offering to hold the frame secured and to continue the seminars, Dr. Green was seen unconsciously by Ms. Walker (as spokesperson for the class) as a creative teacher who nevertheless was trying to capture or entrap his students and annihilate them. Here the unconscious perceptions were of group seduction and of violence to the group.

Dr. Green next asked if there was still another trigger that the group was overlooking. Using the thematic pool as his guide, he helped the students realize that they had not fully accounted for the repetitive theme of groups — as sexual partners and as victims. Ms. Walker added to the mix by saying that she had thought of another association to the dream. One of the children in her dream had been forced by the madman to undress in front of the others. There was a sense of horror in the little girl who had been asked to do it.

Finally, one of the members of the class asked if the missing trigger could be the fact that they themselves were a group. It seemed to him that the dream-associational network was now reflecting an encoded perception of that part of the altered frame as unduly exposing the members of the class to each other — at least for Ms. Walker. Agreeing with this partial interpretation, Dr. Green asked the class to link the other images to this trigger, but they were unable to make any kind of headway. Indeed, self-processing classes characteristically have remarkable difficulty decoding devastatingly critical unconscious perceptions of their teachers — these images usually are barred from awareness.

With time short, Dr. Green stepped in and tried to teach the group how to say themes aloud and then ask how they connect the trigger. The answer is given as a story that begins with the trigger and is completed by the themes. For example, one theme is madness — how can that be connected to seeing the students as a group? One student tentatively wondered if Dr. Green's doing these seminars within a group setting was being experienced unconsciously as an expression of his madness, and the teacher responded, "Of course it was". He went on to acknowledge that, in light of his capacity to hold the frame secured in respect to the time and continuation of the seminars, the group setting certainly was a piece of madness on his part. He added that it also was seen unconsciously as sexually perverse — in the sense of both prostitution and homosexuality — and as murderous.

Dr. Green and the class then linked some of the other themes to the trigger of the group setting. With time nearly up, he asked Ms. Walker for one last association. She went back to the piano teacher and recalled that his three successful students had never met each other. They each had been taught separately and had flourished.

Quickly, Dr. Green suggested that the positive image of the teacher was a form of interpersonal validation. He also recalled the favourable images alluded to earlier, themes that revealed an unconscious view of his work with the class in a favourable light — as creative and talent promoting. Split images of a mixed set of triggers of this kind (i.e., doing effective teaching in a deviant setting) are common in the deep unconscious system — each set of themes touches on different implications of each trigger.

Dr. Green went on to formulate Ms. Walker's last association as the missing *model of rectification* — the decoded message was that creativity and talent are developed on an individual basis. This image spoke for teaching each student separately — for a shift of the class members into private tutorials and a disbanding of the group.

As time was nearly up, Dr. Green asked Ms. Walker to quickly generate a final guided association to an element of her dream. She immediately thought of twins she knew

both of whom played, not the flute, but the piano. Only
when one of them quit taking the lessons that they shared
did the other flourish. Dr. Green suggested that this
encoded image supported (validated) his suggestion for
frame rectification and, as time was about up, he indicated
that this proposal could be explored further by the class
the following week.

It is, I think, fitting that this final vignette deals with a class
that was able to express images from the second unconscious
system that dealt with a basic flaw in the frame of self-processing classes that include multiple students. For some readers,
these unconscious perceptions might raise questions about the
entire classroom process. But I assure you that most of these
students would not have entered self-processing within the
framework of a tutorial. Each had a history of early physical or
psychological abuse or death-related trauma. The deviant
frame of having others in the self-processing class enabled
them to enter the process, and all but one student — whose
brother had been killed just a year earlier — continued to work
with Dr. Green in the tutorial setting after the following group
meeting, which turned out to be their last class.

Many other classes have tolerated this deviation for several
highly productive years before the issue was raised, virtually
always in encoded form, and worked through by means of
trigger decoding and frame rectification. Many students can
initiate self-processing only within the context of a basically
altered frame. Those students who can tolerate the tutorial
setting will find their way into that mode of self-processing —
either from the outset or through effective teaching and
rectification in a group setting.

As for the linking process, we saw how difficult it is for
students to find troublesome triggers — especially when a trigger involves a frame-securing corrective. This brings us to an
important insight that closely connects unconscious meaning
to secured frames. The precept can be stated this way: *decoded
meanings always eventually lead to secured-frames*. This principle stems from the finding that the second unconscious
system is committed to secured frames; it follows, then, that its
encoded messages will always eventually point in that direction.

This tenet brings us full circle by uniting the dread of unconscious meanings and their encoded derivatives to the basic human fear of secured frames — and personal death. Consciously, we fear both deep insight and the secured frames to which they direct us — we fear both meaning and holding.

This insight explains the repeated observation that once a compelling trigger is identified by a class, the class members, as a rule, have great difficulty linking it to the available powerful and disturbing themes; they are reluctant to venture onto the rewarding but feared path to frame securement. The instructor must move in where frightened students fear to tread and make certain that the much-needed healing interpretations and frame rectifications are made — whatever they may be.

Such is the spirit of self-processing, and an honest and forthright spirit it is. At its very core, this spirit is grounded in the abiding belief that we as human beings can cope better with death anxiety than we have until now — and that we need not harm and destroy ourselves in fear of deep meaning and secured frames. To be an effective self-processing teacher, one must find the means of convincingly believing this credo — it is in our nature to feel otherwise. Our pessimism *vis à vis* death anxiety makes us mad and erodes the quality of our lives; it seems also to be destroying our societies and species. At bottom then, it appears that only deep unconscious wisdom can save us from self-harm and self-destruction; in the self-processing class, this same deep knowledge is used to salvage a better life for its students — and coincidentally, for its teachers as well.

Having come full circle now and having developed the fundamentals of the process and how it is taught to students in small groups, it is time to consider the two main variants of the self-processing class — the self-processing tutorial and individual or personal (private) self-processing.

CHAPTER SIXTEEN

The self-processing tutorial and personal self-processing

We have completed our development and study of the self-processing class. We turn now to the two modes of individual self-processing — the self-processing tutorial, which includes the possibility of teaching self-processing by telephone, and personal self-processing. After exploring these two self-processing modalities, I conclude with a few final perspectives related to the vast new territory that we have explored.

THE SELF-PROCESSING TUTORIAL

The principles of self-processing apply fully to the self-processing tutorial. There are, however, some qualifying considerations for this modality compared to the self-processing class, and I will discuss the main ones.

1. *Because of the conditions of the tutorial, secured-frame anxieties are especially intense in this form of self-processing.*

The self-processing tutorial is a one-to-one situation that eliminates all third parties from the self-processing situation. As a result, this modality is in most instances more secure than a self-processing class. The specific frame does, of course, depend on the parameters of a given tutorial experience. The total security of the frame may be altered if the referral source is contaminated or if the tutorial is carried out by telephone (see point 4 below) — the ideal frame calls for a professional referral and direct in-office contact between student and teacher.

In all, the self-processing tutorial has the potential for being set in the most optimal of self-processing frames and for the generation of the most powerful derivatives available in a healing situation — even though an individual situation may nonetheless fall short of the ideal frame. Even then, given the one-to-one relationship and the subsequent consistency with which the instructor maintains the frame, the opportunity for secured-frame moments is always great.

On the one hand, this situation is quite advantageous because it gives students (and teachers) an exceptional opportunity to experience and benefit from a relatively strong and constructive holding environment and to work over insightfully their secured-frame anxieties. On the other hand, these experiences tend to expose both students and teachers to especially intense secured-frame anxieties of the kind that may jeopardize the continuation of the process. As always in the emotional domain, the very best of a situation is the most fearful.

2.   *The self-processing teacher should adhere closely to the basic principles of teaching and frame maintenance.*

Tutorial students, provoked by unconscious anxieties, tend easily to veer off the structure of the standard self-processing exercise and to tempt the teacher to do so as well. It is imperative that the instructor not join in with this kind of defensive misalliance, and that he or she pursue the development of the components of the self-processing exercise in the standard sequence and fashion. The student's resistance should be understood manifestly as such, educationally modified, and eventually illuminated by the linking process.

3. *The instructor should keep in mind the principle that there is no deep insight without a linking of triggers to themes.*

Often, self-indicators and issues arise in the course of a tutorial exercise that might lend themselves to conscious discussion. The instructor must resist the conscious system temptation to engage in this kind of dialogue. After all, the deep answer to any emotional issue is available only towards the end of an exercise when the linking process is successfully completed. Avoiding conscious system dialogues furthers the self-processing exercise and promotes deep unconscious adaptive solutions. Given that a tutorial lasts only ninety minutes, and that there is only fifty minutes for teaching, time should not be wasted with surface exchanges.

4. *The self-processing tutorial can be done by telephone.*

The likelihood of small-group self-processing by telephone is very low in that it requires students who are not otherwise known to each other and who nonetheless come together to do self-processing via speaker-phone. On the other hand, the self-processing tutorial can easily be conducted by telephone if the teacher has the necessary referrals — perhaps through published papers and books, and even through long-distance advertising.

It must be realized, however, that the use of the telephone is inherently deviant in that it modifies the ground rule of face-to-face contact. There may be additional frame alterations as well — the student may own a book by the teacher or have a limited knowledge of his or her professional career. These frame modifications are important early background triggers that should be linked to the thematic material when they are activated — they are certain to come up sooner or later, and many can be rectified.

Because of its inherently deviant structure, the student who does a tutorial by telephone is usually strongly and unconsciously invested in the deviant frame. He or she is therefore highly vulnerable to secured-frame moments and the anxieties that they create. These students often attempt to promote additional frame modifications as the tutorial proceeds, and when these efforts are frustrated because they are counter-manded by the student's own derivatives, the tutorial often faces a crisis. On the one hand, the student in question is secured-frame vulnerable and yet, on the other, his or her derivatives speak for the necessity of securing or maintaining the frame (without which deep healing is impossible).

Under these circumstances, the instructor is advised to hold the frame of the tutorial and interpret the student's secured-frame anxieties. The student then benefits greatly from the deep insight gained through linking and from the strength of the teacher's therapeutic hold. In response, some of these students will renew their contracts with the teacher, but others will flee — unknowing victims of their own silent, secured-frame anxieties even when the teacher has interpreted them quite well with interventions that have obtained encoded validation.

This situation lies at the edge of what self-processing can accomplish with certain vulnerable students. The self-process-ing teacher who loses such a student to secured-frame anxieties can usually rest well in the belief that he or she has given that student a healing experience that is not only exceedingly helpful but of a kind that he or she would not receive under any other conditions.

For a telephone tutorial, it is essential that the student pay his or her tuition in advance of the first meeting and in advance of the start of each additional sequence of four sessions — the usual duration of a tutorial contract. Because usually the mail is involved, the student must take due precautions to allow enough time for the cheque to arrive before the first contact. It follows then that the instructor must be prepared *not* to carry out the tutorial if the cheque has not reached him or her. While some discretion must be used, the teacher must keep in check his own deviant-frame needs and *lean towards frame adher-ence as much as possible* — the deep unconscious system, and the student, expect and appreciate it.

Similarly, if a student owns a book or has a paper written by the self-processing instructor, the work of the tutorial should lead to the frame-securing disposal of this material. In like fashion, if the instructor happens to have anything that belongs to the student — a letter, a book, or whatever — the material should either be returned to the student or destroyed with the student's knowledge. Remember that what seems trivial or even hurtful to the conscious system can be crucial to healing and deeply appreciated by the second unconscious system — the true key to the emotional life of the student.

There are some easily missed details to telephone self-processing. For example, both student and teacher must be in secured-frame spaces. Thus, the professional student should be in his or her office, in a suitably sound-proofed room (if possible), alone and without danger of being interrupted. The non-professional student should be in a private and neutral space. All concerned should be using a telephone without an extension or even call-waiting — uninterrupted total privacy must be ensured. Similarly, the instructor should be in his or her office, with the space secured as if the student were present. Making and paying for the call is, of course, the responsibility of the student.

Finally, once the telephone is part of the self-processing frame, it should be maintained as such. Alternating between the telephone and direct contact makes the frame chaotic and is unwise. However, when circumstances permit, a shift from telephone work to direct meetings, if permanent, is salutary.

Telephone self-processing makes this mode of education and healing available to many people who could not otherwise benefit from its procedures. It is preferable to telephone psychotherapy because far more derivatives are available for the therapeutic work and for the illumination and interpretation of the meanings of the use of the telephone itself — a deviation built into the basic contract. Self-processing therapy by telephone is an endeavour that deserves wide use.

PERSONAL SELF-PROCESSING

The available literature on self-healing is psychoanalytically oriented and centred on discussions of *self-analysis* and its issues. As a result, the few papers and books that have been written on the subject convey an approach to self-understanding that draws its insights from the first rather than the second unconscious system. It was Freud who undertook the first self-analysis only to find that it evoked great resistances within himself — an experience that is pertinent to this day.

The literature that followed Freud has been written mainly by classical psychoanalysts and is highly intellectualized. It is also elitist in that there is a consensus that only analysed individuals can do sound self-analysis (see Chessick, 1990). This may well be true for *self-analysis*, though only in the sense of adopting a particular theory-driven approach, but it is certainly not true for *self-processing*. Indeed, seemingly "well-analysed" individuals are among the students who are most resistant to self-processing efforts.

Personal self-processing is a technique for anyone and everyone — those who have had some form of therapy and those who have not. In truth, no conscious mind is prepared for its ardours and insights, and those who are adept at carrying it out cannot be identified until they have tried to do so. The factors involved are as varied as the basic structure of the human mind (the minds of some people are "wired" for self-processing); the nature of early and later life experiences, with special emphasis on their death-related and secured- and deviant-frame aspects; the extent of deviant-frame trauma in both a person's daily life and in his or her prior therapies (if any); the degree and nature of the traumas that have been suffered; the capacity to tolerate and benefit from a secured frame; the intensity of the need to reach into deeply unconscious meaning; present life circumstances and emotional issues; the nature of the existing psychopathology — and more.

Background literature

Self-analysis began with Freud (Freud, 1897 [1950]; Anzieu, 1986 [1975]; Gay, 1988), who introduced the concept in his letters to Fliess, stressing the high level of resistance and frustration inherent to his pursuit. Nevertheless, he — and others after him (see Gay, 1988; Chessick, 1990) — saw the outcome of his monumental struggle as highly successful. Freud celebrated the results of his self-analysis as the means by which he made many of his early discoveries, including that of the Oedipus complex and the primary role of fantasy in lieu of reality in the formation of neuroses.

The question of whether these insights were matters of sound knowledge or conscious system defensive formations that served resistance far more than genuine insight is still a matter for debate. The communicative approach would see far more defensiveness and denial in the outcome of Freud's self-analytic efforts than deep insight. Certainly, from Freud on, the criterion of *encoded validation* of self-interpretations was not invoked, rendering all of these efforts suspect.

The problem of obstacles to fruitful private self-analysis continues to occupy writers on this subject (see for example, Calder, 1980; Chessick, 1990). Most published reports indicate that the analysts who have been so engaged believe, in general, that they were able to resolve the resistances that confronted them in engaging in self-investigation and that, overall, they were able to carry out effective self-analytic work. Indeed, despite their contention that the absence of a so-called "neutral" psychoanalyst is a detrimental factor, these writers consistently claim that they achieved a greater degree of insight and symptom relief through self-analysis than that obtained through their earlier personal analyses. The very sticky questions of how one can specify definitive criteria for the assessment of the outcome of these efforts — how to create standards and measures that go beyond a therapist's own unreliable conscious system subjective judgement — is not dealt with in any significant way in these studies; that particular issue remains unresolved to this moment.

The subject of self-analysis is so open to biased and erroneous assessment that we are a long way from determining the positive potential and limitations of private self-analytic processes. By communicative standards, all of the efforts at self-exploration described in the literature (see Chessick, 1990, for a comprehensive listing and review) strikingly neglect frame issues and fall short of *unconsciously validated* wisdom — genuine or deep communicative insight. Indeed, *analysing*, which is a highly intellectualized pursuit even with the use of free associations, is one of the most powerful resistances against self-processing. In general, it ensures a fixation in the conscious system realm and precludes entry into the second unconscious system where the greater power over emotional life resides. The differences between *self-analysis* and *self-process-ing* should be evident from the substance of this book and will not be further pursued here — they begin with two radically different ways of carrying out the process and extend from there in many directions (Langs, 1992d, 1992f).

With this as our background, let us turn now to personal self-processing as carried out by an individual — therapist or otherwise — on his or her own. There are again — and for the last time — a number of key points to keep in mind:

1. *The human psyche is not designed for self-processing efforts.*

This theme has been fully developed in earlier chapters and is mentioned here because the personal self-processor must expect resistances, maintain a clear template of the process, and use his or her self-observing faculties to the fullest. When an exercise is not going well, he or she should press for strong narrative themes and intensify the search for frame-related triggers. The pursuit of overlooked omissions and other resistances should be an inherent part of the process. One also must be tolerant of failures, pleased to obtain small pieces of trigger-decoded insight, and persistent — there is no other way to access the second unconscious system and its adaptive solutions.

In general, the greater the emotional pain and need, the stronger the likelihood of a successful personal self-processing exercise. In addition, many individuals who have suffered deviant frame hurts and who are dealing with immediate frame issues of any kind are inclined to be strongly motivated to make this process work, and they too are likely to succeed in their pursuit of deep understanding and emotional growth.

2. *The personal self-processor should do his or her self-processing within a structured frame.*

There is a strong conscious system tendency to by-pass a secured frame for personal self-processing. This is a deviant and self-defeating approach. Personal self-processing requires a clear structure because the frame (i.e., one's management of the ground rules) provides a strong hold for the self-processor (one can indeed hold oneself) and also evokes secured-frame anxieties that enable the private self-processor to experience these issues — and meaningfully work them over.

This precept implies that personal self-processing should be done on a once- or twice-weekly basis, at a fixed time, for the same duration (ideally, forty-five minutes to one hour), and in the same private place — a setting where interruptions will not occur. In addition, the model of the exercise should be strictly adhered to — it is the best guarantor of small and large successes.

3. *One of the most common resistances to personal self-processing is the failure to identify a strong and active trigger and make it available for linking.*

Missing a key trigger is probably the most frequent resistance seen in private self-processing. As stressed before, a key maxim in respect to triggers is that one should search first and foremost for *frame-related triggers.* In so doing, both methods — direct recall and going from themes to triggers — should be used.

4. *Mental health professionals should, as much as possible, work with triggers from their therapeutic work — including their doing self-processing therapy if such is the case.*

The therapeutic and self-processing situations are ideal sources of triggers that can help a self-processor gain trigger-decoded insights — into personal issues of frame management and countertransferences (many of them also related to frame issues). Self-indicators also are common in those who do any form of therapy because there is great vulnerability to conscious system-based errors. Examples are seen when a teacher

or therapist unnecessarily modifies the frame of a class, behaves inappropriately, misses an important intervention, fails
to obtain encoded validation for his or her interpretations, etc.
All of these expressions of countertransference call for a search
for the evocative triggers in students' behaviours and communications and the frame of the class — and for linking triggers to
themes to achieve deep insight.

The frames of the self-processing class and of psychotherapy, and the roles assigned to the teacher and therapist and
to the student and patient, are especially well defined and
powerful. As a result, the transactions within these frames are
exceedingly strong emotionally for all concerned and relatively
easy to explore communicatively. Being placed in the role of a
frame manager, however unconsciously, also renders the treatment situation especially compelling as a source of derivative
communications from the teacher's or therapist's second unconscious system. Still another contribution to the power of
class-related triggers derives from the attempts made by students unconsciously to heal their teachers and to help them to
secure frames. These caring efforts are *unconsciously* perceived
as such by the teacher — and *the second unconscious system
concentrates its focus on healers and frame managers.*

Another advantage of the psychotherapy or self-processing
class as sources of triggers for personal self-processing stems
from the fact that, in these settings, the manifestations of
personal psychopathology are relatively easily identified using
the communicative approach. In addition to the specific criteria
of errant interventions alluded to earlier (see also point 5 below), every anxious or uncertain moment or session speaks for
possible countertransferences in the therapist/teacher and
calls for personal self-processing. These often are disquieting
but marvellous opportunities to gain deep insight. Personal
self-processing can be especially effective after a self-processing teacher has gone through a frame-securing moment with
his or her students. Given that no one is immune from secured-
frame anxieties, these are the circumstances under which
issues of this kind can be moved towards better resolution.

In all of these efforts, it is critical that the self-processing
teacher who is conducting his or her own private self-process-

ing identify his or her *triggers* and not do the initial part of the exercise around self-indicators. *The primary triggers for the teacher are the actions and communications of his or her students*, and especially their frame impingements. The therapist's or instructor's own interventions and behaviours, which are self-indicators, are secondary organizers of the encoded themes — self-perceptions are indeed quite common under these conditions. Still, the self-processor initially must be sure to turn the process around so that he or she works primarily from external triggers rather than from his or her own internal reactions.

5. *Personal self-processing can be effectively used for brief moments while doing therapy or teaching self-processing.*

Self-processing is quite useful when a therapist or teacher is stuck, suffering from intrusive thoughts and/or feelings, inclined to modify a classroom or therapy frame, or in error during a self-processing class or therapy session. At that very moment, the instructor or therapist can engage in a mini-self-processing exercise directed towards trigger-decoded insight.

For example, while listening to a presenting student's material, an instructor in difficulty can create a very brief origination narrative or recollect a recent dream — in part, if need be. There should then follow a few quick guided associations, the identification of the main self-indicators (the therapist's or teacher's error or disturbance), the recognition of the immediate adaptation-evoking trigger within the class and its implications — and the linking of the trigger to the themes.

If time permits — and anything but the most perfunctory effort must await an extended moment of personal self-processing — the background triggers from prior classes and triggers from other aspects of the therapist's work and his or her personal life may be worked into the material. The instructor must use a great deal of intuition in selecting the key elements for processing in order to complete a successful mini-exercise. But if well done, the effort will produce a trigger-decoded (linked) insight for the instructor, who hopefully can then get on with his or her teaching efforts without further noticeable hindrance. It is a lot to handle, but one can become adept at this process and use it wisely and well.

6. *Personal life traumas and emotional issues also are suit-able triggers for the self-processing efforts of a mental health professional.*

The therapist who does self-processing should, of course, be free to work with any kind of significant trigger. However, it is well to recognize that triggers from the therapeutic arena should not be neglected because of a meaningful stimulus from outside life. A powerful origination narrative and thematic pool will provide the ingredients for linking efforts that deeply clarify both situations.

7. *Doing effective psychotherapy and teaching self-process-ing are difficult tasks and should be safeguarded by personal self-processing.*

The healing arena is overcharged with pain, anxiety, and dreaded conscious and especially unconscious meanings, many of which touch on a self-processing teacher's vulnera-bilities and anxieties. Self-processing therapy asks a teacher to surrender much of his or her own conscious system defensive armamentarium and to operate under continuous pressures towards secured frames and their issues. Further, most teach-ers at one time or another suffer from conscious and, more often, unconscious guilt for invoking deviant frames and for interventional errors (many of which attack the patient in some way).

All in all, the self-processing teacher is under perpetual threat of conscious system overload and decompensation. Some of this burden is counterbalanced in self-processing therapy by the exquisite rewards of this work — for both the students and the teacher. Nevertheless, periods of active personal self-processing appear to be the best antidote for the psychic and sometimes psychosomatic wear and tear that such work exacts on its practitioners.

CONCLUDING REMARKS

Having acknowledged and stressed the ardours of self-processing and the major role that resistances play in making this work such a difficult undertaking, I will in these final comments stress the positive side of the picture. Conscious communication is the flawed and uninsightful prose of human expression in the emotional domain, unconscious communication its discerning poetry — and saving grace.

Approaches to the human mind that stay on the surface of communication, much like the gross anatomy of a human organ, are limited and simplistic; they are non-dynamic and on some level so oversimplified as to be of questionable use. On the other hand, studies of the unconscious part of the mind as it is engaged in active adaptation truly stun the imagination and reveal the breathless intricacies and profound wisdom of deep human nature. At a time when we as human beings suffer far more than necessary, and when we, as the prime occupants of this planet, appear to be moving towards self-annihilation, it is reassuring to know that every human being possesses deep within himself or herself the knowledge that can move themselves and humankind towards a far more satisfying fate. It is time we turned to trigger decoding to put this deep wisdom to use.

Doing and teaching self-processing makes an apprentice into a great artist and healer, a privileged soul who is able to enter and negotiate a domain with as much seemingly magical power as seeming terror. As healers, we can only hope that our minds are configured in a way that enables us to enter and stay within this domain — the realm of the second unconscious system. Not everyone has a gift for music or poetry, nor does everyone have a gift for decoding narratives in light of their triggers. Yet if we are to remedy the emotional ills that are so inherent to life and to our fellow humans (and ourselves), then trigger decoders we all should be — to the best of our abilities.

For emotional healers, trigger decoding is the key to a kingdom of kindness and therapeutic loving — a sound kind of caring that resonates deeply within its beneficiaries (and they always include the healer himself or herself). There is an awesome quality and magnificence to this kind of cure that simply is absent in all other comparable efforts. I can think of no endeavour that inherently gives more to both giver and receiver than teaching a self-processing class and conducting a self-processing tutorial. I deeply hope that this book will inspire many mental health professionals to undertake this kind of work and give this new healing method the life it deserves. There is much to gain and, for once, absolutely nothing to lose.

REFERENCES

Anzieu, D. (1986 [1975]). *Freud's Self-Analysis*, trans. Peter Graham. Madison, CT: International Universities Press.

Badalamenti, A., & Langs, R. (1992a). The thermodynamics of psychotherapeutic communication. *Behavioural Science, 37*: 157–180.

Badalamenti, A., & Langs, R. (1992b). Work and force in psychotherapy. *Journal of Mathematical and Computer Modeling, 16*: 3–17.

Bateson, G. (1979). *Mind and Nature*. New York: Bantam.

Bickerton, D. (1990). *Language and Species*. Chicago: University of Chicago Press.

Calder, K. (1980). An analyst's self-analysis. *Journal of the American Psychoanalytic Association, 28*: 5–20.

Calvin, W. (1990). *The Cerebral Symphony*. New York: Bantam.

Chessick, R. (1990). Self-analysis: a fool for a patient? *Psychoanalytic Review, 77*: 311–339.

Freud, S. (1897 [1950]). Extracts from the Fliess papers. *Standard Edition, 1*: 175–280.

Freud, S. (1900). *The Interpretation of Dreams. Standard Edition, 4 & 5*: 1–627.

Gay, P. (1988). *Freud: A Life for Our Time*. New York: Norton.

Goodheart, W. (1993). Between Freud and Charcot: beginning steps from psychoanalysis & folk psychology towards an interactional science of emotional cognition and communication. *International Journal of Communicative Psychoanalysis & Psychotherapy, 8*: 3–15.

Langs, R. (1981). *Resistances and Interventions*. New York: Jason Aronson.

Langs, R. (1984–85). Making interpretations and securing the frame: sources of danger for psychotherapists. *International Journal of Psychoanalytic Psychotherapy, 10*: 3–23.

Langs, R. (1985). *Madness and Cure*. Hillsdale, NJ: Newconcept.

Langs, R. (1986). Clinical issues arising from a new model of the mind. *Contemporary Psychoanalysis, 22*: 418–444.

Langs, R. (1987). Clarifying a new model of the mind. *Contemporary Psychoanalysis, 23*: 162–180.

Langs, R. (1988). *A Primer of Psychotherapy*. New York: Gardner Press.

Langs, R. (1991). *Take Charge of Your Emotional Life*. New York: Holt.

Langs, R. (1992a). *A Clinical Workbook for Psychotherapists*. London: Karnac Books.

Langs, R. (1992b [1978]). *The Listening Process*. Northvale, NJ: Jason Aronson.

Langs, R. (1992c). 1923: the advance that retreated from the architecture of the mind. *International Journal of Communicative Psychoanalysis and Psychotherapy, 7*: 3–15.

Langs, R. (1992d). The self-processing class and the psychotherapy situation: a comparative study. *American Journal of Psychotherapy, 46*: 75–90.

Langs, R. (1992e). *Science, Systems and Psychoanalysis*. London: Karnac Books.

Langs, R. (1992f) Teaching self-processing. *Contemporary Psychoanalysis, 28*: 97–117.

Langs, R. (1993). Psychoanalysis: narrative myth or narrative science? *Contemporary Psychoanalysis, 29*: 555–594.

Langs, R. (in press). Science and evolution: Pathways to a revolution in the world of psychotherapy. *American Journal of Psychotherapy*.

Langs, R., & Badalamenti, A. (1992a). Some clinical consequences of a formal science for psychoanalysis and psychotherapy. *American Journal of Psychotherapy*, *46*: 611–619.

Langs, R., & Badalamenti, A. (1992b). The three modes of the science of psychoanalysis. *American Journal of Psychotherapy*, *46*: 163–182.

Langs, R., & Badalamenti, A. (in press). Psychotherapy: the search for chaos, the discovery of determinism. *Australian and New Zealand Journal of Psychiatry*.

Langs, R. J., Udoff, A., Bucci, W., Cramer, G., & Thomson, L. (1993). Two methods of assessing unconscious communication in psychotherapy. *Psychoanalytic Psychology*, *10*: 1–13.

Newton, P. (1971). Abstinence as a role requirement in psychotherapy. *Psychiatry*, *34*: 391–400.

Ornstein, R. (1991). *The Evolution of Consciousness*. New York: Prentice Hall.

Searles, H. (1959). The effort to drive the other person crazy — an element in the aetiology and psychotherapy of schizophrenia. *British Journal of Medical Psychology*, *32*: 1–18.

Slavin, M., & Kriegman, D. (1992). *The Adaptive Design of the Mind*. New York: Guilford.

Smith, D. (1991). *Hidden Conversations: An Introduction to Communicative Psychoanalysis*. London: Tavistock/Routledge.

Stolorow, R., Brandschaft, B., & Atwood, G. (1987). *Psychoanalytic Treatment: An Intersubjective Approach*. Hillsdale, NJ: Analytic Press.

Weiss, J., & Sampson, H. (1986). *The Psychoanalysis Process: Theory, Clinical Observation, and Empirical Research*. New York: Guilford.

INDEX